D1417626

THE PLAZA

THE PLAZA

Its Life and Times

by

EVE BROWN

A Duell, Sloan and Pearce Book

MEREDITH PRESS • NEW YORK

Third printing, September 1967

LIBRARY OF CONGRESS CATALOG CARD NUMBER: 67-12634

MANUFACTURED IN THE UNITED STATES OF AMERICA FOR MEREDITH PRESS

VAN REES PRESS • NEW YORK

To the late A. M. Sonnabend, to whose faith in a fine New York landmark and the courage to pour millions into improvements and restorations The Plaza owes its survival.

To the late A. M. Sonnabend, to whose faith in a fine New York landmark and the courage to pour millions into improvements and restorations The Plaza owes its survival.

Foreword

THE HISTORY of The Plaza can be said to be a capsule social history of New York itself. A legend in its own time, The Plaza has reflected a way of life during the changing twentieth century. Writing a biography of a hotel that in sixty years of its existence has served as host to thousands upon thousands of guests, among them the great and the distinguished of the world, was a unique task because of the vastness of the human panorama unfolded. Much of the material in this book was gathered from old records and files which were preserved; unfortunately many more records have either been lost or destroyed. Happily the author was able to glean much from the memory of old employees who have marked up a record of forty to fifty years' employment, some now retired, some still at their jobs.

For their contribution with facts and reminiscences I wish especially to thank John Pelay and Ralph Ruggerio, veterans still with the hotel; Romeo Giannini, retired, William Tonetti, also a former employee, and members of the staff. I am especially thankful, also, to Herman Zerriner for the story of his association with the Princess Parlaghy, an early Plaza guest.

FOREWORD

I am most particularly grateful to my former assistant, Rita Irwin, for her help, patience, and understanding. I cannot give too much credit to Leslie Dorsey for the excellent, meticulous job of assembling and coordinating documentary facts. I also wish to thank Miss Julia Edwards for her help and advice and to extend thanks to Mrs. Virginia Sterry Twitchell, Henry Sell, Frank Farrell, Mrs. Harry Allen, Van Buren Thorne, Donald Norris, Kirk Crockett, Donald Stralem, James Gillen, Paul Boiardi, Kay Arendt, Mortimer Brandt, Mrs. Chester Dale, Mrs. John G. McCarthy, Mrs. Cecil Singer, Clyde Harris, and Burt Champion, for their contributions to the material contained in this book.

Contents

Illustrations

ILLUSTRATIONS

THE PLAZA

CHAPTER ONE

Street Scene

"New York, New York, it's a wonderful town,
The Bronx is up, and the Battery's down."

From *On the Town.*

New York was in its most magical autumnal mood on that first brisk day of October, 1907, a serene day in a serene world, when there burst upon the town a phenomenon of such grandeur, a cavalcade of such Edwardian elegance, it sent the press of the nation into journalistic frenzy and left an awestruck public agape with wonderment.

All the elite who made up the social oligarchy of the times were arriving for the gala opening of New York's newest and grandest hostelry, the long-heralded Plaza rising in French Renaissance splendor eighteen stories in the air, where East met West at Fifth Avenue and the southern gateway to Central Park.

They represented the wealth and fashion of the nation, the greatest social and industrial names in the country at the turn of the century. They came in a constant, day-long parade of smart-crested carriages with two properly impressive, properly liveried men on the box, or in the newfangled automobiles driven by haughty uniformed chauffeurs fully aware of the furore their arrival was creating.

At the Fifty-ninth Street entrance curb of the hotel, proud and correct in his spanking new uniform of broadcloth, with gold-lace-trimmed collar and cuffs displaying the gold and fawn colors of the Plaza, stood six-foot, handsome young Tom Clifford, the Plaza's first footman, on the alert to open the doors of each equipage as it drew up. His was the enviable task of helping the socially-great alight—the perfumed, wasp-waisted ladies in rustling taffetas and gleaming satins and huge hats laden down with foliage and inanimate feathered creatures, escorted by bewhiskered or mustachioed gentlemen wearing toppers and carrying the canes affected by the club fellows of the day. Tom Clifford was to perform this chore for the next forty-five years!

His sartorial elegance was eclipsed by the doorman standing at attention just inside the crystal and bronze revolving doors, to swing the arrivals into the great marble lobby. In court attire of black satin embellished with rows of yellow silk braid across the breast, satin breeches, long black silk stockings and snowy white gloves, the doorman was a resplendent picture eloquently expressive of the grandeur that was The Plaza. Even those guests accustomed to European formality gasped and admired; nothing like it had ever before been seen in an American hotel.

Across the street stood hundreds upon hundreds of eager, curious spectators, gazing and gaping at the spectacle of high society and high finance, the millionaires and the moguls of whom they had heard and read so much making their way into the grand new hotel. The crowds had forgathered early, some at 7 A.M., alerted by the clanging arrival of horse-drawn fire engines in a final test and fire drill of the hotel and its personnel before the opening.

Lining the curb, and backed up to the park, they stood and stared and murmured; an orderly crowd as crowds go, not for a moment attempting a better vantage point by crossing over to the hotel sidewalk. They were little trouble, very little trouble, to the corps of policemen on hand to maintain order, for they were a respectful, awed crowd, inspiring one foppish gentleman to comment: "They know their place."

It had been rumored that there would be a rush among those taking permanent apartments to be the first to register at the wondrous new hotel, and oh, the thrill of it when it turned out to be Mr. Alfred Gwynne Vanderbilt, the millionaire sportsman whose father, Cornelius Vanderbilt, was considered the richest man in America. It was just 9 A.M. when Tom Clifford opened the door of Mr. Vanderbilt's limousine, but Mrs. Vanderbilt was not with him at the time. Most people knew why, for the front page of *The New York Times* that very morning had headlined the report from Newport that on the preceding day, September 30, an automobile in which Mrs. Vanderbilt was riding with her niece, Miss Pauline LeRoy French, had collided at an intersection with another car, and "skidded thirty-four feet." The only person injured in the accident was identified simply as Mrs. Moran, the wife of the chauffeur driving the other car. Her world sighed thankfully that Mrs. Vanderbilt had escaped unscathed.

She joined Mr. Vanderbilt later in the day at The Plaza, where the first line on the virgin register was inscribed "Mr. and Mrs. Vanderbilt and servant,"—a now historic "first."

The second name on the register was that of Mr. and Mrs. Wm. G. Roelker of Newport, who had the good grace to add "and maid," instead of "servant." In quick succession came others of equal social significance and industrial prominence, to sign in as tenants: Oliver Harriman, scion of railroad millions and his wife, a Southern beauty; Colonel and Mrs. William Jay, bearing a name of fine Colonial ancestry; Mr. and Mrs. Alexander H. Revell of Chicago.

A loud murmur arose when the legendary "Diamond Jim" Brady arrived, sporting a diamond-and-ruby-headed cane and escorting a beautiful lady who, the whisper went around, was that famed actress Lillian Russell.

The arrival of Mr. and Mrs. George Jay Gould, accompanied by a brood of children, was the signal for another outburst of excitement. All recognized the beautiful Mrs. Gould, the former Edith Kingdon, who had deserted the stage to become the bride of multimillionaire Gould; all had read of the magnificent Gould country home, Georgian Court, at Lakewood, New Jersey, a feudal-like estate designed by Bruce Price, Emily Price Post's father, in the manner of the royal French châteaus on the Loire,

·The Plaza·

FRED STERRY, Managing Director.

MONEY, JEWELS, AND OTHER VALUABLE PACKAGES MUST BE PLACED IN THE SAFE IN THE OFFICE, OTHERWISE THE MANAGEMENT WILL NOT BE RESPONSIBLE FOR ANY LOSS.

ROOM	NAME	ADDRESS
	Tuesday Oct 1st 1907	
521 527-29 23 25	Mr & Mrs Alfred G. Vanderbilt	New York
546	& Servant	
1144 1143-45	Mr & Mrs Wm G. Roelker	New York
1147	& Maid	"
501-07-03	Mr & Mrs B. Beinecke	"
237-9-241	Mrs Jessie Young-Hayworth	Chicago
243	Master Otto Young-Hayworth	"
245	Miss Young-Hayworth	"
611-613	Mr & Mrs Alexander H. Revell	Chicago
615	Miss Margaret Revell	"
617	Master Alexander H. Revell Jr	"
1334-1337	Mr & Mrs Hamilton Carhartt	New York
1335-1333	Miss Carhartt	"
1104-1106	H. B. McQueen	Schenectady NY
503-501-507	Mr & Mrs D O Wickham	New York
507	Mrs Lyman H. Treadway	Cleveland Ohio
505	Miss Elizabeth H. Treadway	do
505	Master Lyman H. Treadway Jr	do
1427	Albert Goodman	New York
333-5	Mr & Mrs Albert Fill and Maid	New York

which boasted sunken gardens, an elliptical staircase of marble and bronze, a private golf course, and a separate building with a great tanbark riding ring.

That the Goulds and their family were to live at the hotel was titillating news, indeed; however, it was but a two-year period of transition for them while awaiting completion of the great marble town house they were building at 857 Fifth Avenue.

Frederick M. Gould, George's brother, was another Gould representative among The Plaza's first tenants; other registrants were millionaire Julius Walsh and his tall, blond wife, Clara Bell Walsh, a Kentucky belle who for fifty years was to make her home at The Plaza—from the day it opened to the day she died there, on August 12, 1957.

The cavalcade continued: John Wanamaker of Philadelphia; Mr. and Mrs. Cornelius K. G. Billings, whose "country home" was up at Fort Washington Avenue and 193rd Street, where now stands the magnificent museum The Cloisters; Benjamin W. Duke of tobacco fame; Mrs. James Henry Smith, briefly married to the legendary "Silent" Smith of Wall Street and mother by a previous marriage of dapper William Rhinelander Stewart and Anita Stewart, who was to wed a member of Portugal's royal Braganza family.

Not the least cause of excitement in the crowd was the sight of John "Bet-a-Million" Gates and his wife and son Charles, whose apartment was reported in the press to have cost $35,000 a year, $10,000 more than the Vanderbilts were paying.

In addition to those arriving to check in, noontime and night found streams of socialites on hand to attend luncheons and gala private dinner parties. Romeo Giannini, who was hired two weeks before the hotel opened and who rose to become bell captain before his retirement on the last day of 1955, recalled to the author with pride "the elite of the town" who came to one or another opening-day function. "All of *Who's Who* was there," said Romeo, in the manner of a society editor reporting a gala event. "I remember Billie Burke, Mark Twain, Charles Dillingham, John Drew, David Belasco, the beautiful actress Maxine Elliott, Fritzi Scheff, who came to live at the hotel, Oscar Hammerstein."

As if all this were not excitement and glamour enough for that

October day, the crowds were equally fascinated by the sight of a fleet of natty new motor taxis lined up on the Fifth Avenue side of the hotel, which was not then the main entrance it was later to become. They constituted the first contingent of metered gasoline-driven taxis to be put in operation in New York by their canny owner, the late Harry Allen, who realized full well the publicity to be derived on this day of days.

The high green-and-red cabs, their chauffeurs outfitted in uniforms not unlike those of West Point cadets, were a dramatic sight; rubberneckers crowded around to inspect and catch a glimpse of the little dials that were to register the fee to the passenger—fees reported to be "very reasonable." The dials were not working that day, however; guests of the hotel were invited to ride free, and many did. Even the rich like getting something for nothing.

Through it all—the crush of onlookers, the distinguished guests arriving to inspect the stunning interior and to partake of any of the five meals served (breakfast, luncheon, tea, dinner and supper) —decorum, although spiked with excitement, reigned. When nighttime came, the curious were still on hand to see the lights blaze in the rooms, and to watch more and more celebrities arriving as the grandeur of the opening reached a brilliant crescendo in a series of glamorous dinner and supper parties.

It was a grand and glorious, a history-making day in the annals of Manhattan Isle.

There is another day, fifty-seven years later, when the eyes of public and press the world over are again focused upon The Plaza.

It is February 7, 1964. The conservative, eminently correct hotel is once again surrounded by a crowd—but how different a crowd! This is a mob, a howling, seething mob, a milling mass of screaming teen-agers suffering from a virulent attack of Beatlemania.

The New York which once turned out to gaze upon the patricians and the socialites with eager, but controlled, curiosity, now roars an uncontrolled, ear-piercing welcome to four tousle-headed youths from Britain, tries to rush police barricades, chants on cue for television viewers—an unbelievable pandemonium.

The first reaction to the news that the very correct Plaza, citadel of conservative elegance, would house the Beatles, of bedlam fame, was incredulity, disbelief.

How could The Plaza do this? was the question asked on all sides. The British press expressed particular surprise and mild consternation. The French press shrugged its editorial shoulders as if to say: "We know. We had it at the George V." The American press went into reportorial tailspins, overwhelmed the hotel switchboard with calls for details, confirmations, whens and wheres. Plaza guests shuddered at the appalling prospect of having the wild ones around —and management held its breath and kept its hotelian fingers crossed.

Dear, unsuspecting Plaza. Who was to know, when a dispatch came from London to reserve suites and bedrooms for a party of six businessmen, that these were the Beatles, their manager, and their press agent. They had insured their reservations by the simple expedient of using their own names. Fifteen rooms they needed, for six days—representing a neat piece of change even by Plaza standards—and the reservations clerk was happy to oblige. He, and many other employees, had never even heard of the Beatles.

With subsequent awareness came consternation; shock waves rippled throughout the hotel when the awful truth dawned. The Four Fringes were reported to have left havoc and hotel destruction (not necessarily of their making but the direct result of their stay) all over Europe. It didn't help much when *Life* magazine came out with a long article and lurid pictures to confirm the reports.

Plaza patrons and managers shuddered to think what might happen to the rare, original Chinese jardinieres in the Palm Court and the priceless crystal girondelle hurricane lamps, copies of those on the balustrade of Chantilly Palace outside Paris; to the beautifully paneled walls and fine rugs; to the expensively upholstered furniture, the satin coverlets on the beds.

But the reservations had been confirmed, the hotel was committed, and there was nothing to do about it except cope with the situation as best it could.

And cope the admirable Plaza did. General Manager Alphonse

Salomone immediately went into action as if he were planning a military campaign, designed to protect regular guests and property and maintain traditional Plaza service as much as possible. He mapped out a program of procedure incredible in that it succeeded even beyond his hopes.

While pandemonium reigned without, within all moved smoothly with a surprising minimum of disturbances except on the twelfth floor, where the boys were quartered, and an overloading of the telephone trunk lines that almost threatened to break down the whole system.

Special security measures were put into effect. To The Plaza's own security staff was assigned the specific task of protecting guests and patrons in their daily comings and goings. Squads of Burns detective guards were hired and stationed throughout the hotel to keep hysterical kids, sensation seekers and autograph hounds out. All was augmented by the city police, who held or tried to hold things in check on the outside, where barricades had been set up at the Fifth Avenue entrance. As the cars bearing the Beatles pulled up, accompanied by police escorts, hundreds of teen-agers rushed the barricades—but not one succeeded in getting into the lobby.

There is on file in the publicity department a photograph that has to be seen to be believed: an Assistant Manager escorting the Beatles to the elevator in the main lobby, with not another soul visible except an elderly lady in the foreground whose expression seems to indicate she couldn't care less.

All days off for the entire personnel were canceled for the duration of the "invasion," all departments were alerted—telephone operators, mail room, maid service, bellmen, elevator operators, restaurants, room service, etc.—to do their best beyond and above the call of duty in the face of possible confusion and harassments. Service, it must be admitted, moved slowly, but it moved, and while there were some complaints by guests, they were surprisingly few, all things considered.

The unsung heroines of "six days in February" were the telephone operators. Theirs was the titanic job of answering thousands of calls from every part of the country in addition to their regular routine—calls from teen-age fans, young editors of high school publications seeking interviews, promoters of every conceivable product seeking endorsements, would-be radio interviewers, reporters claiming to represent obscure publications never even heard of.

The operators, alerted to put no calls through to the Beatles unless they adhered to a code, switched most of the calls to the publicity department, which by this time, besieged on all sides, was about to have the screaming-meemies itself.

The publicity staff's Rita Irwin, unable at one point to get through to the Beatles' manager Brian Epstein on a matter of press importance, abandoned phone call attempts and went up to the twelfth floor to try and locate him. Imagine her horror, on entering one of the bedrooms where a large group of newsmen was gathered, to see a photographer grinding away while instructing one of the Beatles on the fine points of jumping up and down on the bed—with his shoes on! The Beatle was obliging with vigor.

Shocked and horrified, she turned on the lensman with the full force of her Irish temper. "How dare you do this to the Plaza? Why are you manufacturing these sensational pictures? This boy is probably afraid not to go along with the press, and just look what he's doing to our beautiful satin covers. Nobody acts this way at the Plaza, nobody, not even the Beatles. Now you stop this nonsense this very minute."

As gentle applause issued from newsmen who had been observing from the sidelines, the photographer, crushed beneath the fine fury, quickly slunk away.

To tell the truth, the Beatles were rather nice boys; when not on exhibition, surrounded by press and publicity and the necessity of putting on an act, they were exceedingly well behaved and well liked by the staff—by clerks, chambermaids, waiters, bellmen. Said one elderly little Scottish woman, a Plaza chambermaid for many years, "They're bonny lads, neat and clean, who don't leave things laying around," adding with a sniff, "like some other guests do."

Aside from their archaic haircuts and tight Edwardian pants, they were typical of any young people who might stay at The Plaza. They ate lots of chocolates, drank gallons of cola drinks, while having liquor available for those who wanted it, watched television—which they kept going day and night—and ordered tea, tea, tea, in typical English fashion.

Not one shined his shoes with a towel; there wasn't a single cigarette burn on rug or upholstery; nothing was broken, nothing swiped, not even an ash tray. Their hair was shiny clean, their shirts snowy white; they tipped well. One Beatle who had his hair cut in the barbershop at $2.50, declared, "This is the cheapest haircut I've ever had. It will do me until six months from now, when I get my next haircut." He tipped the barber $5.00.

There were, of course, many amusing, even hilarious incidents. Kids tried every ruse to sneak into the carefully guarded hotel; two youngsters actually did get by the guard, walked up the twelve flights of steps, only to be quietly but firmly ushered down—by elevator.

Two other girls tried a unique tack. Walking up to the front desk, they announced they had two gifts to deliver to the Beatles and asked what was their room number. Told that the mopheads were at the moment in Washington, the youngsters walked dejectedly away in the direction of the Fifty-eighth Street exit, discreetly followed by a security man to make certain they left. There, just outside the door, reposed two cartons about the size of orange crates. When opened, out of each popped a girl of about ten or twelve—the "presents" intended for the Beatles.

In due time the Beatles departed, and so did the chanting, screaming teen-agers; the barricades were removed, the telephone switchboard was again back to normal working service, the mail clerks, who had been swamped with sackloads of mail for the incredible quartet, breathed a sigh of relief, and the hotel, somewhat shaken, but unbowed, emerged fairly unscathed by the great onslaught.

From Edwardian elegance to bellowing Beatlemania, The Plaza had managed to span a fantastic arc with superb skill, always the Great Lady.

CHAPTER TWO

How It All Began

ACROSS from Central Park in the 1870's, high-hatted, Lincolnesque gentlemen and gentle, bonneted ladies, beneath whose ankle-length skirts peeped pantaloons, glided over the ice of New York's most fashionable skating rink. This was the New York Skating Club on the southwest corner of Fifty-ninth Street and Fifth Avenue, which drew its water from the little pond in the Park. Here the queen of New York society, Mrs. William Astor, and her coterie indulged in polite winter sports.

The area all around it was fast developing into the most fashionable residential section of the city. Everything was moving "uptown"; the year 1879 found St. Patrick's Cathedral, at Fifth Avenue and Fiftieth Street, being dedicated after twenty-one years of labor, its sculptured, gleaming white stone facade rising as a gesture of noble beauty to transform the Avenue's skyline. It was inevitable that the little skating pond, occupying such potentially valuable land, ten blocks north, would eventually disappear.

In 1883 the property, extending from Fifty-eighth Street to Fifty-ninth Street, comprising 53,726 square feet fronting Fifth Avenue, was sold by its owner, John Charles Anderson, for $850,000. Two builders, John R. Phyfe and James Campbell, chose the site to realize their dream of erecting one of the country's finest hotels.

To build it the partners put $489,000 of their own money into the venture and borrowed $790,000 from the New York Life Insurance Company. But even then, building costs somehow outstripped original estimates, and long before completion of the hotel the builders ran out of funds, could not raise additional capital, and in November, 1887, they were foreclosed by the insurance company, which went ahead to complete the hotel on its own.

Upon completion, the hotel was leased to the brothers David and F. A. Hammond for fifteen years, at a rental of $125,000 per year. On October 1, 1890, the newspapers of the day heralded the opening of "a palatial establishment costing three million dollars to build."

This was the first Plaza, and it bestowed a worthy heritage upon its successor, the elegant Plaza of today. Its eight stories conformed to a law then limiting the height of buildings to ten stories; its pillared front faced Fifth Avenue with architectural dignity; it offered guests all the latest modern improvements in its four hundred rooms. A colored lithograph distributed at the Chicago World's Fair in 1893 proudly extolled such virtues as "the water and ice used are distilled and frozen on the premises."

The society of the gay nineties nodded approval of the mahogany furniture and finishings, the mosaic bathrooms, and the gold and white dining room with stained-glass windows and arched ceilings threaded in gold. The feminine *haut monde* applauded its pink ladies' parlor.

The late Frank Crowninshield, a personage of social and literary distinction, writing in *Vogue* magazine in 1947, on the occasion of the present Plaza's fortieth anniversary, referred to the original Plaza as "the first New York hotel to offer people of fashion the sort of rooms, service, cuisine and wine cellar which, in that simple and fragrant era, made formal entertaining possible." King's *Handbook of New York City* reported that it was "one of the grandest hotels in the world."

The first report that a new Plaza was planned broke in 1902, when it became known that for three million dollars, said then to be the largest cash deal in the history of New York real estate, the hotel had been sold to the George A. Fuller Company.

When the *New York Journal* first reported the sale and the information that the purchasers planned to tear the hotel down when its fifteen-year lease expired in 1905 to erect "the finest and stateliest hotel in the world," at an estimated cost of twelve million dollars, the report was not taken seriously enough to make mild headlines.

Yet history was to prove that the promoters knew what they were doing.

Bernhard Beinecke, known as Ben Beinecke to everyone, has been generally credited with the first vision of building the "world's finest hotel" to replace the first little Plaza, but the actual concept of today's Plaza took place in the minds of a triumvirate consisting of Beinecke, Harry S. Black, president of the Fuller Construction Company, and hotelier Fred Sterry.

No synthesis ever has been created by more contrasting personalities.

Ben Beinecke was a German immigrant who came to America in 1864, at the age of nineteen, by sailing ship, and whose rise to fame and fortune is Horatio Alger at its most fantastic best. The Beinecke Rare Book and Manuscript Library, at Yale, a building worth many millions of dollars, which was given to the university by his two sons, Edwin and Frederick, and by the family of their late brother Walter, is a cultural monument to the immigrant founder of the Beinecke millions.

One of Ben Beinecke's first jobs in the New World was driving a butcher's wagon; it wasn't long before he had saved enough to buy the shop. Some time afterward he sold it at a profit, to go into the wholesale meat business, and in his upward and onward climb was soon supplying many hotels and steamship lines.

A genial, stocky young man, who never lost his German accent, Ben Beinecke made friends with all with whom he came in contact. Always ready to extend a helping hand when possible, he received many a helping hand in return. In 1876, still a quite young man, Beinecke won the contract to supply meat to the World's Fair in

Philadelphia simply by underbidding all competition. Competitors predicted his ruin, but Beinecke figured that farmers would sell their meat to him cheaply just to get it in to the Fair. They did.

Meat bills, as a rule, were the largest bills hotel operators had to contend with in those days, and many depended on Beinecke for credit. They got it, and they rewarded him by faithful patronage.

In time Beinecke rose to command large stockyards in the East, at Fifty-ninth Street and the Hudson River. Cattle cars from the West would move down Twelfth Avenue and be shunted into the yards, their steam locomotives encased so that they would not frighten the horses. England, Scotland and Wales were then getting much of their meat from the United States, and it wasn't long before Beinecke was persuaded to sell his business to the Eastman Company, Ltd. He assumed the presidency, and, with it, the role of international financier.

New interests took hold of his mind, and born of his experience in supplying meat to hotels was a decision to invest in hotels. He built the Manhattan Hotel and raised money to build the one-thousand-room Terminal Hotel at Broadway and Thirty-second Street. The concept of a great, magnificent hotel catering to the bon tons was the beginning of a dream next to come true.

The three Beinecke sons—the Sperry and Hutchinson Green Stamp people, it will interest supermarket shoppers to know—attended the best schools in the East, and they learned to play pool in the Plaza billiard room. Father Beinecke had had little time to play. But his associates did. Harry Black and John "Bet-a-Million" Gates, business friends, each owned a private railroad car, and the White Sulphur Springs and Hot Springs in West Virginia and Virginia and Palm Beach, Florida, were their favorite playgrounds.

Canadian-born Harry St. Francis Black, a heavy-set, handsome, clean-shaven man with a flair for dressing well, had proved his worth as a banker in the State of Washington before coming to New York. Here, he went to work for the George A. Fuller Company, founded by George Fuller, the builders of New York's first skyscraper, the Flatiron Building at Fifth Avenue and Twenty-third Street. He also married the boss's daughter.

Fuller died in 1900, at the age of forty-nine, and the thirty-six-year-old Black succeeded him as president. It was Black's idea that a construction company could use an investment company behind it to finance its projects. By a series of mergers he succeeded in organizing the United States Realty and Improvement Company, with a capital of sixty-six million dollars, with himself as president. The Fuller Company became a wholly owned subsidiary.

Black's wife had inherited $2,500,000 at the death of her father. When the Blacks were divorced in 1905, Harry Black gave her six million dollars as her share of the estate. He later married Isabelle May, and they cut quite a swath in New York society.

Black enjoyed everything his money could buy, and in Palm Beach he met the man with the taste to supply the best of everything, Fred Sterry.

Born in Lansingburg, New York, in 1866, and reared in nearby Albany, where his father, Edwin S. Sterry, was the city's leading photographer, Fred Sterry had already distinguished himself in the hotel field when Black met him. His career began with a job at the historic United States Hotel in Saratoga Springs, famed spa and racing center, to which, every August, flocked the rich, the fashionable, and the sporting element. The contacts he made here stood him in excellent stead, as time would prove.

By the time he was twenty-seven, Sterry was managing director of the socially approved Homestead Hotel at Virginia Hot Springs. Popular as it was, under his management it achieved top rank among America's resort hotels. His skillful direction brought Sterry to the attention of millionaire Henry M. Flagler, one of John D. Rockefeller's associates in organizing the Standard Oil Company, who with the help of his Florida East Coast Railroad, was developing Florida into a great winter retreat.

Palm Beach, which was to become the richest, most fashionable winter resort in the country, was already, at the turn of the century, attracting the wealthy from the North and Midwest during the severe winter months. A small, restricted community, it was a simple place in the beginning, later distinguished by large, pseudo-Spanish architectural monstrosities inflicted in the early twenties upon susceptible millionaires by the redoubtable Addison

Mizner. Planted avenues of magnificent royal palms gave a kind of grandeur.

Recognizing the human yearning for sun and surf, commodities which Palm Beach had in abundance, Flagler built two hotels to lure more of the elite—the Royal Poinciana and the Breakers, the former on the shores of Lake Worth, the latter on the ocean front. The Poinciana is no more, but the Breakers still stands in ornate majesty at the edge of the Atlantic Ocean.

Flagler prevailed upon Sterry to undertake the management of the two hotels, while at the same time keeping his hand in at the Homestead. The still young Sterry, dividing his time between Hot Springs and Palm Beach, brought the Poinciana and the Breakers to the apex of prestige with his very special flair and helped make the name of Palm Beach synonymous with high society.

He did it by playing the role of stage director, leaving stardom to the cast. He was genial without being familiar, a tactful, suave and elegant man of impeccable taste and a passion for perfection.

While in Palm Beach, whither he journeyed each winter in his private Pullman car, Black once mentioned to Sterry that where he really belonged was in New York. "Build me my kind of a hotel and I will come," Sterry answered, with never a thought his remark would be taken seriously. The subject was dropped, but the casual exchange remained in Harry Black's mind, to be recalled by circumstances which developed some time later.

In New York, Black had long talks with Beinecke about enlarging the first Plaza, but its foundation was not strong enough to permit building on to it. Only twelve years after the opening of the eight-story hotel, the needs of New York had increased so much that they even considered building a luxury hotel elsewhere, but not for long. Shrewd businessmen and farseeing, they fully appreciated the value of the site. The city was moving uptown, with both its residential and its business life, and real estate was soaring. Fifty-ninth Street had been widened, and the horse-drawn streetcars had extended their routes. Nor were Black and Beinecke unaware of the strategic excellence of location, with Central Park as a neighbor on one side, and Fifth Avenue, already being hailed as Millionaire's Row, a "front yard," as it were. Why go elsewhere when everything here was in their favor?

The decision to tear down a structure having cost three million dollars, and only fifteen years old, to replace it with a twelve-million-dollar hotel, was typical of the gambling spirit and business acumen of the handful of men who envisioned the most elegant hotel in America.

It is possible they were spurred on by the industrial excitement of the times. The American economy had been expanding at a fantastically rapid pace, and the entire social structure was undergoing drastic change. In 1880 United States production of iron and steel totaled less than seven million tons, but the value of the country's manufactured goods was beginning to exceed its agricultural production by a wide margin. By 1900 the United States was producing nearly thirty million tons of iron and steel, and manufactured products were worth twice as much as those of the farm.

Keeping pace with the industrial and business growth of the country was the population growth in the cities. The biggest boom in people was experienced by New York; by 1900 the population explosion was such that builders could not erect hotels and houses fast enough to meet the demand; by 1907 newspapers were hailing New York as a "city of hotels." One newspaper reported that "with the largest hotel population that any city in the world has ever seen, New York continues to build hotels and to place in them improvements and luxuries few of which were dreamed of . . . a decade ago."

Beinecke and Black visualized a hotel which would be a veritable monument to the new era of industrial wealth, a place where the fabulously rich could live in splendor befitting their millions. Toward this goal they set out to raise what in today's money was the equivalent of sixty million dollars.

A full-dress rehearsal for the building of the great new Plaza was provided by the erection of the Willard Hotel in Washington. Kansas-born Paul Starrett had succeeded Black as president of the Fuller Company, and he named a fellow Kansan, Walter H.

Clough, to supervise the building of that hotel. Both had learned their trade with the Chicago architectural firm of Burnham and Root, who were responsible for the buildings of the 1893 World's Fair. They had the know-how to build superbly; they needed only the money for the new hotel.

It was a red-letter day when Beinecke, Black, Starrett and Clough sat down to luncheon with several other invited guests at Mr. Astor's fine new St. Regis Hotel, which had but recently opened its doors three blocks below the first Plaza, to discuss financing the new Plaza. For all the interest they took in the epicurean delights set before them, they could as well have had a coffee conference. They were too intent on discussion, doodling on snowy napery, making penciled notes, nodding heads or shaking bearded faces. From time to time a voice would rise in excited tones, but for the most part, this was a low-pitched, serious-toned conversation.

Suddenly a deep, authoritative voice broke the tension. "Get Fred Sterry to manage the hotel and you can count on me for all you need. I'll wager my fortune on his hotel ability."

The speaker was John "Bet-a-Million" Gates, speculator, capitalist, promoter, gambler; a Falstaffian character and already a legendary figure who had amassed millions in fantastic deals. Memory came like an electric flash to Black; he recalled Sterry's casual statement about coming to New York if a hotel were built for him, and he enthusiastically seconded Gates's suggestion. The tradition had grown of financial success to anyone who joined the Gates bandwagon, giving a persuasiveness to any project he proposed. With alacrity all agreed with his proposal to get Fred Sterry as supervisor and manager of the new Plaza to come.

Already the sweet smell of success was in the air.

Gates's great talent lay in promotion, in addition to which he possessed an extraordinary money sense. Born in West Chicago, he started out as a grocery clerk, then joined a St. Louis wire-manufacturing company as a twenty-five-dollar-a-week salesman. The first test of his salesmanship came when he went down to Texas to try to interest the ranchers in buying barbed wire for fencing. Nothing doing; rail fencing was good enough for them.

But not for nothing was Gates nicknamed Bet-a-Million. The gambling spirit was in his blood, and he set out to gamble on his barbed wire. He rented a large area of vacant land, built a corral, surrounded it with the wire, and challenged the ranchers to let their liveliest, most ornery steers test its endurance. The wire emerged the victor, and orders came pouring in.

Before long, through sheer business audacity, Gates controlled the barbed-wire industry. In 1880, when he was only twenty-five years old, he succeeded in promoting the formation of the American Steel and Wire Company of New Jersey, with a capitalization of ninety million dollars. He promoted other steel companies and then sold them to the Morgan bank for millions. A live wire, they called him; he gave hilarious parties and would gamble on anything, even which of two raindrops on a window would reach the sill first.

He and J. P. Morgan conducted a running enmity, and it took Morgan to teach Gates about doors. The great Morgan never disguised his dislike of the lusty, pleasure-loving Gates, and once opposed a plan to name Gates as president of a certain steel company. "You get into the newspapers too much," said the publicity-shy Morgan. "It is neither dignified nor good for business."

"I don't do anything you don't do," retorted Gates. "Only, you do it behind closed doors."

"That's what doors are for," Morgan answered dryly.

Gates became one of the directors of the United States Realty Company, together with Beinecke, Clough, Starrett, and George Fuller, Jr., following that historic luncheon conference. Fred Sterry was called in at once.

The first Plaza bestowed a distinguished heritage on the next Plaza to come. Yet no one wept when demolition began in 1905. There was too much curiosity, excitement and speculation about the new hotel. There was no fear the giants at work would be undercapitalized. They were ready, willing and able to create the finest of everything, and they spared no expense to get it.

Like everything else these men attempted, they reached for the top when selecting the architect for their grand new hotel. And the top was Henry Janeway Hardenbergh, who had already proved himself to the United States Realty Company as the architect of the Willard Hotel in Washington.

A descendant of one of the early Dutch families to come to New York in the middle of the seventeenth century, settling at Fort Orange, New York, later renamed Albany, Henry Hardenbergh had a distinguished cultural as well as family background. Born on February 6, 1847, in New Brunswick, New Jersey, son of John and Frances Eddy Hardenbergh, he was a great-great-grandson of the Reverend Jacob Retsen Hardenbergh, one of the founders and first president of Queens (later Rutgers) College in New Brunswick.

Hardenbergh began his career in the office of Detlef Lienau, who had been educated at the École des Beaux Arts in Paris under the famous *Néo-Grec* architect Henri Labrouste. The classical training of his master undoubtedly preserved Hardenbergh from the worst faults of the then fashionable Victorian Gothic. He began to design large city buildings in the late 1880's, which thereafter furnished the bulk of his practice. Joining the American Institute of Architects in 1867, he was elected a Fellow in 1877. He was a founder of the American Fine Arts Society and the Municipal Art Society and became an associate of the National Academy of Design in 1910.

What few knew about the distinguished architect was his suppressed desire to be an actor. This was revealed by the late Judge S. D. McConnell, at a dinner honoring Hardenbergh. "He was once a tragedian," said McConnell, "and I am told he has sometimes regretted that he ever forsook the footlights. He threw up the choice of becoming a great Hamlet and became an architect."

It is doubtful that his histrionic abilities could ever have matched his genius as an architect. Hardenbergh became one of the outstanding hotel architects of his time in the country—designer of such great hostelries as the Waldorf and the Astoria, later to join as the famed Waldorf-Astoria; the Manhattan Hotel at 42nd Street and Madison Avenue, styled in adaptation of the house of Francis I in Paris; the Raleigh in Washington, the old Martinique in New York, the Copley-Plaza in Boston, a United

States Realty property, and the French Renaissance addition to the Windsor in Montreal.

One of his greatest triumphs was not a hotel but an apartment building. For millionaires who wished all the appurtenances of city living in what was then still the countryside, Hardenbergh in 1884 designed the Dakota Apartments at Seventy-second Street and Central Park West, and it is a mark of his architectural distinction that the Dakota, still the home of outstanding celebrities, stands today a Manhattan landmark, while hundreds of newer apartment buildings have been torn down to make way for more "modern" structures. In this building, his talent for compelling composition, coupled with the free use of historical style, first achieved a complete and lasting synthesis.

For the new Plaza Hardenbergh chose the French Renaissance. In adapting the architectural style to his purpose his first concern was perspective. With modest rejection of the first person, he later explained that "an earnest effort was made to embrace the opportunity offered by the exceptional site to allow the building to be viewed in its entirety from many points of view and considerable distances."

Fräuleins and nannies airing their charges in Central Park must have wondered about the tall, slender, reflective gentleman with the bald head, starched high collar and pearl stickpin sauntering through the park gazing over the treetops and into the sky. He saw more than they did; he envisioned a great, elegant French château, eighteen stories high—a mirage fast taking definite shape in his mind.

To give the building base the necessary suggestion of solidity, he planned three stories of marble in bold lines and projections; eight stories above that were to be left bare of ornamentation. From this height his design broke out in balconies, loggias, gables and *tourelles,* with a deeply sloping mansard roof crowning the whole.

Within, he provided eight hundred rooms and five hundred baths, a multiplicity of plumbing sufficient to turn the Saturday-night bath habit into the American fetish for daily showers.

New Yorkers were overwhelmed to learn that the plans provided two whole floors of rooms for public functions, and private suites of fourteen to seventeen rooms. This was no response to popular demand. The builders created the demand, and altered fashions in living by the facilities they offered, refinements of luxury which reconciled even the most confirmed lover of home life to a stay in a hotel.

Men like Beinecke and Black radiated confidence; Gates would gamble on anything. With men like Hardenbergh and Sterry on the team, they could depend on the likes of Starrett and Clough to erect the hotel in record time.

It wasn't easy. In excavating for the new hotel the builders found that some of the pilings for the first Plaza terminated in quicksand and bog, while others had been driven to solid rock and hammered until the lower ends curled up like hooks. According to Hardenbergh, "the new foundation was not completed until it became part and parcel of the eternal anchorage of Manhattan." A statement that became a prophecy.

The George A. Fuller Company completed the building in a record of two years, and on schedule—a feat even in an era not plagued by strikes and labor troubles. Equally remarkable was the efficiency with which every detail of furnishing the hotel was completed.

Even as the old Plaza was being demolished, Sterry called in E. F. Pooley, the interior decorator, to help plan the interior furnishings. Pooley first dispatched a member of his staff to Europe to explore the Old World for all the great furniture and accessories and embellishments it could contribute. With his lengthy report in hand, Beinecke, Hardenbergh, Sterry and Pooley himself later took off on a buying trip.

In Belfast they paused to order a hundred thousand dollars' worth of Irish linen. These linens were exclusively designed for The Plaza and manufactured by William Lidell of Belfast, winner of gold medals at the Chicago and St. Louis World Fairs, and, indeed, at all expositions since the Civil War.

In Switzerland they purchased the embroidered organdy for bedroom curtains that cost $145 a pair. Hardenbergh, to achieve his effects, had not been held to creating enough windows of the same size to make it feasible to order finished curtains in bulk.

At the famed house of Baccarat in France, the travelers found the glassware for the dining rooms and ordered it etched with their own designs. French tapestries and brocades, Savonnerie rugs, Louis XVI furniture—nothing was too good for The Plaza. The largest single order in history for gold-encrusted china was placed with L. Straus & Sons. W. & J. Sloane, then located at Broadway and Nineteenth Street, supplied the carpets and rugs, all made to order. The Savonnerie rugs for the lobbies were handwoven. Four magnificent Aubusson rugs were ordered for the ballroom when it was not in use for dancing.

Little wallpaper was needed, for it was Fred Sterry's conviction that paneled walls with plaster moldings were the only proper background for the high-ceilinged rooms. Walls were painted in soft tones of gray, cream, yellow or rose. These paneled walls are still a lovely feature of Plaza rooms.

The flat silver was made with the soon-to-be-famous insignia of the hotel, two *P*'s back to back, adorning every piece. The candelabra and candlesticks were designed in the period of Louis XVI. Together they totaled four thousand pieces and cost over three hundred thousand dollars.

Vying in sumptuousness with the furnishings were the lighting effects indoors and out. No less than 1,650 crystal chandeliers were bought for overhead illumination. Glittering brackets were attached to the wall. Shiploads of material were imported from Europe to achieve the effect of a French château, within and without, except for one public room, the baronial Oak Lounge, which was paneled with massive carvings of British oak (*Quercus robur*), the same type of fine wood used for the tomb of Edward the Confessor in Westminster Abbey. Ten elevators, an extravagant number for 1907, were installed, and the five grand staircases were lined with gleaming marble, so fine that all are still in excellent condition today.

The mechanical marvels also made the public gasp: a water-filtering system capable of supplying 1,500,000 gallons a day; thirteen electrical dumb waiters, subject to push-button control, to provide almost instant delivery of hot meals from the kitchens to rooms as high as the eighteenth floor; an ice-making machine that could produce fifteen tons of ice a day; a garbage destroyer capable of sorting out and separating silverware and other objects which might have accidently been thrown out.

The promoters had thought of everything. Without having taken a single shortcut, they were on the last mile.

CHAPTER THREE

The Age of the Moguls

THE Plaza came into being in an era of extravagant gestures. Since the late nineteenth century a seemingly never-ending army of newly minted millionaires from all over the country had been invading New York, bringing with them fabulous fortunes amassed in the copper mines of Montana, the gold mines of California, the Comstock lode of Nevada, the abattoirs of Chicago, the timberlands of Michigan, the oil gushers of Kansas and Oklahoma, the railways that had opened up new frontiers.

With them they also brought keen appetites for a grandiose life and ambitious wives with a yearning to get into "society." They had the money to do it, and they went at it with a vengeance. By the turn of the century, Manhattan could boast the greatest population of millionaires in the country. A private house on Fifth Avenue became the coveted status symbol of the new rich; a great marble mansion on Ocean Drive at Newport the crowning point of their careers and ambitions. A seagoing yacht helped.

They built ornate brownstones or impressive limestone *palazzi,* many of them architectural monstrosities, others of exquisite design, such as the Henry Clay Frick home, now a museum. By the turn of the century, Fifth Avenue was known the country over as "Millionaire's Row," and Newport as "The queen of American resorts."

The Gilded Age took hold, rapidly obliterating the well-ordered routine of the Mauve Decade. The afternoon drive in the family equipage up Fifth Avenue to Central Park was still a daily ritual with conservative old families, but the gasoline buggies of the new rich and the daring young scions of the Old Guard were frightening more and more horses; silk-hatted gentlemen and their ladies paraded to church on Sunday, but the country weekend at estates along the Hudson Valley and on Long Island, holidays in the Berkshire hills, were growing lures; the cotillion still held sway at a charity ball, but the waltz was the real craze; the traditional, ever-so-correct assemblies at the Waldorf-Astoria remained the most exclusive social events, but "monkey dinners" and extravagant fancy-dress balls costing thousands of dollars were proving to be much more fun.

A "new" society burst into full flower—a society composed of Vanderbilts, Carnegies, Whitneys, Oelrichses, Belmonts, Goulds, Rockefellers, Harrimans, and the like—names which were already household words throughout the nation.

While Mrs. William Backhouse Astor remained the acknowledged leader of New York society until her death in 1908, the revolt against the dull proprieties of the Victorian era had become more and more effective as rich and vigorous new hostesses were hailed for their lavish entertainments in the ballrooms of their pretentious New York town houses or fabulous Newport palaces. The social game was being played for all it was worth; conspicuous wealth was paraded without apology. If you were rich, you splurged, and no one thought the worse of it or cared what the moral cost.

It is doubtful if ever in the history of the country was there a period to equal such excessive extravagances and vulgar ostentation, such numerous and lavish private entertainments.

The society columns of the day gave full and effusive treatment to the fabulous soirees.

But the year 1907 was also producing other interesting newspaper headlines. In the White House, President Theodore Roosevelt was assaulting the "malefactors of great wealth" and advocating an income tax . . . Secretary of State Elihu Root instituted the political "good-will tour" by making one to Mexico . . . Oklahoma was admitted as the forty-sixth state to join the union . . . an army balloon remained in the air at Princess Anne, Maryland, for four hours, but its proud boast was punctured by dispatches from Friedrichshafen in Germany with the startling news that an aircraft piloted by one Count von Zeppelin had managed to remain aloft for seven hours. . . . The *Lusitania,* largest steamship in the world, the newest sensation of the twentieth century, arrived in New York Harbor in September on her maiden voyage, setting a record speed of five days, fifty-four minutes, between Queenstown and New York.

In the theater and literary worlds purity was being protected. Elinor Glyn's naughty novel *Three Weeks,* which popularized the word "it" as a symbol of sex appeal, was banned in Boston. But in spite of this, fifty thousand copies were sold in less than three weeks. . . . People talked in shocked tones about Richard Strauss's opera *Salome,* which in its first American performance at the Metropolitan, with Olive Fremstad in the title role, brought such an outburst of public indignation that further performances were canceled. . . . The oriental philosophy of Omar Khayyám was at the height of popularity, and the *Rubáiyát* sold in the thousands. The limp leather volume became a favorite decoration for the parlor table, and young lovers sighed, "Ah, Wilderness were Paradise enow!"

On Broadway it was a golden year for the theater. Franz Lehár's *Merry Widow* was playing at the New Amsterdam Theatre on West Forty-second Street . . . Florenz Ziegfeld literally topped it by presenting on the roof of the same theater the first of the Ziegfeld Follies, featuring "the most beautiful girls in the world" . . . The MacDowell Colony was founded in Peterborough, New Hampshire, to encourage and assist writers, artists and composers, and the Fifth Avenue Association was organized in the interests and protection of the most fashionable avenue in the land.

New York, circa 1907, was a city of two moods—paradoxically, both exciting and serene, yet both moods merging in the spirit of the times. All seemed right with a rich and promising world, with nothing more catastrophic than some runaway horses upsetting their wagons when frightened by infernal motor machines. If there were undercurrent rumblings of impending troubles in Wall Street, only a few of the financial *cognoscenti* recognized the signs, knew it and were on the *qui vive*—on that glamorous October day when The Plaza opening took place.

The directors of The Plaza were aware, before the opening, of the disturbing indications of an economic earthquake. The Tennessee Coal and Iron Company was in trouble; the City of New York was rumored, *sub rosa,* to be on the verge of bankruptcy. J. P. Morgan had quietly called in John Warner Gates, one of the builders of The Plaza, and several other financiers to discuss what appeared to be an impending crash. But no word of this could be leaked to the public. It could cause panic. Everything was to go along as planned.

On the day before the opening Fred Sterry gave a luncheon for the outstanding hotel men of New York and a dinner that evening for a handpicked group of about a hundred guests, including tenants who had rented permanent apartments at the hotel, a specially selected group representing the magazine and newspaper press, and a number of distinguished public officials.

The first toast of the evening, by Frank Presbrey, was to Bernhard Beinecke and the directors of the United States Realty and Improvement Company for their "foresight and financial bravery." Glasses clinked again to the genius of Henry Hardenbergh and his greatest architectural triumph, The Plaza.

"There is nothing to compare with it on earth," raved Judge McConnell, general counsel of the George A. Fuller Company. If he was swept away by the occasion, he was not the only one.

After dinner Sterry, as he had done earlier in the day with the bonifaces, conducted the guests on a guided tour of the hotel, and the press kept faith with its public the next day with a blast of publicity that was heard around the world. What had begun as an inspection tour, by morning had turned into a tidal wave of news.

"The great eighteen-story building was lighted from top to bottom," reported the *New York World.* "But the exterior gave only a faint hint of the glorious interior. Marble and gold and wonderful tapestries vied with each other at dazzling the sight, under thousands of electric lights."

The great marble foyer with its fine rugs; the exquisite china and elegant silver service, the gleaming crystal chandeliers, the mosaic floors, the magnificent Tea Court facing Fifth Avenue, finished in Caen stone and Breche violet marble, with a high Tiffany dome of harmoniously tinted glass; the marble mantels in the beautifully appointed rooms, the great kitchens, the handsome restaurants—all were described in glowing detail.

Of all the wonders of the hotel the ballroom created the greatest sensation. All white and gold, with huge crystal chandeliers, and panels on the walls covered with exquisite yellow silk, the room was ringed on all sides by a balcony equally resplendent in white and gold decor. What fascinated everyone was the section at the south end of the room, which was lowered in five minutes to the level that transformed it into a forty-five-by-eighteen-foot stage for dramatic or musical performances. It was a mechanical marvel; nothing like it had ever before been heard of, no less seen.

Cornices of some public rooms were decorated with real gold leaf, at a total cost of twenty-seven thousand dollars; the effect was so blinding, however, that several days after the opening Sterry had the precious gold leaf covered with bronze varnish at the request of guests who thought it too glittering. Greater love hath no manager for his flock.

Estimates of the cost of the hotel soared as high as seventeen million dollars, probably inspired by Frank Presbrey's statement at the preview dinner that the directors of the hotel had "voted millions more than the original estimate called for." The owners, however, were quick to deny that they had exceeded their original budget. The hotel cost twelve million dollars—and that was that.

The press continued, day after day, to extol the luxury of the great new hostelry, as reporters discovered more and more news items. *The New York Times* listed the first tenants neither alphabetically nor in line of prestige, but in order of their reported incomes—and again the Vanderbilts came in first. One writer estimated that "when sleep time came to The Plaza each night . . .

$387,000,000 worth of slumber would be represented." How this odd figure was arrived at is one of the unsolved mysteries of the twentieth century.

"FIFTY MILLION DOLLARS OF HOTELS" was the banner headline over a full-page montage in another newspaper, with illustrations of New York's ten most expensive hotels, dominated by a huge photograph of The Plaza. Price tags attached to each hotel illustrated the fact that The Plaza exceeded all in cost—even the combined cost of nine million dollars for the St. Regis and the Gotham. "It takes a thousand people to run the Plaza," headlined another story.

The then fantastic rates were printed for the edification of the masses. All unprecedented elegances considering, they weren't so bad. Single rooms were priced at $2.50 to $4 without bath, $3 to $6 with; double rooms were $6 to $10; suites cost $12 to $20 per day, and for from $16 to $25 per day a transient could obtain a suite with parlor, two bedrooms and two baths.

Ninety percent of The Plaza was reserved for permanent guests, ten for transients. Within fifty years the situation was to be reversed. Curiously enough, permanent guests were charged more than transients, percentagewise. The stiff rental prices were designed to keep undesirables of possible permanence out.

So far as the newsmen of the day could see, a room at The Plaza cost as much for one night as a shopgirl earned in a week, but the Philadelphia *North American* attempted to soothe its readers with the observation that the annual rental price "is not really in excess of what it would cost to maintain a Fifth Avenue home."

With arched brows the newspapers reported that Plaza tenants, between them, owned two hundred automobiles, worth a total of $1,200,000. Cornelius K. G. Billings, the financier, was reported as owning twenty of different makes, and chauffeurs were described as living at the hotel as "the pampered servants of the rich with nothing too good for them so long as they can drive the devil machines of the rich." The French chauffeur of one tenant was sketched reclining on a velvet couch in his own private apartment, ordering champagne. So far the chauffeurs had no personal valets, but the writer speculated the time might come. The social commentators of the day could forgive the rich their wealth, but not the sin of sharing it so unevenly.

The height of journalistic hysteria was reached when an enterprising editor published a mock-up photograph of the Central Park side of the hotel, where the most desirable apartments were located, with cutouts identifying several specific apartments of the multimillionaires by name. Head shots of the wives were superimposed on each to give more impressive identification. It was a perfect blueprint for any adventurous raffles.

Two weeks after the opening the newspapers again splurged with superlatives in reporting the first great public celebration at The Plaza, The Pilgrims' Dinner, on October 15, to honor the Lord Bishop of London, the Right Reverend Arthur Foley Winnington-Ingram, spiritual adviser to King Edward VII. Since this was the first large banquet of The Pilgrims of the United States, which had been organized in 1903, it was an occasion doubly worthy of reams of linotype.

Several hundred of democracy's nobility paid $15 a ticket to attend the stag dinner and to see the English cleric who had but recently beaten President Theodore Roosevelt in a rigorous game of tennis, and gleefully boasted of it. Assistant Secretary of the Navy Truman Newberry came from Washington for the event; Senator Chauncey M. Depew, with his bright whiskers and sparkling wit, graced the long dais on the balcony-lowered stage of the ballroom.

Ignoring the Lord Bishop's disapproval of liquor, Nicholas Murray Butler, the forty-five-year-old president of Columbia University, toasted him in champagne. If anyone besides the Lord Bishop refrained from imbibing, he missed the joy of sampling some of the finest vintage wines, which flowed throughout the banquet: Brauneberger, Viño de Pasto, Pontet Canet and Beaune. Industrial giants, financiers and socialites for their $15 dined on a ten-course epicurean repast rich enough to cause the beginning of gout in those who were not already inflicted with that "rich man's disease."

The menu was, of course, printed in the newspapers, and several editors, fully aware that the majority of its readers were not knowledgeable even of "menu French" in a Berlitz-less era, gave the English translation of this repast:

Huîtres

Tortue verte Oloroso Crème Argenteuil
Amandes Salées Feuilles Farcies Céleri, Olives
Diablotin à la duchesse
Flétan farci de Homard Newburg
Pommes de terre persillade
Filets de Boeuf à l'Arlequin
Haricots verts sautés au beurre
Médaillon suédois
Perdreaux rôtis sur canapé
Salade Panachée

Glacè Napolitaine
Petits fours Gaufrettes aux amandes
Sweets Pièce montée
Café

And so it went, day after day, with reporters and photographers on watch for every exciting item of news they could glean.

But a sad new day was dawning, and the press soon changed its tune. Financial storm clouds were gathering, and on October 21, lightning struck. The Knickerbocker Trust Company collapsed; the panic was on, sparked by a run on the bank which lasted until its reserves ran out in less than two days. Other banks throughout the country were also forced to close.

Financiers of the day, including "Bet-a-Million" Gates, were among those conferring for weeks in the study of J. P. Morgan, in a mighty move to halt the panic. But not until early November were they able to stem the tide. By November 2, the worse seemed over when Morgan and his group combined resources to import a hundred million dollars in gold from Europe.

But the damage was done. Depression deepened the poverty of

the masses; many of the rich were seriously affected, and those who were not, sharply pulled in their horns. The spree of giddy intoxication with the splendors of The Plaza turned into denunciation of the millions "squandered" on it. The same newspapers which had sung its praises now shouted deprecations; the rave reviews curdled into editorials against the conspicuous spending epitomized by the hotel.

Was history repeating itself? The first Plaza had ruined its builders. Would the new Plaza drag its backers down the drain? They had tremendous resources, it was true, yet even if all the individuals involved weathered the storm, there was danger that the splendid hotel, born in luxury and nurtured with exquisite care, might fall victim to the financial depression. The hotel was fully booked long, long in advance, but for how long would guests be able to pay rentals of twenty-five thousand dollars a year and more?

They soon learned. Some of the city's rich continued to live high on the hog, but at The Plaza three hundred thousand dollars' worth of bookings were canceled. It was not only a bitter blow; it could be serious enough to prove catastrophic.

With admirable faith and determination not to lower their standards, the operators of The Plaza never bowed to the public outcry for austerity to match the gloom. On the contrary, they recognized the fact that the hotel could go under unless it held steadfast and lived up to its original concept of the *ne plus ultra* in elegance and service, a place to attract the wealthy who still had wealth. If they could just hold on, recovery was bound to come. Here was the test; it took courage.

Fred Sterry had all of that, and he had the wholehearted backing of his board of directors. Instead of compromising, cutting corners, lowering rates and restaurant prices, reducing its staff, The Plaza recharged its energies. Sterry continued to make trips to Europe to bring back the greatest of delicacies and the finest of wines; the most correct service was maintained with the help of dedicated personnel, as every effort was made to keep up the high standards of the hotel.

But with his rare instinct, Fred Sterry knew that something more was needed to keep the hotel going, to bring whatever business was still to be had to his caravansary, rather than to any other. What The Plaza needed, as it would never need again, was a social entrepreneur to lend éclat by giving the smartest of parties and entertainments for the most fashionable of society's elect. It would follow, as a natural sequence, that they, when entertaining, would do so at the most fashionable place in town, The Plaza.

In Frederick Townsend Martin, Sterry found his man.

CHAPTER FOUR

One Man in His Time

THE "Four Hundred" of Mrs. Astor's day had their Ward McAllister. Proper Victorians bowed on cue from their social arbiter of New York and Newport, who avowed that only Mrs. Astor's guest list of four hundred, just the number who could be accommodated in the ballroom of her town house, mattered in New York society.

More than half a century later the International Set danced to the tune of the extraordinary Elsa Maxwell; the tune, a medley of heterogeneous celebrities, social and theatrical, and the more mixed, the merrier.

In between these two remarkable characters who made partying their life mission was the *arbiter elegantiarum* of the Edwardian era, Frederick Townsend Martin. In him the lavish-living Edwardians had a social impresario of impeccable background, so splendid and fastidiously fashionable that an invitation from him became a mark of immediate social acceptance. His special contribution, in an era when actors and actresses were socially out of bounds, was to break down a prejudice against stage people by introducing the proper Edwardians to the shimmering stars of the theater and the arts—in the most carefully selected fashion. The Plaza became his bright particular bailiwick.

A fascinating tale of personal triumph emerges from a life of contradictions. Freddy Martin, born to wealth and social position, became the friend of Skid Row derelicts and a subject of veneration for the society reporters. He entertained the cream of society and the not always deserving poor, while the less colorful enjoyed it all vicariously. While cultivating royalty, he wrote books denouncing those of his class—the idle rich, the social climbers, the snobs.

His enthusiasms ranged from slumming to collecting family crests from stationery. On his way to the opera, he would drive by a pawnshop to retrieve some poor old woman's household possession.

The discretion of all concerned was such that there remains no proof The Plaza ever paid Martin a dime. Nor is there any doubt that he cost the Plaza plenty.

Town Topics, a naughty keyhole publication, gave the clue by publishing a story that the managers of the new Plaza "apparently" had secured the services of Frederick Townsend Martin as "social organizer and agent in general." A newspaper columnist reported that Martin was paid on a percentage basis for the celebrities he drew to the Plaza, and irreverently compared him to a circus barker.

Martin was much more. By the time he came to The Plaza he was a dignified bachelor socialite, aged fifty-eight, intimate of society leaders on two continents, a host of distinction. Whether he needed the money has been debated. He inherited wealth. He also spent it lavishly. Regardless of money, the job he undertook was a challenge, to help save The Plaza from the disastrous consequences of the panic of 1907. As his accomplishments show, he did much to assure its success, to establish its social popularity and prestige.

Freddy Martin's father, Henry Hull Martin, a leading lawyer and banker from Albany, New York, was as dignified as he was wealthy. His mother, Frances Townsend Martin, needed no ladder of social rungs; she had an established and assured position in the New York and Newport of pre-Civil War days.

The Martin boys, as boys will be, were irrepressible. For years brother Bradley, older than Freddy, stole the show. From Bradley,

Freddy learned how to give a ball, and from Bradley's mistakes he learned even more.

Mrs. Bradley Martin has gone down in social history as the socialite who created sensational headlines as the hostess of two extravagant balls, equaled seldom before and seldom after. Early in the 1880's, the Martins gave a great Circus Ball, and Freddy joyfully shared the wine with the coachmen and the footmen waiting in the cold. The horse chauffeurs imbibed so generously that many departing guests found no one in condition to drive the equipage home. Freddy did not escape blame from the columnists, or the ridicule of the public.

On February 10, 1897, the Bradley Martins gave the ball to end all balls, the fabulous Versailles Ball at the old Waldorf-Astoria, which stirred up such a storm of protest for its extravagance that the Martins were practically forced to flee abroad.

As Freddy defensively told the story years later, it was a drab winter in Manhattan when his brother thought to brighten it by giving a concert. His wife, observing that this would serve to give employment only to a "few foreigners" who would play or sing, came up with the idea of having a fancy-dress ball—but to issue invitations on such short notice that the guests would have to obtain their costumes quickly in New York instead of going to Paris for them—so helpful for the local tradespeople.

If Mrs. Bradley Martin did not actually originate the notion of pump priming for charity, Freddy Martin justified it in his explanation of how it happened.

The ballroom of the Waldorf-Astoria had never presented such a magnificent sight. At a cost of twenty-five thousand dollars, the Martins had it transformed into a replica of Versailles, with a backdrop of rare tapestries, orchids, roses, and huge arrangements of growing greens to form formal hedges—the whole illuminated by thousands of softly glowing lights. Mrs. Martin, gowned as Mary Stuart, dazzled her court in a gold-embroidered creation trimmed with pearls and other precious stones. Her husband, disdaining the role of Mary Stuart's sickly husband, Francis II, appeared resplendent in court brocade as Louis XV.

Having adorned their ladies with priceless gems, the gentlemen dazzled them by wearing diamond buttons. Mr. August Belmont took the honors for the men in a suit of gold-inlaid armor valued even then at ten thousand dollars. Miss Anne Morgan supplied a note of barbaric color by arriving as Pocahontas.

"The power of wealth with its refinement, and its vulgarity, was everywhere," Freddy Martin later described the scene in a revelation of his schizophrenia. As for the flowers, he said, "The fragrance was like incense burned on the altar of the Golden Calf."

He might have known, though he confessed he never could understand it, that the Church would not approve. Granted that the tradespeople benefited, the clergy thought the guests might have done better to drop a few diamond buttons in the collection plate. Some of the guests were to leave great fortunes to charity when they died, but this was before it became fashionable for millionaires to be philanthropic with millions during their lifetime.

Headlines described every elegant and extravagant aspect of the ball. In the pulpit the clergy raged, editorial writers took up the cry, and an outraged public stormed. But the sharpest sword was ridicule. Cartooned and literally mocked out of the country, the Martins retreated to a hunting lodge in Scotland and never came back. Their daughter married an English lord and thus Uncle Freddy Martin obtained his entrée to English society.

In American society, Freddy stood his ground and did the correct thing at the correct seasons of the year in the correct places. In Palm Beach, he did much to ensure the social success of soirees given by Mrs. Henry M. Flagler, whose husband built the two hotels operated by Fred Sterry. Freddy Martin's talents properly impressed Sterry.

By 1907 Freddy Martin was a short, stout man with thinning brown hair, always dressed in good taste, but no dandy. His enthusiasm for people—all sorts of people, from pretty actresses to dowagers, from elevator boys to potentates—won him many friends. Riding up in the Plaza elevator to escort a princess to dinner, he would tease the Irish elevator boy about his great shock of black hair and suggest they trade.

Martin's first great social coup was in the early winter of 1908, and The Plaza again made nationwide headlines.

The outstanding event of that season in New York—as in all seasons—was the opening night at the Metropolitan. Naturally, Mr. and Mrs. George Jay Gould had a box, No. 12, and in top hat and opera cape went Freddy Martin as their guest. The conversation during entr'actes touched, as conversations often do, on the subject of friendship, and all agreed it depends on deeds, not words.

"Freddy," said Mrs. Gould, "I'll prove I'm one of your best friends. I will act in a private play for you, if you will make arrangements for a tea. This is something special, you know, because Mr. Gould doesn't care for me to do any acting, but I'm sure he'll agree to this."

As an actress who had appeared in comedy roles on Broadway, the former Edith Kingdon of Brooklyn had consented to give up the stage when, in 1886, she became the bride of multimillionaire George Gould. By 1907 she was not only one of the reigning beauties of society, but a famed hostess. But nostalgia for the stage never left her.

After some urging, Mr. Gould agreed to the idea of his wife's appearing in a private theatrical performance, and gleefully Mrs. Gould and Martin began planning for a tea gathering with not more than two hundred guests invited to see Mrs. Gould perform.

Elisabeth Marbury, society play-broker, who, together with Elsie deWolfe, later to marry Sir Charles Mendl, and Mrs. William K. Vanderbilt, was instrumental in establishing Sutton Place as a fashionable neighborhood by taking up residence there, sent Freddy nineteen plays to choose from. Their choice settled on *Mrs. Van Vechten's Divorce Dance,* a one-act play by Edward Van Zile. The plot was simple. Mrs. Van Vechten is giving a dance to celebrate the first anniversary of her divorce from her husband, and has hired the detective who secured the evidence to guard her fortune in jewels while the dance is in progress. Through a comedy of errors she and her husband are reconciled.

There were just three parts, and Mme. Nordica, the distinguished diva, made headlines by volunteering to play the role of

Mrs. Gould's maid in the play. Next, Mme. Nordica made headlines by withdrawing from the cast, having failed to get a release from the San Carlo Opera Company in Chicago. Her role was taken by Mrs. Francis Pruyn of Albany, where the name Pruyn was synonymous with "first families."

The ups and downs of rehearsal—every up, every down—made news and built tension. The clamor for invitations rose day by day —the fact that matinee idol Kyrle Bellew, star of *The Thief,* then playing on Broadway, was to have the male lead opposite Mrs. Gould but added to the excitement and the appeals for tickets.

The day the guest list reached six hundred (and sixteen years after Mrs. Astor's ball the population explosion left no chance of reducing it to four hundred), Freddy wrote a letter to the *Times* to print, urging the ladies to come hatless or be prepared to remove their hats to permit those behind them to see. Naturally the *Times* printed it.

On the afternoon of January 24, 1908, the most elegant carriages in Manhattan and the new automobiles of the elite formed a line in the direction of Fifty-ninth Street and Fifth Avenue that suggested the opening of the opera. Outriders of mounted police and an inner guard of patrolmen and footmen in hotel livery defended the main entrance. The steps of The Plaza were freckled with major-domos; detectives of the Pinkerton and Park Row corps eyed each other suspiciously.

In the elevators talk centered on whether or not to remove hats, the most flamboyant hats French designers ever succeeded in foisting on American womanhood. Some ladies heeded Martin's plea and left their enormous chapeaus in the ladies' parlor; the majority sailed into the ballroom in full plumage to the chagrin of women now hatless and the consternation of the men—of whom there was a considerable number present.

Young and radiant Ethel Barrymore, the dramatic star of the play *Alice Sit by the Fire,* wore the largest hat of all. It did not obstruct the view; she occupied a box. La Barrymore was upstaged by the lady who wore six pins in her hat, three of them with diamond heads the size of pigeon eggs. Everybody who was anybody among the women wore orchids; those who wore gardenias were suspect.

The most eligible young men in New York stood ready, in black velvet knickerbockers and velvet jackets embroidered in gold, to escort the guests to their seats. They included Bradley Martin, Jr., Frederick Martin Davies, Kingdon Gould, son of the star; Bertram Cruger, William Whitehouse, Stephen Van Rensselaer, Rupert W. K. Anderson, Seymour Johnson, and two Englishmen of the Honorable variety—Reginald A. Fellowes and J. J. Astley. Anyone who knew their society needed no introduction to their names.

Whatever was happening behind the curtain, a big show went on in front, with society in the cast. Mrs. Payne Whitney wore a hat of osprey feathers. The dowager Mrs. Vanderbilt (Mrs. Cornelius of the château across the street), wore mauve chiffon trimmed in sable; another Mrs. Vanderbilt—Mrs. William K.—wore a black velvet coat costume with a white lace jabot and a large hat of white crim with white plumes; Mrs. Ogden Mills was in royal purple velvet, as befitted one born to the purple, combined with sable; Maxine Elliott, stately and magnificent, loomed amid a crown of chatterers; Elinor Glyn settled the momentous question of hat or no hat: being a guest of the hotel, she had left hers in her suite.

The assemblage was out of a society editor's dream; a combination of *Social Register, The Blue Book,* Burke's *Peerage* and *Who's Who in America.*

Present from Broadway in addition to La Barrymore were Margaret Illington, Augustin Daly, in whose company Edith Kingdon Gould had once acted, and Daniel Frohman, who had "loaned" the male star, Bellew. To add international glamour, there were present a Mr. J. deThal, gentleman-in-waiting to the Czar of Russia; Fernando Mesia y Stuart, a nephew of the Empress Eugénie; the Countess Denes Szechenyi, whose son was to marry Gladys Vanderbilt a few days later; Viscount Middleton, Count Paul Esterházy, Count Anton Sigray—the printed list was formidable.

At five o'clock the curtains were pulled aside by George Jay

Gould, Jr., and Arthur Hamilton, dressed as pages in rich Colonial costumes. The audience gasped, then applauded the scene—a Louis XV boudoir replete with a dressing table Marie Antoinette reportedly had used in the Trianon Palace. Every piece was an *objet d'art*. Lord Duveen, the art dealer, freely admitted that he had loaned the tapestry chairs and some of the pictures on the wall, and had given personal attention to carrying out the ensemble of a perfect Louis XV boudoir. The bureau loaned by him was worth four thousand dollars. ". . . but please," said Lord Duveen to a *Herald* reporter, "don't mention the price. It sounds so shoppy." Needless to say, the reporter ignored the request.

The French maid, on stage when the curtains parted, tantalized the audience with her lines, and tension built until Mrs. Gould made her grand entrance to an outburst of applause. Her appearance revealed a carefully guarded secret, the gown she had chosen for the occasion. It was of rose-point lace covering cream satin and chiffon and profusely trimmed in pearls. Around her throat and descending almost to the waist was the star's famed rope of egg-sized oriental pearls—and from the jewel case reposing conspicuously on the dressing table splashed pearl and diamond chokers, emeralds and diamonds worth a fortune, all Mrs. Gould's own personal gems.

"Mrs. Van Vechten" immediately realizes that the detective she has hired to guard her jewels during the dance isn't the right man. She levels a revolver at his back; imagine her surprise to discover, by a coincidence so prevalent in stage plays, that the "detective" is her former husband, eager for a reconciliation, who had arranged with the real detective to take his place. His persuasiveness wins her over, especially when he suggests the novel idea that they enter the ballroom together and surprise the guests.

To one of the lines that she was not "modern," Mrs. Gould brought laughs with the retort, "I got my divorce in New York." This, of course, was no laughing matter in real life in 1908, when a divorcee was looked upon as something of a social leper in most circles. It was to take fifty-eight years longer, and countless bitter controversies later, before the state amended the law to recognize other factors besides proof of adultery as grounds for divorce.

The climax of the play came when the maid delivered a letter from the real detective, who admitted he had lied in presenting the divorce evidence to justify his fee. The husband was a good guy after all—and the Van Vechtens presumably lived happily ever after.

This short little theatrical gem took thirty minutes to perform. It took as long at curtain call to deliver the bouquets to Mrs. Gould. Those newspaper critics privileged to "review" the play agreed she was a resplendent actress, and the aftermath of publicity was all that could be desired—by Freddy, Mrs. Gould and The Plaza.

It would be difficult to compute in cold dollars and cents the sum represented by this trifling drawing-room comedy, but the New York *World* tried. An eight-column headline the next morning read: A $20,000,000 ACTRESS POINTED A $100 PISTOL AT A $1,000 ACTOR AND A $100,000,000 AUDIENCE APPLAUDED. THE ACTORS SAT ON AN $18,000 SOFA, LEANED ON A $4,000 BUREAU AND WALKED ON A $3,000 RUG. The *World* succinctly summed it up as a truly "swell affair."

The question remaining was: What can Freddy Martin do to top this?

He showed his daring by inviting not six hundred, but a thousand guests to a soiree—not to see a society actress but to honor a genuine actress, Miss Billie Burke. Many of his guests had never attended a social function with an actress worth less than twenty million dollars, and few had attended a reception honoring one. For these were the days when authors were dismissed as "merely literary" (of course this didn't apply to Edith Wharton, for she was born "in society"), and actresses were frowned upon for showing their ankles. Yet on November 24, 1908, Martin made some kind of social history by bringing stage and society together at what *The New York Times* (which seemed to keep a constant watchful eye out for Plaza happenings) described as perhaps the largest reception ever given by a private entertainer for a public entertainer.

In two brief seasons the exquisitely fine-featured Billie Burke had captured the imagination of all New York. Some years earlier she had married Florenz Ziegfeld, creator of the famed Ziegfeld Follies; not one of the celebrated Follies beauties could match her in glamour. Long before she was to become famous in her movie roles as the fluttering mother of the bride, Billie Burke was John Drew's radiant leading lady in *My Wife*.

Tradition-bound society reporters briefly skipped over her pretty presence at the reception and mentioned in the long lists of guests only one other representative of the theater, the indomitable Miss Barrymore. The guest list was another carbon copy of the bon tons at all Freddy's parties. Mr. and Mrs. Charles Dana Gibson were mentioned among those present, for he was, after all, a socially accepted artist, who had married a Langhorne of Virginia, and whose "Gibson Girl" was the symbol of a new vigorous femininity. The guests listened to gypsy music, Miss Edith Rodgers made her debut as a soprano solo, and there were "several recitations."

All in all a very proper affair—even if it was in honor of an actress.

A jewel in Freddy's party crown was a dinner he gave in 1909 in honor of Lady Paget, a leading hostess of London, who was visiting New York. Her Ladyship's dinners for King Edward VII and Queen Alexandra had set a high mark for such functions, and Freddy was determined to outdo the British Empire. He conferred with Fred Sterry on giving a dinner for fifty in as novel a setting as possible—and it was all to be a great surprise for the guests.

To set the scene Sterry put fifty designers and decorators to work, and they labored for thirty-six hours. When the guests arrived at the ballroom they entered a veritable Garden of Eden of azaleas, japonica and smilax; they walked through passageways formed of bending ferns and palms, hedged together with bridal wreath, lilacs and marguerites. In the center of the ballroom, a cornucopia of exotic fruits decorated a table a hundred feet in circumference. Over all a tall cherry tree spread its blossoming branches, the result of a four-day forcing process.

This was not the dinner table. The guests dined at a long, magnificently appointed table lighted by shaded yellow candelabra. They dined on the rarest of delicacies, but the gossip columnists did not miss the fact that they later ate the decorations too—peaches from the groves of South Africa, Malaga grapes from Spain, pears from southern California, tangerines, kumquats and Indian River pineapples from Florida, strawberries from South Carolina as large as crab apples.

An orchestra played, and at Lady Paget's request a Negro singer, Harry T. Burleigh, who had performed for King Edward VII, entertained.

And so it went. The guests of honor at his various dinner parties kept Freddy continually in the headlines:

> Frederick Townsend Martin gave a dinner at The Plaza last evening for Lady Sarah Wilson, an aunt of the Duke of Marlborough. . . . The Count de Keogorlauer, who will arrive today on the *Kaiser Wilhelm der Grosse,* will be the guest of Frederick Townsend Martin. . . . F. T. Martin entertains for Count Apponyi. . . .

In the midst of such glamour Freddy Martin found time each year to give a New Year's dinner at the Bowery Mission for the down-and-outs. With tears in his eyes he told Bowery bums of his friendship for them and of the plight of the rich. "Where idleness and extravagance creep in, decay begins." He brought them entertainment, too—Mme. Nordica and the great comedy actress Marie Dressler.

He did not hesitate to use the rich to help the poor, and he did it in a way that made the socialites feel wonderfully righteous. One of his unique ideas was a doll auction, just before Christmas of 1910. All dolls were donated, and he even persuaded Mrs. William Howard Taft, wife of the President, to donate one.

It was displayed at the White House for the benefit of the press before being sent up to New York to be auctioned off for charity.

The "First Lady doll" wore billows of lingerie and hand-wrought lace, a cap of Irish lace and sky-blue slippers. There was something of pertness in her expression, as if to say, "It isn't every doll that makes her debut at the White House."

Miss Dorothy Whitney, sister of Harry and Payne Whitney, who was to become Mrs. Willard Straight, headed the charity committee, and the *New York American* sponsored the event. Freddy himself, well aware of the bank accounts of the bidders, served as auctioneer and kept the bidding going until handsome prices were paid—two that went for large sums were the dolls contributed by Mrs. Leslie Carter, representing the dual roles she was playing in *Two Women* at the Lyric Theatre.

The next Christmas season Martin outdid himself by raising $2,400, a very handsome sum in those days, for the *New York American*'s Fund for Poor Children. Edwin Markham, the poet, recited a poem he wrote for the occasion, "The Bolted Door." The guests purchased seats, boxes, flowers and souvenir copies of the poem. Goetz-Hocky, the violinist, performed on his twelve-thousand-dollar Stradivarius, and two French dancers performed "the most amazing and barbaric Apache dance ever seen in New York." Who stole the show, however, was Enrico Caruso, who did not sing, but was on hand to do some of the caricatures for which he was famous. Those caricatures are prized by some of the greatest collectors in the country. The Grand Ballroom, naturally, was the setting for what the *American* described as "perhaps the most resplendent audience" that ever assembled for "a worthy cause."

This event inaugurated a custom some generous performers have since found cause to regret, the national habit of calling on entertainers to perform free for "sweet charity." But with social leaders like Mrs. Stuyvesant Fish and Mrs. John Jacob Astor "among those present," it was a sought-after privilege to be permitted to perform —then.

As The Plaza prospered, Martin found more time to spend in England, more time to write books lecturing the social personages he dominated, which bore such titles as *The Passing of the Idle Rich* and *My Personal Experience of Meeting Snobs.*

While no snob himself, Martin fully realized the value of "snob appeal" for climbers and was not above using it to achieve his objectives, whether social or for the benefit of the underprivileged. He championed the cause of woman suffrage, urging women to play a more active role in charity and community affairs. He told American women that the British and French were far ahead of them in organizing hospital drives and improvement programs; he succeeded in luring one of his Great Ladies, Mrs. Stuyvesant Fish, into lecturing college students on their responsibilities to the community.

Freddy Martin was busy moving his collection of old prints, Chinese porcelains and Chippendale furniture into a house he had leased in London's fashionable West End when he suffered a heart attack and died on March 5, 1914, at the age of sixty-five. The newspapers front-paged news of his death, and the obituaries revealed hitherto unsuspected facts of many directorships he had held.

He outlived the man who gave the era its name, Edward VII, by four years. By just a few months he missed seeing the first ship pass through the Panama Canal and escaped witnessing the outbreak of World War I in Europe.

Frederick Martin died as he had lived, an enigma, a man of curious inconsistencies, of strange distinction. He responded to all of life, to the glitter of luxury and to the grimness of poverty. Both the "idle rich" he enjoyed and exploited, and some thirty Bowery derelicts for whom he had provided some semblance of better living flocked to his funeral.

A potent force on two diametrically opposed fronts, he was in a large part responsible for the social aura and distinction which was attached to The Plaza from its very beginning, while at the same time allied with the dregs of humanity in the Bowery. He spent one night in a Grand Ballroom—the next in the warrens of the poor.

The two worlds of Frederick Townsend Martin provide a fascinating chapter in the annals of Edwardian New York.

CHAPTER FIVE

Splendor on the Park

It has been said and written of The Plaza that its Old World elegance and entrenched aura of the rich and the celebrated are equaled by few hotels in the world.

It is equally true that few hotels in the world command such a magnificent setting, in the very heart of the great metropolis of New York, where town meets the country mood of Central Park in a myriad of seasonal changes. The location has been described as the Place de la Concorde of America, and indeed the late Joseph Pulitzer, in willing fifty thousand dollars to the City of New York for the erection of a fountain, must have envisioned it as such, for he directed that it be located in the square near Central Park in surroundings "as far as practicable like those in the Place de la Concorde" of Paris.

That now lovely square was little more than an open, treeless expanse of asphalt and curbing when the Hotel Plaza was erected on its western front sixty years ago. The immediate surroundings, however, could not have been more impressive. In an era when Fifth Avenue, from the Fifties up, was an avenue of great town houses, the greatest and most splendid of all was the hundred-room mansion of Mr. and Mrs. Cornelius Vanderbilt, which stood just to the south of the Plaza and was, like it, French Renaissance in architecture.

The mansion occupied the entire west side of Fifth Avenue between Fifty-seventh and Fifty-eighth Streets. Two pairs of huge wrought-iron gates defended the driveway and porte-cochere at the Fifty-eighth Street side and were opened only for the most formal occasions, such as the wedding reception of Gladys Vanderbilt and Count Laszlo Szechenyi in 1908. The Fifty-seventh street entrance was the "everyday" entrance. After the Château de Blois, as it was called, was demolished in 1927, the mammoth gates were presented to the city by Mr. and Mrs. Vanderbilt's daughter, Mrs. Harry Payne Whitney, and they presently stand guard at the entrance to the Conservatory Gardens at Fifth Avenue and 105th Street.

The mansion was one of the great tourist attractions in the early 1900's, and the widely published news that the owners' son, Alfred Gwynne Vanderbilt, was the first tenant to take up residence at the grand new hotel just across the street gave but added spice to the stories of the fabulously rich who were to make The Plaza their home. Young Vanderbilt was building a hotel bearing the Vanderbilt name on the site of his parents' first home at Park Avenue between Thirty-third and Thirty-fourth Streets, which opened two years later.

In later years The Plaza named a newly decorated suite in honor of its first tenant. Former Governor William H. Vanderbilt of Rhode Island, in a letter expressing appreciation of the hotel's thus honoring the memory of his father, wrote: "one of my earliest memories is staying at the Plaza with my parents when I was a very small boy—a long time ago."

Next to the Vanderbilt mansion, on Fifty-eighth Street, was the large town house of Mr. and Mrs. Charles B. Alexander, one of whose daughters married Winthrop Aldrich, former Ambassador to the Court of St. James, and brother of the first Mrs. John D. Rockefeller, Jr. Across the Avenue was the old Savoy Hotel and nearby the old Netherland; a few blocks down was the great mansion of Collis P. Huntington, one of the rich and powerful robber barons of railroad fortunes. The area was distinguished by other town houses of the very wealthy, and there's wasn't a shop in sight on Fifth Avenue.

Today Fifth Avenue is dream stuff realized as a boulevard of fine hotels and apartment houses, home of some of the world's most fashionable and expensive shops, backbone of the richest urban area in the world.

Above Fifty-ninth Street its development as an avenue of great private mansions built by the new millionaires just before and right after the turn of the century was largely due to the creation of Central Park. The story of its rise as a wonder street of the world is a capsule history of New York City; The Plaza contributed history-making chapters.

Less than a hundred years ago the area to the north of the hotel was a region of stagnant ponds, unkempt woods, and squatter's shanties. Andrew J. Downing, a landscape architect who had studied the fine parks of Europe, envisioned that area as a great park, with lakes and winding roads and walks, and proposed its development. He was backed up by such leaders of public opinion as Washington Irving, William Cullen Bryant and George Bancroft, who enthusiastically took up the cause, and the first step toward creating Central Park was taken in 1856, when the city bought 7,000 lots totaling 776 acres. Inevitably land values around the proposed park soared, particularly on upper Fifth Avenue. A tract at Sixty-ninth Street, which sold for $3,000 in 1852, brought $40,000 in 1857, and twelve years later William H. Vanderbilt could not get it for $1,250,000.

Of thirty designs submitted in a contest the judges selected the plans prepared by Frederick L. Olmsted and Calvert Vaux. Richard Hunt, the architect who had designed a number of Vanderbilt homes, also contributed to the final design.

Half a million trees, shrubs and vines were set out in a manner to harmonize with the natural conformation of the land. The Plaza's verdant neighbor was completed in 1876, and some hundred varieties of trees now flourish in the present 843 acres. The fan-shaped leaves of the ginkgo trees wave at the windows of the hotel; the drives, the walks, the lakes, the bridle paths lend a country atmosphere to a hotel in the very center of a teeming city.

It was to be some time before the little *piazetta* in front of the Plaza became a beautiful square of gaiety and beauty, which has

The city's first metered taxicabs line up at the 59th Street entrance.

The Plaza, General Sherman statue, and Vanderbilt mansion c. *1925.*

W YORK HISTORICAL MUSEUM

NEW YORK HISTORICAL SOCIETY

Central Park c. 1895, showing the first Plaza hotel, demolished in 1905.

The wireless room was established in 1907 to facilitate transatlantic reservations.

D'ARLENE STUDIO

A view of Grand Army Plaza before the trolley tracks were removed.

The Fifty-ninth Street lobby in 1912.

D'ARLENE STUDIO

Crystal chandeliers sparkle throughout the hallways.

The Persian Room in 1934 with decor by Joseph Urban.

D'ARLENE STUDIO

Mrs. Walter Abel with a model of the figure atop the Fountain of Abundance, which her father, sculptor Karl Bitter, designed.

The Rose Room provided a setting for Edwardian Era dinner parties.

The Fifth Avenue lobby was originally a summer dining room.

D'ARLENE STUDIO

A sitting room-bedroom designed by Christian Dior.

The Terrace Room, added in 1921, carried on the grand tradition.

served these many years as a monument to the vision and inspired taste of Thomas Hastings, the architect of the New York Public Library, to whom fell the task of producing this lovely city square from a number of scattered and unrelated elements.

The first step was taken in 1908. Just north of Fifty-ninth Street, he provided space for Augustus Saint-Gaudens' golden statue of General William Tecumseh Sherman astride his horse. This famous statue, which was unveiled at the Paris exhibition in 1900, had been ineffectively placed a full block north of its present location.

The southern half of what is officially the Grand Army Plaza, directly in front of the hotel, was reserved for the fountain provided for in Pulitzer's will. The Pulitzer sons, Joseph, Herbert and Ralph, commissioned Hastings to design the fountain, which was completed in 1912.

Hastings created a broad base of five marble basins, stepped back one above the other, and rising from the top basin a pedestal pool supporting the bronze nude of a woman holding a basket of fruit. Karl Bitter, the sculptor who designed this and made the sketch of the model, died before he could complete the work, and Isidore Konti finished the statue as it now stands. This is the Fountain of Abundance, a theme carried out by the cornucopias on each side of the base.

A game still played is trying to find out who posed for the figure. Legend had it that it was a schoolteacher, whose beauty otherwise would have remained forever hidden under voluminous skirts. Janet MacFarlane, former director of the Albany Museum of History and Art, believes the lady with the fruit was "Suzy," a famous artists' model. Only as recently as April 1966 another name came into the picture. Eighty-four-year-old Mrs. Doris Doscher Baum, who posed for the Miss Liberty twenty-five-cent piece designed by Hermon Atkins MacNeil and first minted in 1916, declared, when appearing on the *I've Got a Secret* TV show, that she had posed for the Abundance figure. But whoever the model, the Lady of Abundance is now one of New York's most famous characters, to be seen in hundreds of thousands of snapshots taken by tourists from all parts of the world.

Nowhere in New York is there a place of such enchantment. It is a place for all seasons: in spring, when the populace emerges from winter hibernation like butterflies from a cocoon; in summer, when sun worshipers are lolling on the steps, dipping toes in the pool; in fall, when nature takes on its glorious raiment and the city is in an exhilarating mood in anticipation of a new social season; at Christmastime and on snowy nights, when the illumination of hundreds of gleaming lights shine like a halo around the lady of the fountain and make it what Ed Sullivan had called "the most beautiful sight in New York."

It is a place of international flavor and contrasts: a tiny Japanese woman in kimono and obi; a bearded, turbaned Sikh; a towering dark man from Ghana in his picturesque robes; a stunning East Indian woman in a sari of beautiful silks. It is a place of familiars, too: gentle old ladies feeding the pigeons; young lovers strolling by, holding hands; a mink-clad socialite walking her dog; a young man in morning coat and striped trousers escorting a pretty young girl with shiny hair to a wedding reception in the hotel; a bright red Jaguar nudged close to a silver-gray Rolls Royce, whose chauffeur is chatting with a Plaza doorman; a tall, sophisticated young beauty striking a pose as a camera grinds; two young girls in shorts giggling as two bearded youths pass by. . . . Everything fuses into a kaleidoscopic picture one seldom sees anywhere else in the world.

Conspicuous are the horse-drawn hansom cabs standing at the park curb, supplying a link between past and present, a nostalgic note harking back to a more serene and gentle era. Three generations of sightseers have taken delight in climbing into these ancient, sometimes shabby, vehicles, drawn by ancient horses with a plastic rose, a spring of wax lilies of the valley, stuck jauntily behind their drooping ears. The driver, looking as ancient as his horse, is a colorful sight with his high hat and long whip, and he knows it. Sightseers ask questions, and as Dobbin clop-clops along, many a carriage driver has made up a romantic story of himself and the city for the benefit of fascinated tourists. A good story often makes for a good tip; posing for pictures for the folks back home is good for another tip.

A most generous tipper was the late Errol Flynn, the dashing actor, who enjoyed a leisurely ride in the Park as much as his swashbuckling movie roles. Sophisticated Barbara Stanwyck had her special driver, "Old Bill," whenever she came to town. The sharp-tongued Alexander Woollcott softened enough to take a small niece to see *Alice in Wonderland* in a carriage from The Plaza.

As mansions disappeared over the years, great changes came to Fifth Avenue. Hotels, stores, banks, office buildings took their places on ground whose value ran to astronomical figures. A new Sherry-Netherland sprang up where once there had been the Netherlands Hotel; replacing the old Savoy, a Savoy-Plaza rose in 1927, and the Hotel Pierre at Sixty-first and Fifth Avenue joined the most luxurious hotel area in New York.

Into the neighborhood came the greatest shops in the world. Bergdorf Goodman moved up from lower down the Avenue to the Fifty-eighth Street site of the Vanderbilt mansion, and the Tailored Woman opened for business on the Fifty-seventh Street corner. Children gaze in rapture at the animal kingdom of F. A. O. Schwartz; hard by is chic Bonwit-Teller; just nearby, in the Tiffany windows, women young and old stare at jewels fashioned for a queen; in the windows of Van Cleef & Arpels are gems fit for a maharani. Today the list of shops, banks, and corporation buildings bearing world-known industrial names around the perimeter of the Plaza reads like an international directory of fine living.

Steadfast through all the changes stood The Plaza, holding to the line of its first design for fine hotel living. Her outward appearance has changed slightly, but so subtly that few except some old-timers are aware of it.

When the hotel first opened, the main entrance was on the Fifty-ninth Street side, through whose doors streamed the elite on that glamorous initial day. But the Fifty-eighth Street entrance afforded a more exclusive approach for permanent residents as the excitement of the opening calmed down. Facing the little square at the Fifth Avenue facade was a low, broad terrace opening onto what is now the Fifth Avenue lobby but which was, in those days, a restaurant. Flower-bedecked trellises converted it into a summer garden, a favorite gathering place for society on warm afternoons and evenings in pre-air-conditioning days. The terrace was nicknamed the Champagne Porch.

Two carriage entrances on either side of the open terrace gave access to the garden restaurant known as the Louis XVI Summer Garden. The garden effects were removed in the winter, the area reenclosed and redecorated in winter dress. When a new addition of three hundred rooms, a penthouse, and new ballroom were built on to the Fifty-eighth Street side in 1921, the terrace disappeared to make way for what is the Fifth Avenue entrance, but the original doors at either side are still there. If one looks closely, one can see them, camouflaged by large bins of evergreens.

Six tall, bronze *torchères,* each with five frosted ball globes encircling a clear lamp, originally graced the first-floor balcony overlooking the Avenue. They were removed in 1921 and put in storage. In the forties two of these great *torchères* were brought out to command the Fifth Avenue entrance, and four were placed at the Fifty-ninth Street doors. They have become as much a symbol of the Plaza as the double-*P* insignia, which has been etched in glass, reproduced in bronze, repeated on napkins and stationery and matchbook covers, and which graces every ad. Its originator and designer is lost to history, but is as dear to Plaza patrons as a family coat of arms.

Something new was added in 1963, a proud testimonial to The Plaza's place in the history of New York. Attached near the corner joined by Fifth Avenue and Fifty-ninth Street is a bronze plaque, erected by the New York Community Trust, which reads:

LANDMARKS OF NEW YORK

THE PLAZA HOTEL

Designed by Henry J. Hardenbergh in French
Renaissance style. The Plaza opened its doors
on October 1, 1907, and among the original
residents were members of the Gould, Harriman
and Vanderbilt families. An earlier Plaza Hotel
opened at this location in 1890 and was demolished
in 1905 to make way for the present structure.

Long before being declared a landmark, the Plaza was described by *Life* magazine as "an indestructible and slightly incredible link with another age . . . which, transcending mere success . . . has mellowed into a New York tradition."

Interestingly enough, the plaque provided the Plaza with its first and only exterior identification sign. It is one of the few hotels in the world which never has displayed its name on the building. This is The Plaza! One is expected to know it.

CHAPTER SIX

The Tempestuous Years

The decade that followed the brilliant opening of the "world's costliest hotel" was a time capsule of wondrous and terrible happenings. It was to see American economy reach the soundest in its history; it was to see war and destruction such as the world had never known before.

The nation weathered the panic of 1907, and the warm glow of renewed prosperity spread over the land as a new industrial age opened up and new financial giants appeared on the economic horizon. All sorts of exciting things were happening; all sorts of causes were springing up to occupy public attention.

The women were kicking up their heels in every direction. Suffragettes waving yellow umbrellas and braving the hoots of the mob paraded from Union Square to the Plaza. In the vanguard of the "Votes for Women" fervor was Mrs. Oliver Belmont, the former Mrs. William K. Vanderbilt, who directed a two-day bazaar at the hotel to promote and raise money for the cause.

Everyone was talking of the world automobile race from New York to Paris, by way of Alaska and Siberia, sponsored by *The New York Times* and the French *Le Matin*. Six cars—French, German, Italian and American—left New York on February 12, 1908, in relays, en route to San Francisco; thence by boat to Valdes, Alaska, on to Nome by road, and then to East Cape, Siberia, by boat. Two cars rolled into Paris from East Cape by road on July 30, a huge German Protos and an American Thomas Flyer, driven by George Schuster. The German was disqualified and the American declared the winner. President Roosevelt received the victorious driver at the White House, just as astronauts were to be welcomed a half century later.

On October 1 of that same year, Henry Ford introduced his famous Model T car, at a cost of $850, which only a few years later was to be reduced in price to $350. When, by 1915, one million of these had rolled off the assembly line, American economy was at its peak.

Even while the newspapers of 1909 were headlining the story of Peary's discovery of the North Pole came the thrilling news that a Frenchman, Louis Blériot, had flown his plane across the English Channel to land at Dover, the first time any traveler had reached Britain other than by water.

Champion heavyweight Jack Johnson defeated Jim Jeffries in the ring in Reno, Nevada, on July 4, 1910, and a new phrase was added to the American vernacular. Declared his mother upon hearing the news: "He said he'd bring home the bacon, and the honey boy has gone and done it."

An event that provided columns of news that year was the dinner at The Plaza on November 1, sponsored by the Aereo Club of America to climax the International Aviation Tournament. Hawley and Post, who had made a fantastic balloon flight into Canada, were honored guests. Claude Grahame-White, the famous British aviator who later married Ethel Levey, former wife of George M. Cohan, congratulated the honor guests, and among those present were aviation pioneers Wilbur and Orville Wright. The presiding officer was August Belmont who, in an impassioned speech, warned the aviators that they might one day be asked to risk their lives for their country. An awesome prophecy—in 1910.

The British monarch who had given his name to a gentle era died, and in June 1910, there was a gala Coronation Dinner at The Plaza celebrating the elevation of George V to the English throne. The press reported that Fred Sterry, "Earl of The Plaza," and "My Lord" Harry Black refrained from making speeches, but nobody could stop Roy McCardell, "Viscount of New Rochelle and Earl of the New York, New Haven and Hartford Railroad" from cabling His Majesty. The King, reportedly, responded warmly. And who is to say that this was a practical joke?

The town went wild over a new tune, "Alexander's Ragtime Band" by a young, unknown composer, Irving Berlin. Over at Reisenweber's the "original Dixieland Jazz Orchestra" introduced their "Tiger Rag," and at the Plaza the rafters rang with cheers when on a New Year's Eve Enrico Caruso, the world's greatest tenor, burst into glorious song.

A young dancing couple, British-born Vernon Castle and Irene Foote Castle, of New Rochelle, New York, destined to become the most glamorous dance team in the world, created an overnight sensation in the American debut of an English musical show, *The Sunshine Girl.* Irene Castle bobbed her hair, and a whole world of young people followed suit forever after.

The Plaza, which gave the nation a new standard of hotel luxury and sophistication, gave it something else in 1912 by introducing tea dancing in the Grill and dinner-dancing in the Rose Room. The town went tea-dance mad, and the new "animal dances," the bunny hug, the grizzly bear, the turkey trot, the foxtrot and the kangaroo dip were scandalizing the conservatives.

It was a time, too, for simple pleasures. Guests at The Plaza went horseback riding and ice-skating in Central Park. At 5 P.M. of a wintry afternoon a flying squadron of waiters from the hotel would execute a flanking maneuver on the ice across the street to present pink-cheeked skaters with warm drinks and little cakes.

Season merged into season, and who is to judge when twilight descends on a serene era and the dawn of a tragic era rises?

William Howard Taft had succeeded Teddy Roosevelt as President in 1909. Roosevelt, declaring "My hat is in the ring," tried a comeback to the White House four years later, but it was Woodrow Wilson's tragedy to become the twentieth century's first wartime President.

The Taft Administration had been marked by difficulties with Mexico. Troops were on their way to the Mexican border in March 1911, after the revolution there when a most important conference was held between Señor José Yves Limantour, Mexican Minister of Finance, and Henry Lane Wilson, American Ambassador to Mexico, in Limantour's Plaza suite. Newspaper headlines told of other important conferences. "Señor Limantour never left his apartment in The Plaza yesterday," reported the *Herald*. "Financiers consult Señor Limantour; his suite has been the scene of all the meetings" said the *Times*.

That American troops were recalled shortly after these conferences was merely delaying a war crisis that erupted a few years later, in April 1914, when diplomatic relations between the two countries were severed and President Wilson ordered an Atlantic fleet to Tampico Bay.

For many American soldiers this was but a rehearsal before the volcano of war between Austria and Serbia erupted in Europe in July 1914, bursting into a flood of violence that engulfed most of Europe and sucked America in a few years later.

A European trip was becoming a status symbol in an era of great transatlantic luxury liners, and the early summer of 1914 found thousands upon thousands of Americans vacationing abroad. When in August Germany, France, and England were in the fray, pandemonium reigned in the United States embassies of those countries as they were besieged by Americans frantically seeking aid in securing passage home. At The Plaza, Manager Sterry was deluged with cables; fully half of his tenants were among those caught in the European war whirlpool, and appeals for emergency funds and help in other ways came by the hundreds. As ships bearing returning Americans reached these shores, Sterry sent squads of bellmen and assistant managers down to the docks to assist Plaza patrons in the ensuing confusion and bedlam. The docks of New York, the largest neutral port in the world, presented a fabulous sight with the merchant and passenger ships of belligerent nations also anchored, fearful to chance crossing the Atlantic without naval protection.

Dispatch after dispatch from abroad brought news of death and destruction, and Americans were shocked and horrified when in May 1915 the *Lusitania,* queen of the Cunard fleet, was sunk by the Germans without warning off the coast of Ireland. With it went many Americans—among them Alfred Gwynne Vanderbilt, the first guest to register at The Plaza. Still, America maintained its neutrality until February 1917, when the United States liner *Housatonic* was sunk by German subs.

The German Ambassador and Countess von Bernstorff were longtime Plaza patrons. Annual horse shows at Madison Square Garden always lured them up from Washington, and many dinners had been given at the hotel in their honor during the equine sessions.

Little honor, social or otherwise, was accorded them when the von Bernstorffs sailed from New York on February 5, 1917, with 149 members of the German ambassadorial and consular staff—two days after the sinking of the *Housatonic* and the severing of diplomatic relations. On April 6, President Wilson signed a joint resolution of Congress proclaiming a state of war with Germany.

Patriotic zeal reached its zenith. Olive drab became the fashionable new color for men. At The Plaza white tie and tails gave way to Sam Browne belts and spiral leggings; the playboy gave way to the doughboy, and the flowing headdress of the Red Cross replaced the chic chapeau of the debutante and the tiara of the dowager. Dishwashers and Ivy-Leaguers, truck drivers and tycoons, bellmen and bankers all marched off together to make the world safe for democracy, parading proudly to the tune of the nation's most stirring song, "Over There."

George M. Cohan, author of that song, is probably the only man in history to receive a Congressional Medal for composing a popular song. His contribution to the winning of World War One was recognized by Congress on the eve of World War Two. The composers who came after him who tried to capture the mood of the Second World War produced nothing so stirring.

George M. Cohan was also the first man to be commemorated with a plaque at The Plaza. The Lambs of theater fame, after his death in 1942, erected a bronze tablet in a corner booth of the Oak Room, the now famous "Cohan Corner," where the "Yankee Doodle Dandy" of Broadway for years held forth at cocktail time. The inscription reads: "Here in this corner, where he spent many happy hours, The Lambs have placed this tablet in honor of the most brilliant versatile gentleman in the theatre of his day."

By October 1917, ten years to the day after The Plaza opened, the lobbies were awash with uniforms. French, English, Italian and Belgian uniforms mingled with those of Americans as pretty girls danced with Allied officers at teatime in the Grill. Women brought the sweaters they were knitting for doughboys to lectures and bond rallies. Lee Nichols, an Englishman who lost his right arm up to the shoulder, told humorous war stories at a war benefit in the ballroom. His empty sleeve conveyed his message of courage and sacrifice.

Because of its particular location The Plaza became a focal point for visiting military and government dignitaries as war-bond rallies were launched in the Grand Army Plaza square. Mary Pickford, Marie Dressler, Mrs. Oliver Belmont, perched on platforms, were supersalesmen in the Liberty Loan Drives. So, too, was Fred Sterry, chairman of the Liberty Bond Drive at the hotel. Tenants and staff demonstrated both their patriotism and their affluence and helped Sterry win a prize by purchasing the record sum of thirty million dollars' worth of bonds.

Like so many other hotels, and so many homes, The Plaza suffered with the soldiers in the Spanish flu epidemic of 1918. Doctors in uniform or mufti rushed through the lobby carrying small black bags. Both Red Cross and hospital nurses were everywhere. Civilians as well as the military were victims, and many were the incidents.

One of the most curious was recalled in later years by Mrs. Clara Bell Walsh, who received a phone call from a total stranger with a most unusual request. Mrs. Walsh, who lived at The Plaza from the day it opened, was constantly featured in the society columns, and calls from strangers came as no surprise. But this one startled her. Over the phone came a cultured voice, heavy with grief: "I wonder if you know some young man who owns striped trousers and a morning coat?"

"Why, I must know plenty," Mrs. Walsh replied. "But why do you ask?"

"My son died yesterday and is being buried tomorrow morning. I do want a proper funeral for him. So many of his friends are sick with the flu that I can't find enough pallbearers. It occurred to me that you might know somebody with striped trousers and a morning coat who would be willing to serve as a pallbearer."

As it happened, Mrs. Walsh did. She also attended the funeral herself.

As from a nightmare, all of The Plaza awakened to the blaring sound of music at 3:30 A.M. on November 11, 1918, three days after the false Armistice had set off a happy demonstration. The news of the real Armistice had just reached New York, and The Plaza management broke the first rule of hoteldom, which is, "Let them sleep." It was "over, over there."

Sterry had hastily corralled a big brass band and sent it through the corridors to awaken everybody. The startled guests responded with frenzied enthusiasm. The news, of course, touched off the greatest demonstration the United States had ever known, and at The Plaza the consumption of champagne to celebrate the Allied victory reached an all-time high.

The statistics that became known soon after had a sobering effect on the country. Of total mobilized forces numbering 4,355,000, casualties numbered 364,800, missing persons 4,500, and the deaths stood at 126,000.

As if to further sober up the nation, Congress lost no time approving the Eighteenth Amendment bringing prohibition to the land. Several states had already adopted prohibition—Maine, Kansas, North Dakota, Georgia, Oklahoma, Mississippi, North Carolina and Tennessee. Although mighty moves were made to block national prohibition, the amendment had already been approved by the Senate in 1917, and adopted by the House with minor changes a few months later. It was the first amendment to have a time limit placed on its ratification. On October 28, 1919, the Volstead Act, prohibiting all liquor traffic in the United States, became law—and prohibition, effective the following January 20, ushered in the roaring twenties.

"The Era of Wonderful Nonsense" Westbrook Pegler labeled the twenties. There are those who would hardly agree that an era which saw the rise of gangsterism and the greatest scourge of lawlessness the country has ever known could be termed "nonsense," no less "wonderful."

People didn't drink less because of prohibition. They only drank worse. Many died of bad booze, and college youths bragged of their recipe for "bathtub gin." As legitimate bars closed, speakeasies flourished, and "Joe sent me," became a password, if not a joke.

Like all other bars, the Plaza bars, where ladies and gentlemen imbibed with decorum and the word "drunk" suggested only the ungrammatical past tense of drink, celebrated—if that is the word—their closing the night before the Volstead Act went into effect. That was a night to remember. It was like New Year's Eve all over again, all over town. Only this was a wake.

Shortly thereafter the Oak Bar off the Oak Lounge was converted into a brokerage office for E. F. Hutton and Company, and the beautiful Rose Room, scene of some of the town's most elegant parties, became the home of an automobile sales company.

For some people directly associated with The Plaza, the closing of the bars proved something of a bonanza. Donald Stralem, whose father, the late Casimir Stralem, was for a time a director of United States Realty Company, recalls that the entire contents of the liquor and wine cellars of the hotel were distributed, for free, among the directors and some favored others. "I still have one single bottle of Plaza gin left," gleefully reported young Mr. Stralem. By which it can be gathered that father's share of the alcoholic loot was considerable.

The thought of what The Plaza had to replenish when prohibition was repealed staggers the imagination.

Champagne still flowed in the suites of those who had stocked up in anticipation of prohibition and liquor was plentiful at private parties over which the hotel had no control. Silver hip flasks became as *de rigueur* as pearl studs for evening wear, and the code for many a dinner party was B.Y.O.—"bring your own." A reporter covering the first New Year's Eve of prohibition in the New York hotels, The Plaza included, described it as "Hip, Hip, Hooray; more hip than hooray."

When the drys the next day proclaimed a victory for their side, the other side winked an eye and agreed, it was dry all right—extra dry—like Moet and Chandon used to dry it.

Historians of the twentieth century will undoubtedly record the teeming twenties as one of the most uninhibited, frenzied eras in the annals of our country. Writers called it "the Aspirin Age." References to the "Lost Generation" were constant; the war was blamed. The press got into the act with worried editorials about the antics of a new young breed, the flappers. "Nowhere in America has the elder generation been so hysterically upset over the problem of the flapper as in New York City," observed the *New York Journal.* According to its exposé, prep-school boys and girls as young as sixteen were behaving in incorrigible fashion.

If this has a familiar ring to those deploring the mores of today's teen-agers, it is but history repeating itself.

Jazz, cigarettes, Papa's money tossed away at craps or "red dog" between fox-trots, cocktails sipped in cozy corners, highballs spiked from the flapper's own little silver stocking flask, petting parties and crash dances were among the evils cited by the *Journal.* The crashing of coming-out parties sans invitations did indeed originate in the twenties. It's a custom that still flourishes today.

The Southern Society, at a dance in The Plaza ballroom way back in 1912, put its foot firmly down after several young couples made a spectacle of themselves doing the fox-trot, that "grotesque adaptation of Terpsichore." By 1922 it was too late to stop the shimmy, a dance introduced by Gilda Gray, and when the Charleston craze swept in, in 1925, it marked the total breakdown of adult resistance to the age of the flapper. Everybody was doing it, from small boys who stood in front of The Plaza and danced for pennies, to buxom matrons. One evening in the Grill the hectic dance turned into a snake dance, and as the line grew longer and longer, the leaders headed out and up the steps, across the square to Fifth Avenue, in and out of two other hotels, gaining gleeful recruits as they snaked and leaving only the police staring in blank amazement.

If it brought speakeasies, prohibition also brought tea dancing to a new high of popularity, and the Plaza Grill, where tea dancing had first been introduced, became the gayest, most fashionable rendezvous for New York's younger set. The flappers and philosophers immortalized by F. Scott Fitzgerald flocked there every afternoon, swaying and fox-trotting to the syncopated music of the unforgettable Joe Smith and his orchestra.

Beauty met brilliance in the Grill. Boys from Harvard, Princeton and Yale brought their dates there, girls from Vassar and Bryn Mawr and from New York's fashionable Spence and Finch schools. Acknowledged queen of the Grill was the glamorous Constance Bennett, who tangoed with an endless succession of admiring partners before her little sisters, Barbara and Joan, were old enough to go to dances, and long before either she herself and Joan achieved movie stardom. La Bennett was fully aware of her feminine charms and popularity; when cut in on during a dance (which happened constantly), she would archly say to her new partner, "You know who you're dancing with? I'm Constance Bennett." As if he didn't know!

Other beauties and indefatigable dancers who became Grill habitués were Mae Murray and Gloria Swanson. The latter, still a frequent and familiar visitor to The Plaza, has, in the opinion of some old employees, hardly changed at all. The sight of Rudolph Valentino doing a tango sent debutantes into ecstasy.

The Plaza Grill remained a center of gay life all through the war and postwar periods and became the most glamorous legend of the twenties—to which F. Scott Fitzgerald contributed a large part in fact and fiction. After romping at the tea dances he and his wife Zelda would go dunking in the Plaza fountain to the musical accompaniment of police whistles. When they could afford it, the Fitzgeralds lived at The Plaza. At parties Scott Fitzgerald could be seen mixing with everyone, or generally misbehaving. Along with the gin, available at $7 a bottle, he was soaking up atmosphere for his novels.

In his most famous, *The Great Gatsby,* published in 1925, a golden-shouldered girl named Jordan Baker "sitting up very straight on a straight chair in the tea garden at The Plaza," tells the story of Daisy Fay's heartbreak over Gatsby. Fitzgerald's characters wandered in and out of The Plaza as often as he did.

Ernest Hemingway, while living in Key West, once wrote Fitzgerald to "come on down," not to soak up sun, but to cover a Cuban revolution. Aware of Fitzgerald's fitful moments of despair, he added, "If you really feel blue enough, get yourself heavily insured and I'll see you can get killed. I'll write a fine obituary—and we can take your liver out and give it to the Princeton museum, your heart to the Plaza Hotel."

Not only the collegiates and the coeds tea-danced. The idea spread to their parents, and one of society's great ladies, the late Mrs. Huntington Tappin, started the Saturday Tea Dance Club —"an exclusive tea dancing club for persons of all ages"—which met weekly at The Plaza. Such proper bon tons as Mrs. William H. Rockefeller and Mrs. J. Prentice Kellogg were among the patronesses.

The Plaza tea dances set a style copied by society in a number of other cities. Many families with higher social than financial standing adopted the *thé dansant* as a more appropriate fashion than a ball for daughter's debut in society. And eventually families with higher financial than social rating introduced their daughters at tea dances which cost more than a ball.

Mrs. Tappin and Mrs. William H. Tew conducted the leading social-secretarial bureau in New York, which was housed for years at The Plaza. To them was accorded the distinction of deciding who among the collegiates, even if unknown to the hostess, should be invited to make up that debutante dance phenomenon, the stag line. Theirs was the most coveted list among many, and Ivy League undergraduates vied to have their names included.

If the list at times produced young gentlemen of good family but exceedingly bad manners—well, you had to shrug that off. Extra men at dancing parties were at a premium then, as now; the length of the stag line determined the success of the ball. The Tappin-Tew office still controls the so-called "best list."

Next to dancing, football was the great enthusiasm of the younger crowd, and the wealthy hired railroad cars to take their parties to Princeton or New Haven and get them back to The Plaza in time for late dinner and dancing. Donald Norris, a gay blade of the twenties, sharing his memories with the author one day in the sixties, recalled winning $50 from Scott Fitzgerald on the outcome of the Harvard-Princeton game. He also related some of the uncurbed shenanigans that went on. It was after a Colgate-Columbia football game, during an all-night party at The Plaza, that Norris walked off with a small gold chair belonging to the hotel. No one stopped him, and at the time he credited his self-possession for the lack of interference. A few years later he might have wondered if the management simply decided to wait for a proper moment to get even.

Norris was best man at the wedding of Mildred Bedell, retail-store heiress, and Edward Quinn, in 1924. Besides handling the ring, he was charged with the responsibility of delivering a thousand dollars and two train tickets for a California honeymoon to the newlyweds in their suite at The Plaza the next day. Like bridegrooms before him, Quinn had given his room number only to his best man. In the excitement of things, Norris forgot the number of the suite.

When he arrived at the hotel and asked for the Quinns, the desk clerk, following instructions, denied that they were registered. Norris insisted they were, but to no avail. The Plaza clerks, so adept at adapting their accents to the Oxford tones of English guests, could say "No" to an intruder as firmly as they could say "Yes" to a welcome guest.

In desperation Norris called the bride's father, who hurried down to the hotel to put on his dollar pressure. A threat to buy the hotel and fire the clerk failed to reunite father, daughter and son-in-law and best man. Only a demand to see Fred Sterry produced action. Sterry knew when to ignore even a honeymooner's request, and recognize that of a millionaire.

The newlyweds got their tickets, their money, and took off for their California honeymoon, but just barely on schedule.

Yet all was not frenzy and frivolity in these razzmatazz speakeasy days. The disabled, the widows and the orphans of World War One were not forgotten. The national observance of Poppy Day was made possible largely by the success of the first Poppy Ball held in the Plaza ballroom on St. Valentine's night, 1921. The American Legion, acting as treasurer of the dance, took in enough to order one million poppies to be made by disabled veterans and war orphans in France. Fashioned of silk, the flowers were sold by Legionnaires throughout the United States on May 30. In later years, poppies were made by American veterans out of crepe paper, and eventually the money raised each year went to help the victims of other wars—World War Two, the Korean War and the war in Vietnam.

As prohibition agents were scurrying around trying to discover violations of prohibition, many disturbed, serious-minded citizens were trying to discover ways and means of having the Volstead Act repealed. When Columbia University President Nicholas Murray Butler, in a speech before the Missouri Society of New York, made a powerful frontal attack on prohibition at The Plaza, he was backed up by many important people, who had up to then remained publicly silent, no matter what their private opinion. Later the Rockefellers deserted the dry cause, and then along came Franklin D. Roosevelt to administer the *coup de grâce* in 1933.

By that time, however, the country was in even worse trouble.

Caught in the postwar frenzy, everyone was playing the stock market. By the late twenties even waiters and barbers were gambling in the market on margin. The little man in the street, which was not Wall Street, invested his savings and dreamed of getting rich in a hurry.

The pace grew faster. The stock market went up and up. Harry Black, expanding on all fronts, was building the Savoy-Plaza across the Avenue. His friend and associate Ben Beinecke did not approve of the financial risks Black was taking. As the building went up, the venerable Beinecke would stand at the window of his twelfth floor suite, which was overlooking Fifth Avenue, and shake his head worriedly. Forty years later his son, Frederick Beinecke, told the story and sighed in recollection.

Frederick Beinecke, who had joined the Plaza staff as treasurer in 1911, recalled the twenties as a fantastic period of great wealth and great risks. Regarding the wealth, he told of a woman guest who had left nearly a million dollars' worth of jewelry with the desk clerk. Recognizing the tremendous responsibility for the hotel, the desk clerk called Beinecke, who in turn called in Sterry, who in turn called the bank in which the Beineckes also had an interest and rented a hundred dollar safety-deposit box.

When Madame called for her jewels the next morning, she did not hide her annoyance at the time it took to bring them upstairs. She was never told that her jewels had spent the night in the bank instead of the hotel vault.

Of the risks, Beinecke recalls being told by the management, "There is something wrong in the accounting department. Find out what it is." Without a clue as to what was wrong or where to start looking, young Beinecke sat down at the desk of the auditor and opened a drawer. He found it filled with margin calls and that was his clue. The auditor eventually went to jail for stealing to meet his margin calls and doctoring the books.

As butchers, bakers and dressmakers gambled in the market, the conservative, financially knowledgeable Ben Beinecke watched, with long memories and genuine concern.

Early in October 1929 the stock market began the fatal decline that was to culminate in the greatest depression the country had ever known. Not even J. P. Morgan or John D. Rockefeller could halt the panicky wave of selling which reached its peak on October 29. Sixteen million shares were dumped on the market and stockholders lost thirty million dollars in one day.

The ticker in the Oak Lounge of The Plaza was jammed with stunned onlookers; the brokerage office of E. F. Hutton and Company in the adjoining room was swamped with worried investors, many of them millionaires who saw their fortunes being swept away in a tidal wave of frenzied selling.

Another panic was on. For the nation, and for The Plaza, it was the end of another era.

CHAPTER SEVEN

A Bitter Age

BROTHER, can you spare a dime?"

The thirties staggered into the century hand in hand with gloom and despair. Fright and panic seized the nation as financial empires tottered, banks closed, unemployment figures reached into the millions, and tycoons leaped from windows or ended it all with a bullet. No one was spared. The Plaza suffered with the rest.

A succession of blows—the Wall Street crash, the bank closings, and its aftermath of industrial depression—were hard enough to take. After close to a quarter of a century of uninterrupted prosperity, through two depressions and a world war, the luxurious Plaza was operating deep in the red. Even harder to take were the personal blows. In quick succession the hotel lost its founding triumvirate, Harry Black, Ben Beinecke, and Fred Sterry.

Harry Black's death was tragic. Black was a wealthy man; he had survived two depressions—the panic of 1907, and an industrial recession in the mid-twenties—and undoubtedly could have survived another. But Black was a builder, and he could not bear to see the cards come tumbling down. He foresaw the inevitable before many others.

Eleven days before Wall Street's house of cards collapsed entirely, Harry Black was found unconscious with his head under water in the bathtub of his Plaza penthouse. He was revived after many hours—but his spirits did not revive. He succeeded in committing suicide on July 19, 1930. At the age of sixty-six he shot himself in his Long Island home, Allondale, at Lloyds Harbor, Huntington.

At his death he was director of a dozen corporations, and in his will he left six million dollars to his wife, Isabelle May Black. There was no note, no motive the world could see; it could only guess. *The New York Times,* that very morning, headlined the story: INDUSTRIAL SLUMP SEEN NEARING END. Black knew better. Some friends and asociates found consolation in the fact that he did not live to see what was to happen to his country and to his beloved hotel.

Bernhard Beinecke, the conservative, with his fortune virtually intact, died quietly in his Plaza apartment on December 20, 1932, at the age of eighty-seven, leaving three sons to carry on for him. He lived to celebrate fifty years of happy married life with a Golden Anniversary party in 1925. His wife and daughter continued to live in the Beinecke suite; son Edwin took over the Black penthouse.

In the depths of its own depression, The Plaza suffered yet another blow. Death came to Fred Sterry in 1933, at the age of sixty-seven, while he was on a year's leave of absence because of illness. Ill health had necessitated an earlier leave in 1923. On his return in 1924, as president of the Plaza Operating Company, he had plunged back into work with his old-time vigor. In 1927 he became president of the new Savoy-Plaza Hotel, a United States Realty Company property, costing twenty million dollars, which rose on the site of the old Savoy Hotel. The cost of constructing that hotel in the twenties demonstrated that the day had passed when it was economically feasible to ignore price and produce a hotel as sumptuous in every detail as The Plaza.

Plaza partisans, as deeply concerned with the loss of three great oaks as with the fire raging through the economic forest, argued that Black, Beinecke and Sterry could have kept the hotel in the black, as they did in 1907. Actually the performance of The Plaza remained remarkable in spite of everything. During the dire thirties, more than 80 percent of the hotels in the United States went bankrupt; during that decade of depression not a single large new hotel was built. The new Waldorf-Astoria, occupying a full city square, opened its magnificent doors to a solemn city in 1931, but the construction was planned before the Wall Street crash.

The cushion which helped The Plaza survive was its roster of permanent, forever loyal, and in some cases, still financially substantial guests. Many wealthy widows continued living there with fortunes fairly intact; indeed, "the thirty-nine widows of The Plaza" achieved a measure of fame around the hotel as a slogan. In a display of financial solidarity the hotel's permanent guests carried on without as much as reducing the size of their tips. These diehards could not be pushed out of The Plaza. They would only be carried out. Unhappily, they were not as young as they had been in 1907.

But the times were grim enough at the hotel. John Auguste Pelay, who joined the staff in 1914 and was still serving in 1966, as bell captain, recalled a time when the staff waited three weeks for its pay, and transient guests were carrying their own luggage. Even the limited revenue derived from the Rose Room, which the Studebaker Company used as an automobile showroom during prohibition, ceased when the company moved out in 1930. The Grill Room of tea-dancing fame was converted into a furniture storeroom. No one was dancing in those days. Frequently only the Fifth Avenue Café, later to become the Edwardian Room, remained open for dinner.

They were desperate years for the entire country. The only people who seemed to be making money were the bootleggers, and the cult of Al Capone flourished as the country's economy was on an alarming downgrade.

Unemployment in 1930 stood at four and a half million; by 1932 over ten million people were unemployed, and United States industry was operating at less than half its maximum of 1929. Thousands of banks throughout the country had closed since the crash; the Bank of the United States in New York (no connection with the government despite its name), with 60 local branches and 400,000 depositors, collapsed in December, 1930, and with it went the funds of some of New York's richest. Yet that same year, when one of the largest rings of bootleggers was broken at Chicago, it was estimated that seven million gallons of whiskey had been sold to speakeasies all over the country, to total a business of some fifty million dollars.

President Hoover tried desperately to stem the floodtide of the depression by granting generous credit to industry and ordering a stern check on government spending. Congress in 1932 voted $116,000,000 for construction of public works to aid the unemployed; the Reconstruction Finance Corporation was established that year with two billion dollars at its disposal to advance loans to failing banks, building and loan societies, railroad and insurance companies and farm-mortgage associations. But Hoover didn't have a chance to see the outcome of his program; his time as the country's leader was running out. The public was demanding a change of administration, and the Democratic nominee, Franklin D. Roosevelt, was swept into office by a landslide in the 1932 elections.

Despite the change of administration, conditions remained desperate, and the low-water mark was reached on Inauguration Day with another tidal wave of bank failures. A special session of Congress was called on Sunday, March 5, 1933, to proclaim a national bank holiday, beginning the next day. Not until March 13 did the still solvent banks across the country begin to reopen. In the meantime hundreds of thousands of people were caught stranded, without available cash for even bare necessities. Guests at The Plaza were in a more fortunate position than many; credit was extended to all.

Spurred on by the dual calamity of depression and prohibition, the nation's leaders were loudly demanding repeal. Nicholas Murray Butler was constantly in the vanguard with impassioned speeches; that redoubtable "dry," John D. Rockefeller, sufficiently aroused by the scourge of prohibition which had brought with it an unprecedented crime wave, made urgent pleas for erasure of the Volstead Act. Other influential citizens, public-spirited women as well as men, raised their voices with his. With powerful forces against it, prohibition was doomed, and on December 6, 1933, another national milestone was reached with ratification of the

Twenty-first Amendment, repealing the Eighteenth Amendment.

With repeal came a brief lift in national spirits, as countless bars and hotel restaurants serving liquor reopened, and many new restaurants and bars came into being, creating new jobs as more revenue was put into circulation. The legalized liquor industry lumbered into high gear in 1934, as distillers lawfully satisfied an American thirst that took thirty-five million barrels of beer and forty-two million gallons of hard liquor to slake.

Henry A. Rost was operating manager of The Plaza in 1933, and the repeal of prohibition gave him his chance to revive the hotel as a scene of celebration and a gathering place for celebrities.

He first reopened the bar in the Oak Lounge. Women immediately flocked to it, and Rost recognized the need for a room with a setting attuned to feminine appeal both as a cocktail lounge and a fashionable place for dinner and supper dancing. The beautiful old Rose Room seemed like the ideal place.

Carefully he took his time to make it the most elegant and exciting room of its kind in New York. In Joseph Urban, a Viennese painter and scene designer who had taken Hollywood and Broadway by storm with his movie and stage sets—particularly his sets for Ziegfeld's Follies—Rost found the man he wanted. Urban didn't disappoint him.

From the splendors of Persia he took inspiration for what was to become the famed Persian Room. The exquisitely dramatic frescoes he designed were like dreams out of Omar Khayyám. Five murals, portraying in luminous colors the pleasures of dancing, singing, hunting, eating and drinking in Persian fashion, were transferred to the walls by Lillian Palmedo; red velvet draperies replaced the onetime rose; chairs were upholstered in rich crimson; brilliant blues gave dramatic accent here and there; and a twenty-seven-foot bar along the west wall was a happy reminder of Old Man Volstead's demise.

Rost then went into action on plans to make the Persian Room debut a great social occasion. Like Sterry before him, he fully appreciated the publicity and dollar value of the "society" label, and The Plaza had to have the tops. It was a social coup when he arranged for the opening to be a benefit for the impressively sponsored New York Infirmary for Women and Children. It also established a precedent for other smart supper-club openings. "For the benefit of" became the slogan that assured success for any society project—and this before the admission price could be deducted from income tax.

It was a great day for The Plaza when the Persian Room officially opened on April 1, 1934, with a glamorous cocktail dance attended by the *crème de la crème* of New York, Newport and Tuxedo Park. It could be nothing less, with Mrs. George U. Harris as chairman of the benefit. The former Lucile Baldwin of Tuxedo Park had been hailed as the greatest beauty and one of the most popular debutantes of her season. Later, as the wife of the very rich George Harris, whose socially exalted parents had long maintained an apartment at The Plaza, she was one of the leaders of the fashionable younger married set.

The press photographers snapped pictures of Lucile Harris, wearing the latest long-skirted import from Paris and a turban draped around her raven hair. The pictures were syndicated, and immediately a new fashion trend swept in. Persian turbans were featured by shops and fashion editors all over the country, and Persian blue became the popular color for accessories.

The opening was acclaimed by the press as the first great gala since the end of prohibition. It was a brilliant social occasion still remembered with nostalgia by many who were in attendance, the author included, and is constantly recalled in newspaper and magazine stories about The Plaza. The incomparable Emil Coleman, the most popular maestro of music in society's ranks, conducted his orchestra, and Tony and Renee DeMarco, appearing as featured dancers, created an immediate sensation that was to keep them in the limelight for years.

The DeMarcos that afternoon brought ballroom dancing out of the doldrums in which the low taste of the Charleston era had left it, and resparked the national enthusiasm for exhibition dancing, an earlier vogue dominated by Irene and Vernon Castle, Florence Walton and Maurice Hughes, Margaret Hawkesworth and Basil Durant. As they danced to the accompaniment of "Tea for Two," or a Chopin or Debussy musical arrangement, they chatted and laughed with each other, with the orchestra and with the customers, and society applauded their informal gaiety as it did their exquisite dancing. Later Tony and Renee were divorced, and a new marital and terpsichorean union was billed as Tony and Sally DeMarco. Both of the DeMarco teams became a legend of the Persian Room.

If the afternoon made headlines, the evening made social history of a sort. The inaugural dinner dance was top-heavy with "names." With so much going for it—society, Emil Coleman and the DeMarcos—the Persian Room was an assured success from the beginning. The fashionables flocked there nightly—and if the glamour didn't lure them, the prices did. In depression days the Persian Room menu featured dinner for $3.00, supper for a minimum of $1.50. At dinner, evening dress was "suggested"—for supper it was "respectfully stipulated," and respectfully society responded with gala parties that might number from thirty to forty guests in a single group. This was the era when society discovered it could be more fun, and cheaper in the end, to entertain in public than at home, thus inspiring the late Maury Paul, the famed Cholly Knickerbocker, to coin a phrase that has become a familiar in the American lexicon—"Café Society."

Patrons of the room were a new social generation, attractive debutantes and post-debs with their beaux, and "younger marrieds" restrained by the seriousness of the depression, but hungry for gaiety. Celebrities and socialites mixed and danced side by side. Mr. and Mrs. James Forrestal entertained for Gary Cooper; the Marchioness of Dufferin and Ava provided champagne for a party of forty just before dashing to see some of the guests off on the *Berengaria* in one of those jolly midnight sailings; Mr. and Mrs. John V. Bouvier were often there before their divorce, and at home, where she belonged, was their little daughter Jacqueline, the future Mrs. John F. Kennedy, who in so short a span of history was to become the First Lady and all too soon the First Widow of the land.

The fall of 1934 was even more brilliant, when Eddy Duchin and his orchestra followed Emil Coleman, and again with Tony and Renee DeMarco featured. Engaging Duchin for the Persian

Room's first formal winter season was another coup of Rost's, calculated to attract the smartest of the town's chic younger-married set and debutante crowd. The handsome young orchestra leader had first captured the fancy of society—with his infectious smile and good looks as well as his syncopated music—at the Central Park Casino of cherished memory, where his romance with the glamour girl of her year, Marjorie Oelrichs, flourished. Their marriage, shortly after his first Persian Room engagement, made the headlines of the nation: The bride had an impeccable social pedigree with the stamp of Newport, where the name Oelrichs ranked in distinction with Belmont, Vanderbilt, and Astor; the bridegroom was a self-made man of modest, simple background. It was the dream stuff of which novels and movies were made—and Hollywood did years later with *The Eddy Duchin Story.*

In his 1935 season in the Persian Room, it was "Mr. and Mrs. Duchin," and every evening found the young bride entertaining at ringside. Her guests, usually post-debutantes and young married friends who had come out with her in a season that produced a flock of glamour girls, gave special éclat to the room. Frequent guests and close Duchin friends were Mr. and Mrs. Averell Harriman. When Marjorie Duchin died in 1937, six days after the birth of her son, it was Marie and Ave Harriman who sheltered with family love and affection the baby Peter, while professional commitments took Eddy Duchin all over the country. Eddy was to meet a sad death in 1951, after a long, lingering illness, but his musical talent lives on in his son. Peter Duchin and his orchestra are a society favorite today.

There is no doubt that the Persian Room helped The Plaza out of the financial doldrums. In its first year, the still depressed 1934, gross receipts of the Room were in the vicinity of twenty-three thousand weekly. It was beginning to look like old times again—gay if not altogether carefree times.

The Grill was still closed to tea dancing, but the Tea Court, renamed the Palm Court, flourished again as a gathering place for all ages, where the waiters served dowagers, debutantes and small-fry with equal deference.

The Oak Lounge was converted into a dining room, officially

named the Oak Room, but always to remain for old-timers "the Back Room of The Plaza." George M. Cohan appeared promptly at five every afternoon in, by now, "his corner," to be joined by celebrity friends. An average afternoon would see fifteen to twenty men and women gathered around the Grand Old Man of the stage. No one was allowed to pick up a check; none was presented. Headwaiter Cesar Boyer, at The Plaza since 1925, knew to whom the bill was to be charged.

The thirties saw The Plaza becoming more and more of a transient hotel. As older tenants died, great apartments were broken up into small suites and transient rooms to provide additional revenue, and it was slowly beginning to pay off.

The country was not yet singing "Happy Days Are Here Again," but here and there a break appeared in the economic clouds. Henry Ford made a confident gesture by restoring the five-dollar-a-day minimum wage to 47,000 of his 70,000 workers in 1934; more gains in the nation's economy were registered the following year. In 1936 commerce was 12–15 percent higher in dollar totals than the previous year. Farm prices were up, metals were up, production of automobiles increased by 20 percent. Things were looking up.

Yet even as the public confidence was rising came ominous rumblings of approaching catastrophe. As in 1914, they were again emanating from Europe. Nazism and Fascism were on the rise, and a Spanish civil war broke out. Much public sympathy in the United States was on the side of the Loyalists, and young men by the hundreds voluntarily transported themselves to Spain to join the anti-Franco armies. It was but a hint of things to come.

Dispatches from abroad brought more and more disquieting reports as the menace of Hitlerism rose. A free world was shocked when in September 1938 the Munich Pact was signed by Hitler, Mussolini, Chamberlain and Daladier. The Sudetenland and all important Czechoslovakian military strongholds were yielded to Germany in an attempt to avoid war. Anthony Eden, then British Foreign Secretary, resigned in protest of Prime Minister Neville Chamberlain's policy of appeasement.

Up went the market, down went the market—and everyone was

saying prosperity was just around the corner when the New York World's Fair opened in April 1939. For The Plaza, as for other New York hotels, it was a heaven-sent bonanza as international exhibitors with large accompanying staffs and visitors from all over the country flocked to New York with money to spend.

Almost simultaneously with the Fair opening came the blow; the prophecy of doom was realized in Europe. After ceaseless aggression, German armies invaded Poland without declaration of war; two days later Great Britain and France declared war against Germany. Soon almost every European nation would be involved in total warfare.

The tremendous volume of war orders that flooded the country's factories brought an upswing in recovery, but a troubled, watchful United States, officially neutral, unofficially solidly behind England, could no longer delude itself that it could keep out of the conflict. Yet when the Japanese struck at Pearl Harbor on December 7, 1941, the shock to the nation was as sudden as the blast which totally destroyed or seriously damaged nineteen American ships and cost three thousand American lives.

Barely twenty-five years after one world war, America was enmeshed in another. A divided, fearful nation, after a year of fence-straddling for "peace at any price," responded to the disaster of Pearl Harbor with angry dedication and a single-minded unity it had not known since 1917.

Overnight it looked as if the whole country had gone into uniform. The scene at The Plaza was 1917–1918 all over again, but something new had been added. The distaff side was now in the thick of it; the "best dressed" were not ten, but thousands of women in uniform—debutantes and their sisters and their cousins and their aunts who had joined the WAC's, the WAVES, even the Marines. Their uniforms mingled with those of volunteer groups, the AWVS, the Red Cross Aides, countless others.

Suddenly everybody was traveling in all directions: to and from boot camps and aviation training centers; to and from Washington, to, but not from, the battlefields.

The Plaza lobbies took on the characteristics of Grand Central Terminal, and many of the faces in the crowd, men and women on official wartime missions, were familiar ones—Colonel Oveta Culp Hobby, director of the Women's Army Corps; Ambassador Myron C. Taylor; Beardsley Ruml, whose famous tax plan was one of Washington's controversial war issues; Secretary of the Navy Frank Knox; former Secretaries Josephus Daniels and Truman H. Newberry.

Hotel space in wartime was so scarce that The Plaza, like other hotels, was setting up emergency cots in the ballroom and smaller function rooms, even in executive offices. The office cot-occupiers were warned they'd have to vacate before the 9 A.M. arrival of an assistant manager or an accounting executive. In all hotels a five-day rule went into effect: transients could not be accommodated for a longer period and were forced to look for another hotel and another five-day stay.

Again The Plaza was in the vanguard of war-relief fund-raising efforts and entertainment projects for the men in uniform. Even before America's involvement, the hotel had been the scene of numerous benefits in behalf of Allied war-relief organizations. The first "Bundles for Britain Ball" was held in the Grand Ballroom under the direction of one of society's most indefatigable young matrons, who as Natalie Wales was a "do-and-dare" debutante before "causes" became fashionable. Violently pro-British, she had sparked the "Bundles for Britain" movement at the beginning of World War Two in Europe; when the United States entered the war, she turned her efforts to "Bundles for America." Today, as Lady Douglas-Hamilton, she is still in the forefront of causes.

The Grill Room now came into good use, to be reopened in the war effort. There, in 1942, Mrs. Marshall Field and Mrs. Charles C. Auchincloss inaugurated the first in a series of tea dances for officers of Allied nations. The Plaza also donated its ballroom for weekly dances for servicemen, and benefits to provide funds for canteens were many and often. Among those most socially sponsored were the dances for the Soldiers' and Sailors' Club, headed by Mrs. Donald Tansill, later Mrs. Gustav Rainville, and Mrs. William Woodward, one of New York society's Great Ladies.

The surface still shone in the Persian Room, flourishing in the boom of wartime traffic. On September 22, 1942, the seasonal opening was a Navy League benefit for the families of both the Navy and the Merchant Marine. The sponsoring group was headed by Mrs. John Jacob Astor. In long kid gloves, the incomparable Hildegarde played the piano and sang naughty songs with the air of a youngster eavesdropping. "She pinched young soldiers on the cheeks and kissed old soldiers on their bald spots," wrote reporter Harriet Van Horne in the *World-Telegram*. With audacity she introduced generals to privates, admirals to sailors. "Will you salute this enlisted man?" she would ask the brass, and the officers always played along.

"War money flowed. So did champagne," reminisced Hildegarde later in her book *Over 50—So What?* And added with no false modesty: "I drew a champagne crowd."

The war bond drives were on again. One evening during her performance Hildegarde was inspired to ask for someone in the audience to purchase a really big bond, and warmed up the room by singing, "The Last Time I Saw Paris," as only she could. She got what she asked for—a twenty-five-thousand-dollar war bond was sold on the spot. Aware of the publicity available, large corporations soon responded to a Hildegarde song and a request by purchasing what mounted to a total of a million dollars' worth in bonds.

In the sixth of many war bond drives staged during World War Two, the Plaza won another prize for selling $1,400,000 worth, close to $1,500 a room and, as the newspapers reported, a "record." Many of the reporters were too young to recall World War One, when the Plaza sold $35,000 worth of bonds for every bedroom in the hotel—but then, there were three hundred less rooms at that time.

In some upper-case New York nightclubs a private or ordinary sailor found it difficult to get a table. They never had a hard time at The Plaza. Headwaiters recognized many a GI, even out of evening dress, as Yale, Harvard or Princeton boys who had made up the debutante-dance stag lines. Wartime replacements among the waiters were impressed by management with the importance of treating enlisted men as well as officers with respect. At The Plaza, every customer was a personage; the GI of today might be the industrial leader of tomorrow.

Like The Plaza, Mrs. Charles O. Maas was a lady with the capacity to rise to the occasion. The widow of President Woodrow Wilson's naval aide, who died in 1919 leaving her only modestly provided for, she was then living in a first-floor suite, part of the famed Guggenheim apartment which had been cut down to a number of small suites, each retaining its semblance of original elegance. She was able to continue there because of a special low rate. With her small inheritance she undertook to give a series of parties for servicemen.

To her first party, on Washington's Birthday 1942, she invited three hundred soldiers, and as the war continued she made a habit of entertaining some half-dozen soldiers every Sunday night. She did not import girls for the boys, and she discouraged war stories.

Those lucky enough to get an invitation were content to dine with her in the elegant Persian Room and return to her apartment to wander, as in a museum, gazing at paintings and antiques.

No stone monument would do for Mrs. Maas or her husband. She wanted a living memorial. When the emergency ended she retreated quietly into favored shadows, cherishing a book in which the boys had inscribed their names and expressed their thanks.

In March 1945 Morton Downey was the singing star in the Persian Room when fourth-term President Franklin D. Roosevelt asked for a midnight curfew for soldiers and sailors.

"He's running the country, I'm running the city," said New York's Mayor Fiorello La Guardia, and set the curfew for an hour later. Playing it safe, however, the Persian Room closed down at midnight, time enough to take in enough, the press remarked, while restaurateur Toots Shor made his immortal crack, "Any crumb bum who can't get stewed by midnight, ain't tryin'!"

La Guardia was dining at The Plaza on the evening of April 12, 1945, when a waiter brought him the news of President Roosevelt's death. When victory in Europe was achieved on May 4, the reaction at The Plaza was in subdued contrast to November 1918, both

RICHARD AVERILL SMITH

Everett Shinn's Oak Room mural, depicting a wintry night in 1908.

John Warner ("Bet-a-Million") Gates, among the Plaza tenants who helped finance the hotel, with Mrs. Gates.

UNITED PRESS INTERNATIONAL

Hetty Green, who once stayed at The Plaza for a month, with her family.

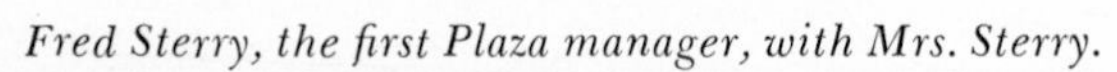

Fred Sterry, the first Plaza manager, with Mrs. Sterry.

HAVENS

Mrs. Clara Bell Walsh in the suite she occupied for fifty years.

The Plaza's first public event, honoring the Lord Bishop of London, 1907.

IRWIN DRIBBEN

Hungarian author Ferenc Molnar resided at The Plaza, 1940–52.

UNITED PRESS INTERNATIONAL

Frederick Townsend Martin and Mrs. Charles Alexander at a costume ball in The Plaza's early years.

IRWIN DRIBBEN

Operatic star Mary Garden at the hotel in 1952.

Virginia Sterry Twitchell, center rear, *in a Spence show.*

D'ARLENE STUDIO

Art collector Chester Dale and Mrs. Dale.

Mrs. John Lindsay and brother-in-law Robert Lindsay at a 1950 benefit.

IRWIN DRIBBEN

IRWIN DRIBBEN

Helen Hayes, Charles MacArthur, and William J. Hunt.

Peggy Wood, Lillian Gish, and Gertrude Lawrence.

IRWIN DRIBBEN

Jose Ferrer, Milton Baron, Georgette Cohan, George M. Cohan, Jr.

IRWIN DRIBBEN

François Gouron, Plaza chef during the mid-forties.

Elizabeth Taylor inspects the kitchen with Nicky Hilton.

IRWIN DRIBBEN

out of respect to Roosevelt and an awareness that the war was yet to be won in the Pacific. But it was joyous enough.

But on V-J Day—victory in Japan—on August 14, with President Truman's announcement of the unconditional surrender of Japan, it was the 1918 Armistice all over again at The Plaza—as everywhere—a frenzy of joyous celebration from cocktail hour long into the dawn of another day, when the last newspaper was on the streets and the confetti was swept out of the lobbies.

On September 26, 1945, a gala Victory Ball was staged in the Persian Room for the benefit of the Soldiers' and Sailors' Club—the first festive formal dance since the beginning of the war. As reported in the society columns, "Everybody who was anybody was there." Chairmen Elsie Woodward and Milly Tansill didn't even have to try.

CHAPTER EIGHT

Heartbeat of a Hotel

NORA SULLIVAN, Annie Sullivan and Mary O'Sullivan established such a tradition of generations of Irish maids and Irish wit at The Plaza that in no time at all a newly engaged advertising agency was inspired to create a correspondence between a pixie chambermaid and some thirty thousand top business executives. The by now famous "Mary O'Sullivan letters" turned out to be the most hilarious direct-mail campaign of the century; it brought increased business and won awards from the advertising fraternity for the hotel.

Annie Sullivan had no equal when it came to the delicate task of ironing girls' party dresses, and it was her personal delight to see that little Lorraine Manville Gould, Mrs. Cornelius Dresselhuys' daughter and Tommy Manville's niece, who was born at The Plaza, was the most exquisitely dressed child in New York's small-fry social set.

It took Nora Sullivan, a chambermaid as Irish as the Blarney stone, to make the discovery of a lost wallet at The Plaza something to write about. When Nora left County Cork en route to America, where she would seek to settle, she lost her passport in England—and what a time she had to get another!

"I found to me great surprise," she said in her emerald brogue, "that you can't go nowhere without a passport."

So, when one day in May 1963 she came upon a forgotten wallet in a bureau drawer containing among other items two passports, she rushed to the executive housekeeper, Kay Arendt.

"Oh, ma'am, I do hope you can find the poor man. He'll be in the divil's own mess without these passports."

"Good Lord, did you see all this money?" replied Miss Arendt, as she counted out a thousand dollars in greenbacks. Her standards of values differed; she had never had passport trouble.

"Yes, yes," wailed Nora, "but it's the passports that's important." She chafed at the "inconvenience the poor man must be sufferin'."

Through identification cards Arthur Dooley, then a Plaza manager, located the owner, happily not caught in immigration at Kennedy Airport, but safely at home in San Antonio, Texas, whither he had traveled on borrowed funds, and with no idea of the whereabouts of his wallet. While on the telephone with him, Dooley mentioned the chambermaid's concern over the passport, rather than the money; with typical Texas largesse the owner directed Dooley to give Nora five hundred dollars and mail back to him wallet, passport and the remaining money.

"Aw, he needn't have done a thing like that," said Nora, shy and embarrassed at the attention. Interviewed later by columnist Norton Mockridge, who asked if she had had any moment of temptation, she replied in shocked tones: "Oh, no, no. It's part of our religion to be honest; it's part of our job."

"It's part of our job" exemplified the spirit of responsibility and unswerving loyalty of more than half a century of Plaza employees. Everything is relative, and the Plaza always has claimed one of the most satisfied staffs in New York, as well as boasting of having retained more employees for a longer length of time than any other hotel. Hundreds who joined the hotel in 1907 worked there until they retired. Dozens who came a few years later are still there.

Service pins commemorating twenty, thirty and forty years on the staff have to be mass-produced, and company parties celebrating retirement after forty and fifty years occur almost annually. Silver-haired veterans already retired are invited back as special guests.

John Auguste Pelay, Plaza bell captain, who has been described as "five-feet-three of quiet dynamite," was honored with a gala party celebrating his fiftieth anniversary year at the hotel in March 1964. To the surprise of John and The Plaza alike, the City of New York recognized the importance of the occasion by presenting him with an award. The citation reads:

> To John Auguste Pelay, who has served for fifty years at the Plaza Hotel in New York, one of the world's most renowned hostelries, and who through his relationships with countless thousands of visitors brought credit not only to the hotel, but to New York, through his kindness, energetic service and unfailing courtesy.

High-priced publicists have worked for months, sometimes years, to achieve such an accolade for an important client. In this instance, it was a story in *The New York Times,* by Philip Dougherty, who interviewed Pelay, that inspired Commissioner Richard C. Patterson, Jr., of the Department of Commerce and Public Events to suggest the citation. Commissioner Patterson, representing the Mayor of the City of New York, was invariably on hand to greet heads of state and diplomats arriving at The Plaza, and remembered warmly the services and attention to their needs of the bright-eyed little bell captain and his assistants.

Romeo Giannini, Pelay's predecessor, who rose from elevator operator to bell captain, belonged to the class of 1907 and was one of the last to retire, in 1955. A decade later, at the age of seventy-six, he sighed in happy reminiscence. "What beautiful women! And how they dressed! They were a sight to see on an opera night."

With total recall he rattled off not only the names of the elite roster, but identified the tenants by floors and suites: John Wanamaker of Philadelphia in Suite 1001; Mr. and Mrs. Isaac Gimbel, also of Philadelphia, parents of Bernard Gimbel, in an eleventh-floor suite; Colonel Sosthenes Behn, head of I.T. &. T., and Mrs. Behn, occupying an apartment on the fourth floor (tall, handsome Mrs. Behn is still in residence at this writing); Howard Gould on the fourth floor, and so on. There was no mistaking his pride in being a Plaza alumnus.

The Plaza today has a little more than a thousand employees, not much over the size of the staff when it opened, and they constitute a storehouse of fascinating tales and incidents not only of guests, but concerning themselves. The stories would fill volumes and afford a footnote to history; many, of course, must be buried in discretion and consideration for personal feelings. When, after the departure of a "Mr. and Mrs. X" a chambermaid discovered a small fortune in jewels in a bureau drawer and turned them over to the housekeeper, discretion dictated the management's handling of their return. Before notifying "Mrs. X," the security officer first got in touch with "Mr. X" at his office. The lady of the jewels, it developed, was not his wife. It is quite possible a divorce was averted.

Ralph W. Ruggiero was an attendant in the Turkish baths when he first came to The Plaza some thirty-five years ago and his first thrill was receiving a tennis racket belonging to international tennis champion Jay Gould, from the late George Jay Gould. Today as an assistant manager, he greets the grandchildren as well as grandnieces and grandnephews of the sundry Goulds who made The Plaza their home in earlier days. Edith Kingdon Gould Martin, Mrs. George J. Gould's granddaughter and namesake, and her husband Guy Martin are frequent visitors from their home in Georgetown; "regulars" at The Plaza on their trips from their Maryland estate are her brother, Kingdon Gould, Jr., and his wife, often accompanied by several of their brood of nine children.

For many years a Plaza laundress arrived for work very early in the morning in a chauffeured limousine. Anna Tynan, who was in charge of the laundry, was married to Mayor Jimmy Walker's chauffeur, Charles Brown, and such were the merry Mayor's social habits that often Brown would arrive home in the wee hours just in time to drive Anna grandly to work.

Anna was a Plaza veteran of fifty years before she retired in 1960, thereby generating a flood of syndicated press stories. The bare fact that she survived a half century of laundry service caused a Philadelphia columnist somewhat removed from the scene to envision poor Anna toiling untold years bending over a washtub. "Does it bother her that some members of the staff get all the recognition?" he wondered.

The writer could have saved his crocodile tears. Few employees in The Plaza's history received more publicity than Irish-American Anna, and she fully appreciated her place in the hotel picture as well as in the laundry. She was an interviewer's dream, and reporters listened to her tales of love, marriage and remarriage with a twinkle and a ready pencil. Her first job was ironing the beautiful delicate Irish curtains, and she did not fail to see what was behind them.

Anna Tynan ran one of the largest, best-managed and most expensive laundries in the country, and her large staff of assistants included four sisters—Cecelia, Ellen, Mary and Agnes. Her father was in the employ of the contractor who supplied much of the marble for the hotel. All of which made Anna's pride in The Plaza akin to family pride.

The father of the late Prime Minister Nehru is said to have sent his best personal laundry to Paris to be properly done. While guests at The Plaza have not gone quite so far, one guest continued to send Anna her laundry long after she left. In a letter, from her summer home at Fisher's Island, Mrs. W. D. Campbell wrote: "Dear Miss Tynan: Thank you so much for doing the laundry for me. I always love the Plaza laundry work and during the war sent all my sheets, etc., from Oklahoma . . . I had no idea the kitchen laundry went too. . . . The shirts came back beautifully done."

Thomas Pappas, headwaiter in the Palm Court and a forty-year man before his retirement in 1961, was a favorite among debutantes and college girls.

"Before they become engaged, they bring in their future husbands and say, 'What do you think of him?' They listen to me more than to their own fathers and mothers," he boasted.

One Southern belle brought three suitors to Pappas for inspection; the fourth passed muster. "This one is all right," he said. At the invitation of the parents of the bride, Mr. and Mrs. Pappas attended the wedding in the South as their personal guests.

Jack Koch, who started as a busboy in 1908 and rose to become headwaiter, could have retired long before he did, in the middle fifties. When he left, he was a rich man as a result of Wall Street tips from some of the guests. One was industrialist Orlando Weber; another was Frederick Bedford, a founder of the Standard Oil Company. Bedford asked him once how he invested his savings. Koch told him he had bonds and some corporation stocks, among them Bush Terminal stock. Bedford advised, "Hold your Bush Terminal for a while, sell when it gets to fifty dollars; buy some A.T. & T., and put all you can in Standard Oil of New Jersey and Standard Oil of California. Don't sell this oil stock. Your children and grandchildren will be able to live off them."

Said Koch to the author, "I took his advice and I still have all my stock." He left a substantial inheritance when he died in October 1965 at the age of seventy-five.

John Christoforon, supervisor of the employees' cafeteria, in October 1963, received fifty shares of Hotel Corporation of America Stock from Vice President Paul Sonnabend in recognition of fifty years of "dedicated and fruitful service."

Gold is where you find it, and a Plaza chef found plenty in a book loaned to him. Chef François Gouron, king of the kitchen in the Hilton administration, was an inveterate reader, and it was the custom of the late Boyd Hatch, one of Floyd Odlum's associates in Atlas Corporation, who was living at The Plaza with his family, to send down to Chef François books and magazines which he had read and no longer had need of.

Staying at the hotel, too, was Federico Bemberg of Buenos Aires, one of the world's richest men, whose brother Otto had married Mr. and Mrs. Hatch's daughter Georgia. The Bemberg family owned the internationally known Argentinian banking firm of O. Bemberg and Company, and their fortune was estimated at over a billion dollars.

So when Chef François, in glancing through one of the books sent by Hatch, came across a scrawled memorandum, obviously to be removed but forgotten, from Bemberg to Hatch, advising him to buy Rheingold stock, he sat up and took plenty of notice. "If it's good enough for them, it's good enough for me," he reasoned with good cause, and acting on the accidental tip bought enough stock to yield him a neat profit—sixteen thousand dollars—when he sold it.

Like all hotels, The Plaza has cultivated celebrity guests; unlike most, its efforts have no direct connection with the publicity to be had. The image of The Plaza, the caliber of the clientele, is what matters. And beyond this, individual employees have found time to cultivate their personal enthusiasm among the great.

A man named Smith was the object of a campaign on the part of a staff executive such as has seldom been launched to win the patronage of a head of state. David Smith, famed metals sculptor, rated by art critics among the greatest of modern sculptors in steel, had been coming to the hotel for years on his numerous trips to New York from his home at Bolton Landing in the Adirondacks. Sheila Lee, for two decades head of the credit department, looked forward to his visits. One day the ebullient Sheila inadvertently learned that Smith was in town but registered at the St. Regis, and, sleuthing around, she discovered the reason why. It seems that bills from The Plaza, intended for another David Smith of considerably less than A-1 credit, were being sent to sculptor Smith with those certain polite, but firm, requests that he pay up. Confused identities multiplied the confusion of bills, which so annoyed the artist that he switched allegiance.

Irish and determined, Sheila made it her business to get him back. She knew his reputation and his work, and was aware that a number of his creations were on exhibition in New York at the time, so off to the museums she hied herself, to the Museum of Modern Art and others displaying his work. She studied and took notes, and armed with this as ammunition telephoned Smith at Bolton Landing to explain what a natural error had been made—"Smiths are as numerous as Lees." She was so sad, she wailed, that he had deserted The Plaza, for she was one of his greatest admirers, and to prove it launched into conversation about the specific works she had seen, and pelted him with questions and critiques on sculpture in general, all of which she managed to make both discerning and admiring. Who would not be flattered?

Smith was charmed as well as flattered, and promised on his next visit to New York to come back to The Plaza.

A few years later, when the hotel was discarding an ancient addressograph for a more modern one, Sheila thought that "The Vulcan of United States Art," as Smith was known, might like it for some of his metalwork inspiration, and it was dispatched to Bolton Landing, much to his delight. Later, on a postcard from Italy, he sent his thanks. "Most grateful am I. I loved that machine. I'll make something with it in due time. Strange for me to be in with the A-cups and party girls, but it was most complimentary." This last was in reference to the Spoleto Festival of Two Worlds, "Sculptures in the City," which he had been invited to judge.

Smith died May 23, 1965, only a few months after having been appointed by President Johnson to the National Council on the Arts. That last card he sent her is one of Sheila Lee's most cherished mementos.

Another famous sculptor, Carl Milles, came to The Plaza one time to discover there was no room for him at the inn; the clerk regretfully said he had no record of a reservation, and the hotel was full. In despair Milles sought out Sheila Lee, of whom he had heard from Smith.

"I'm Carl Milles," he said.

"You are!" she exclaimed. "I am so glad to meet you."

"I wish the room clerk were as impressed," he sighed and told his sad tale. Somehow, by some magic hocus-pocus known only to her, Sheila managed to secure a small room for the elderly, white-haired Milles.

While at the hotel Milles contracted pneumonia and was confined to his room for weeks, with Sheila a frequent visitor. His wife had joined Milles during his illness, and one day during his convalescence she took him to Rockefeller Center to watch the ice-skating. Enchanted with the whirling of a little seven-year-old girl, Milles sought out her parents and asked permission to sculpt her. While in bed he completed one of his loveliest little figures, the well-known "The Skating Girl." Sheila received one of the first to be cast in bronze, and it occupies a place of honor in her apartment. Sheila Lee left The Plaza in 1965—but her memory lingers on.

Naturally, not all the best people stay forever. Harry, an early bartender, quit to go to Paris after World War One and there opened the famous Harry's New York Bar, which became the haunt of American Bohemians. William O'Dwyer, a young law student, eked out his limited funds by working as a bartender in the Oak Room. He was to visit it often in later years as the Mayor of New York City.

William C. Tonetti joined the staff in 1924 as secretary to the maître d'hôtel and rose to become a banquet manager. After twenty-nine years the Plaza lost him to the Metropolitan Club, the club created by J. P. Morgan after the Union League Club black-balled one of his friends. "Bill" Tonetti is a walking history book on The Plaza; an hour or two with him is an experience in nostalgia.

In the early days Plaza waiters were to be seen and not heard, while Plaza maids were neither to be seen nor heard. They would tiptoe around and rush into the bedroom when Milady left for the day, complete their job before her return, rush in again when she left for dinner, to turn down the sheets, and dash quickly out again before being seen.

All this has changed with "Operation Name," a recently inaugurated management campaign to train personnel in the importance of addressing all guests by name—how to obtain and remember the names. A guest leaving a call with the telephone operator for a certain hour the next morning will be flattered on hearing a cheery voice say, "Good Morning, Mr. Jones, it is eight o'clock."

Katherine Thompsen, Plaza manicurist since 1912, with a now fifty-five-year service record, is among those who needed no "Operation Name" training. She can reel off half the names in the New York *Social Register* in total recall of her customers. Harry Symes Lehr, who came down often from Newport, was a dandy and an egotist with feminine mannerisms; John D. Rockefeller came in about every ten days and true to legend was a dime-tipper; Henry Clay Frick commanded her services up at the Frick mansion on Fifth Avenue and was a prodigal tipper who gave her a twenty-dollar gold piece over the three-dollar barbershop charge.

Carl Zahn, first owner of the shop, paid her eight dollars a week —but there were compensations. Davies Warfield, president of the

Seaboard Airlines in the twenties, and uncle of Wallis Warfield Simpson, who became the Duchess of Windsor, remembered her handsomely in his will, leaving her fifty thousand dollars and two seven-carat diamond rings. "Not bad for a poor working girl," she remarked with a gleam in her eyes.

Customer generosity, but not of such munificence, helped the first manicurists survive a seven-day week at eight dollars. But Pauline Szabo, among the unsung heroines of the labor movement, went on strike way back in 1911, for more money and a half day off, and lost her job. Pauline should see The Plaza today. In this thirty-five-hour a week era, the chef cannot fire a cook for spoiling the broth without consulting the union.

The barbershop is symbolic of the enduring relationship between the barbers and the customers. When in 1947 a redecorating job was completed under the direction of socialite Mrs. W. Dorland Doyle, they celebrated with a huge, ever-so-social cocktail party to which the male patrons were privileged to bring their ladies. The party featured the original 1907 beer keg, and the world's champion barbershop quartet, the St. Mary's Horse-shoers. The late Anthony J. Drexel Biddle, and his step-son-in-law, Prince Hohenlohe, were among the first to arrive among several hundred guests who represented the *Social Register, Who's Who,* top industrial and Wall Street tycoons, the majority of them old-time barbershop customers.

Reminisce with Ralph Sclarace, head barber, whose first job there was in 1916, and you learn that barbers then were paid $14 a week; that haircuts were forty cents as against $2.50 today, that a shave was twenty cents compared to today's $1.50. But the tips were larger then.

Other things have changed too, including the location of the shop, which, to make way for the Trader Vic Restaurant, was moved in 1965 from its original lower lobby space to mezzanine quarters overlooking Central Park. Long, long ago the barber chairs had connections for telephones, but there are none today. Many guests used pomades and lotions they brought over from Europe for their own use; today the shop stocks a variety to satisfy every male taste. The stories of the greats who were shaven and shorn there are many: Chauncey Depew would permit only owner Carl Zahn to trim his whiskers; Florenz Ziegfeld would give out free tickets for his famous *Follies,* but the barbers were more interested in the beauties who often came to meet him there; Jimmy Walker was a sport and a generous tipper; Damon Runyon was "one of the finest men to patronize the shop," and even when suffering from cancer of the throat was cheerful to the last; the advent of the Gillette safety razor had much to do with the Sunday closing, since men began to shave themselves; and only two women were ever permitted to have a haircut in the Plaza barbershop—the indomitable Clara Bell Walsh, who sacrificed her long, blond hair to the "bob" of the twenties, and her pal, Mary Martin, who had to "wash that man right out of her hair" for years.

The "mutual enthusiasm society" going for staff and tenants since 1907 was never better illustrated than in the relationship between Mr. and Mrs. Arthur Lipper, who took up residence in 1933, and their floor maid, Margaret Alford (the same who wrote poems to Celeste Holm's son Danny). Mr. and Mrs. Lipper were a devoted couple who celebrated their golden wedding anniversary with a party at The Plaza in 1950; everything was coming up golden, even to orchids dipped in gold. When Mr. Lipper died in 1956, maid Margaret, a painter whose artistic efforts had won her many prizes in amateur contests, sought to console the widow with something she knew would please her. From memory and from photographs the chambermaid painted two portraits of the late Mr. Lipper. The venerable Mrs. Lipper, who could afford orchids dipped in gold, was delighted with the paintings, which hang on the walls among her precious personal furnishings—one in the living room, the other in her bedroom.

Dukas Stavros, a Greek waiter, and Stavros Livanos, a Greek shipping magnate, became friends on the basis of a name and language in common. For a vacation one year, the shipping magnate shipped Stavros, his wife and two children off to their native land as his guests.

There is larceny of a sort even in the hearts of the rich, dignified and elegant guests who occupy the rich, dignified and elegant Plaza rooms. A Plaza housekeeper divided hotel guests into two types—those who leave everything behind and those who take everything not nailed down. Petty thefts have added up to as many as seventy thousand washcloths in six months; guests wrap things in them. Ball-point pens disappear by the thousands; silverware, towels, coffeepots, cups, embroidered sheets, even blankets and bathroom rugs disappear in the luggage of some departing guests. The room check is sufficiently thorough that the housekeeper usually knows who has appropriated what—before the bill is presented by the cashier. It is, of course, expected that guests will take matches and soap, pens and pencils. But the mammoth unsolved mystery is who managed to get away with a still missing piano from the ballroom—and *how*.

Guests forget the oddest assortment of possessions—trusses and dentures, furs and evening gowns, eyeglasses, nighties and pajama bottoms galore. When possible, all are mailed back to the owner—but informing the departed guest of some types of property left behind calls for tact and diplomacy. Some women would rather lose a set of dentures than admit to wearing them.

Catering to the special tastes of tenants is more in the Plaza line. The sort of thing the housekeeper learns from experience is that the Gregory Pecks want a double bed, and the Egyptian delegation to the United Nations wants no beds at all. Joan Sutherland always eats well after a concert, and a woman executive heading one of the country's largest aviation companies, who gave her patronage to another hotel because she couldn't stand the red accents in her Plaza suite, is now back in the fold, happy in the all-blue suite management makes it a point to reserve for her.

A color-blind tenant asked for a green sofa, then swore, when it arrived, that it was blue. Without a word, the weight lifters picked up the green sofa, and a blue one was substituted. This the lady saw as green, and everybody rested happily.

In an operation of the size of The Plaza, crises are bound to occur. A military aide to the President of a South American country once called the desk and, using his own name, requested quick laundry service. The clothes were returned the same day—with the lieutenant's name stenciled on every piece of the President's underwear. The anguished aide was sure he would be relegated to jungle duty. With ingenious tact, Mrs. Nina Lytle, head of the International Department, convinced him that with the lieutenant's name before him every day, the President would be continually reminded of the officer's good qualities.

There are gripes, too, plenty of them. Even in Sterry's time the hotel had its share of complaints to keep it on its toes. One complaint even made the headlines in 1910: "GLOBE-TROTTING MILLIONAIRE PUTS THIS CITY ON GRILL."

Peeved at The Plaza, Randolph Berens, a globe-trotter and Egyptologist, had this to say to the press: "In all your life you never saw anything like the treatment I got. . . . I paid six dollars a day for my room and two dollars a day for my man's room, and when I asked for a place to play a little game of solitaire, why, the big, pompous man in charge said, 'Mr. Berens, you'll have to play in your room.' "

For every Randolph Berens, there are a multiple of Eleanor Powells. The famous dancing star, who was appearing in the Persian Room, took time to write a note of appreciation to Mrs. Helen Carey, her chambermaid. ". . . How can I ever thank you enough for all your kindness. What a wonderful person you are. . . . You just don't know how much you are helping me to give a good performance each evening. Your warmth and smile and just the you of you each night is part of the applause I receive. It takes many people to make a star sparkle. You are an important part of my success here in New York."

Like Sullivans and O'Sullivans, like Alfords and Lees, like Pelays and Christoforons, Helen Carey epitomizes the spirit of loyalty and pride of Plaza employees throughout its long and elegant life.

CHAPTER NINE

People Are Funny

KAISER WILHELM once caused something of a royal controversy by declining to sanction the annual award of the Art Gold Medal to Herr Paul Wallott, designer of the Palace of the Imperial Parliament in Berlin. The Kaiser decreed that this highest of honors should be given, instead, to the artist who had painted his portrait six times, the Princess Vilma Elizabeth Lwoff-Parlaghy. This may have been enough to start the rumor that she was his mistress.

If medals were awarded for the most fabulous of personalities ever to have stayed at The Plaza, the greatest of the free spenders and the most eccentric, the Princess Lwoff-Parlaghy would win them all. She had more dash than the Prince of Wales; she spent more at The Plaza than "Diamond Jim" Brady, who gave his favorites gold-plated bicycles, or "Bet-a-Million" Gates, generally considered top tipper. And before women won the right to vote, she won recognition as the world's leading feminine painter. By keeping a pet lion cub at The Plaza she outdid the eccentric who could afford to indulge his fear of germs by renting empty rooms above and below him to avoid contamination.

Arriving to paint the portraits of the most prominent men in America, the Princess swept into The Plaza in 1908 accompanied by a retinue consisting of a royal surgeon, a private secretary, a chamberlain resplendent in blue military coat with coronet embroidered on his hat, two butlers, three maids and a bodyguard attired in a magnificent green uniform of military cut with gold epaulets. In her arms, the Princess carried her pet spaniel, Bübchen. Her menagerie of bears, wolves, monkeys and reptiles she had diplomatically left abroad, but her two riding horses pranced into the Sixty-seventh Street Riding Academy simultaneously with her descent upon The Plaza.

For herself, the Princess engaged a suite of many rooms on the third floor, overlooking Central Park, at a cost of $1,333 a month. This was only the first of her many trips to the United States, and the next time she came she did better. She chose a larger suite of rooms costing three thousand dollars a month. At dinner parties, the butlers, clad in crimson satin coats and black satin knickerbockers, served guests from platters and salad dishes of solid gold. The value of the art she brought along to decorate her suite was variously estimated at from three to ten million dollars. Art connoisseurs particularly appreciated a carving of an archbishop by the greatest of all wood sculptors, Tilman Riemenschneider, the only one of his works outside a European church or museum.

For special privileges the Princess paid lavishly, and she gave strict orders that no person outside of her own friends and staff should be allowed to ride in the elevator with her. None of the guests objected to the Princess' monopolizing the car until the day the American-born Duchess of Manchester stepped into the elevator with her. The former Helena Zimmermann, a great heiress from Cincinnati, was unknown to the Princess, who was visibly annoyed.

Princess Parlaghy whispered to her footman, who whispered to the elevator operator, who whispered to the Duchess to vacate. The Duchess boarded the next car, and witnesses reported she was quite perturbed, if not actually simmering. Within minutes, the Duke himself descended upon the management with fire in his eyes.

"I never heard of the Princess Parlaghy. . . . It is all most annoying," *The New York Times* quoted the Duke. The Duke later was seen consulting various red- and blue-bound books. Whether he found Princess Parlaghy among the peerage is not recorded, but he did calm down somewhat when he learned of her artistic repute.

Born in Hadjudorog, Hungary, in 1865, the Princess obtained her title by marrying a Russian prince. A divorcee by the time she came to The Plaza, she reputedly possessed an income of a million dollars a year. Far from denying it, the Princess looked sweetly modest when she told reporters she managed to spend only $250,-000 of it a year. Her bills at the hotel were always paid in cash, and rumor had it that it came from the Kaiser through the German consul.

She arrived on the scene in New York already hailed as a most eminent painter of kings and princes of Europe. Not only the Kaiser, but King Edward VII had posed for her. She had painted the Czar and Czarina of Russia, King Christian of Denmark, the Empress Eugénie, King Leopold of the Belgians, Queen Elizabeth of Rumania, and the King of Italy. She traveled from St. Petersburg to Persia to paint Ali Asghar Khan, Grand Vizier of Persia (Iran). In 1904, King Edward traveled to Marienbad to open an exhibition of her paintings.

No one doubted her talent. At the age of fourteen she had gone to Munich with her mother in hopes of studying under the famous German master Franz von Lenbach, who was noted for his powerful interpretations of men of strong character. Lenbach told her he took no students, but the young girl's distress was so genuine and her pleading so touching that he put her to the test by asking her to copy one of his paintings—sure in his mind it would be pretty bad. But so exactly did she copy it that Lenbach was amazed; few could have told which was the original. He took her on as a pupil, and while she emulated his strong style, she displayed her own individual talent for capturing a likeness in oils. At the age of sixteen she created an art sensation with her painting of Kossuth, the Hungarian patriot.

America's most prominent men were as ready as royalty to pose for her. Her subjects included Andrew Carnegie, August Belmont, Seth Low, Chauncey Depew, Ogden Mills, the poet Edwin Markham, Supreme Court Justice Joseph Choate, Thomas Edison, and Robert W. De Forest, president of the Metropolitan Museum. All but Edison came to pose in her studio suite at The Plaza; his portrait was done from a photograph. The portrait of Choate is now in the American Museum of Natural History.

Such a lady felt she had her reasons to be haughty, and perhaps even her rights, when she was paying for the privilege. For a trip from Boston to New York, she naturally rented a private railroad car. How else would a princess travel? But the railroad made the error of hooking her car up not to the end of the train but right in the center, between the coaches and the smoker. This time, the Princess could not keep strangers out of her preserve. Her footmen did collect the calling cards of those going to and fro, and these were later presented to the railroad with a cascade of accented outrage. The Princess had paid $160 extra for her privacy, and before World War One this was a considerable sum.

Yet she could be wonderfully friendly, particularly toward animals. On a visit to the Ringling Brothers Circus at the old Madison Square Garden she fell in love with a lion cub, which she coveted. But the Ringlings refused to part with it at any price. So the Princess resorted to strategy.

She had just completed painting the portrait of General Daniel E. Sickles, a veteran of the Civil War and old war lion of the United States Army. Correctly, she guessed the Ringling Brothers would deny him nothing, so she appealed to him. When the General sought to buy the lion, the Ringlings tried to make a gift of it. The General insisted upon paying $250. Circus press agents were then making their place in history, and the press witnessed the transaction when Princess Parlaghy arrived to claim the cub. The war lion presented the circus lion to the Princess, a gesture which raised him to the status of a social lion.

The Princess sent for champagne and promptly officially christened the pet "General Sickles," but very probably she already knew she would call him Goldfleck. Wrapped in a fine wool blanket, "General Goldfleck Sickles" was whisked by limousine to The Plaza. Guest and tenant eyebrows rose an inch when Manager Sterry allowed the Princess to keep the lion in a separate room of her apartment—but under the care of a trainer.

Herman Zerenner, a well-known photographer of the time, tells of his meeting with the Princess and his subsequently being hired by her to photograph her subjects and their portraits. She had rented a summer retreat at Elka Park in the Catskills, an extensive estate. The neighbors labeled her mysterious, and Zerenner had no idea the fashionable lady walking her dog would speak to him the morning he met her and murmured, *"Guten Morgen."* His use of German brought an immediate response, conversation revealed his trade, and soon he was engaged as photographer at $150 per month. He was promptly put into court uniform, one for daytime, one for evening wear. A darkroom was also put at his disposal.

Goldfleck behaved as a very proper lion should until the day Zerenner snapped a picture while he was in the room. At the flash of the bulb Goldfleck panicked, raced through a partly opened door into the hall and down the corridors of the hotel, while guests and staff scattered wildly. Finally, raw meat lured the upset lion back into his royal lair.

Goldfleck was still young, but fast growing into a lion-sized lion when he fell ill and died. At the request of the Princess, Zerenner took a picture of the wake, Goldfleck on The Plaza rug surrounded by vases of flowers, his toys and his dishes. He was buried in a pet cemetery in Westchester, and a headstone was erected with the inscription: "Beneath this stone is buried the beautiful young lion Goldfleck whose death was sincerely mourned by his mistress, Princess Lwoff-Parlaghy, New York, 1912." A photograph of this is among Zerenner's prized possessions.

Before she came to The Plaza, the Princess painted for the joy of it. While there, she learned to charge prices running up to $15,000 for a full portrait. Although she specialized in painting men, the Princess made a gracious exception for queens. "I have never painted young women. The strong men of America appeal to me. When you are painting strong men, you are painting character," she explained.

To the press she was always diplomatic. When she gave some fine old lace to the Brooklyn Museum, she delighted a reporter for *The Brooklyn Daily Eagle* by saying, "I can well see how Brooklyn some day can be the art center of this country, for its position is unique in that it retains its quiet and refined atmosphere, notwithstanding the rapid rush of the growing metropolis." That was before the rapid rush caught up with Brooklyn.

World War One spelled Waterloo for Princess Parlaghy. Her funds stopped coming from Europe, and America's leaders were too busy to have their portraits painted. She still cut an elegant swath as she pranced through the hotel lobby, thanks to her love of color in dress. But her finery could not hide her problems from the staff. She sought to economize by cutting out the extras, but nobody had taught her how. As politely as possible, the management suggested that Madame pay her rent or move to more modest quarters; not until she had run up a bill of twelve thousand dollars did the management reluctantly but firmly insist that she give up her apartment.

The Princess was able to move her most beautiful possessions to a house at 109 East 39th Street, and she remained surrounded by them until her death on August 28, 1923. She did not escape several court appearances concerning debts of more than $205,000. The day before she died, only her physician, Dr. Edward Fiske, prevented the deputy sheriff from entering her home armed with three writs of seizure. She is buried in this country—at Woodlawn. She was a fabulous, stranger-than-fiction personality, remembered today only by one or two Plaza old-timers.

Some who followed her at The Plaza were just as haughty and not half so talented or charming. Not easily forgotten was the Near East potentate who arrived in the middle of night accompanied by a staff even larger than Princess Parlaghy's and 250 pieces of luggage. Bellmen had distributed more than a hundred to the rooms of the party when an attaché called down to the desk to complain that the luggage of His Majesty had not arrived in his suite.

"Coming right up," the efficient bell captain assured him. But that was not enough. Indeed, it would not do at all. The luggage of His Majesty had to be delivered first, by all rules of royal protocol.

So down came the hundred pieces of baggage, up went the luggage of the chief. After which, for the second time that trying night, bellmen were distributing the bags and suitcases of the rest of the party. Nothing was said of an extra tip.

Perhaps the oddest character ever to stay at the Plaza bothered no one but himself. This was a wealthy Philadelphian with an exaggerated fear of germs, but happily possessed of finances to indulge his phobia.

In addition to a room for himself, he rented the rooms to the left, to the right, across the corridor, above and below, and he slept in each room in rotation, following a theory of his own on how long it takes germs to die out.

Waiters put his meals on a food wagon, covered the food with a white cloth, rang his doorbell and took care to depart before he answered. He ordered whole roasts of beef and whole hams, then cut himself only a small piece out of the uncontaminated center of the meat. He was never seen without white gloves, never seen to shake hands. Every morning the chambermaid had to deliver fifty white towels. Letters and cables were read to him over the telephone.

But the staff liked him. He tipped generously, and he was invariably polite. But so alone. It had not always been thus. When younger, this same gentleman had stayed at the venerable Bristol Hotel in Vienna, and was reported to have behaved much the same way he later behaved at The Plaza. At the Bristol, a lady came all the way from Paris to see him, and the staff rejoiced. At last the poor fellow's isolation would end. Alas, the lady stayed on the floor below. During her ten days there, they had some very nice chats—all by telephone.

As long as they did not make a public spectacle of themselves, however, eccentrics were endured at The Plaza. For years, each winter season brought the return of a gentleman attended by two Negro maids. In the privacy of his suite he would bedeck himself in lace and satin evening gowns and long ropes of pearls.

One of the most colorful of Plaza guests, but no eccentric, was Evander Berry Wall, the American Beau Brummel of the Edwardian era, with a pedigreed background. To Berry Wall's valet fell the job of hanging eighty-five pairs of trousers in the closets of his suite, and it was said that he possessed a different scarf for every day of the year. In evening cape and high silk hat, he cut a dashing, debonair figure for the society photographers of his day; the title bestowed upon him by the press, "King of the Dudes," was well merited. His moustache was always carefully trimmed, occasionally he wore a monocle; he deplored a growing tendency toward the wearing of dinner jackets to balls and other evening affairs. A dinner jacket was for informal dinner only.

Berry Wall and his wife divided their time between Paris and The Plaza—where their pet chow was almost as much of a personage as E. Berry himself.

His preoccupation with fashion was no youthful fad. Berry Wall was forty-eight years old when The Plaza opened and a stickler for correct dress. He wore collars four inches high and as rigid as the ramparts around a medieval castle. Wall had his rivals. Robert Hilliard, the actor, once purchased a purple satin waistcoat embroidered with green stars in his campaign for sartorial supremacy over Berry Wall. Louis Newman, a broker, made an entry at a party in purple evening tailcoat and white-topped patent leather shoes. Wall never viewed these peacocks as competition.

Neither Pest nor Puritan was the title of his memoirs published in 1940. No puritan certainly, he seldom drank water, and rumor had it that he rinsed his mouth in champagne. Indeed, his capacity for champagne became a Plaza legend.

In 1923, aged sixty-four, Wall returned from Paris to The Plaza wearing a black slouch hat and lamenting the passing of the good old days when a man could live elegantly on an income of $25,000 a year. He admitted running through the fortunes left him by his grandfather and his father. Fortunately, his mother had put hers in trust for him, and he continued to live well, if more modestly, in his old age.

As an elderly man, he reverted to the fashions of the Edwardian era, a pale-gray derby at the races, fitted overcoats and his perennial high collar, winning only a reputation for eccentricity. No one could miss him strolling down Fifth Avenue with his chow dog. In his biography he wrote, "I have loved horses and chow dogs but only one woman, and so I am something of an anomaly these days." His was a happy marriage, for his wife made no attempt to compete with him on the fashion front.

Of The Plaza's site, Berry Wall said, "This is where the Metropolitan Opera should have been built." He recalled that when the Met was planning to move from the old Academy of Music on Fourteenth Street, the directors had the choice of three locations: the site of The Plaza, a site on Sixty-first Street between Broadway and Central Park, and the site it chose, on Broadway at Fortieth Street.

"But wouldn't this have been the place for a great opera house?" asked Wall, sipping his champagne in the Oak Room. Having lost out on The Plaza site, the Met eventually moved to Lincoln Center, close by the second site it originally rejected.

Plaza guests have a habit of tipping generously, some lavishly. The prize for carefree generosity, however, belongs to Manuel Ugarte, who in 1908 was secretary of the Honduran Legation in Washington. He dreamed of blazing his trail down the Great White Way, and to prepare his feet for the expedition he called a chiropodist several times a day to his room at the hotel. His pockets filled with jewels, he strolled forth, handing out gems to the lovely ladies and little nifties of New York. The girls all too eagerly accepted his gifts. Ugarte not only ran out of jewels, he ran out of money to pay a five-hundred-dollar order from Tiffany's. For his own protection, his uncle, Urcano Ugarte, took him to Bellevue. The twenty-four-year-old youth was placed in the psychopathic ward, where he babbled interminably of love.

Other diplomats have made a spectacle of themselves merely by behaving at The Plaza as they would if they were in their own homes. The creation of the United Nations has not only filled the halls of the hotel with colorful costumes, it has introduced equally colorful customs. An African visitor breakfasting in the Edwardian Room surveyed the menu and failed to find his favorite dish of rice and meat, food which lends itself to dainty, even delicate, use of the fingers. So he bowed to local eating habits to the extent of ordering a huge platter of eggs. Then, disdaining fork or spoon, he scooped them into his mouth with his hands, a feat his gaping neighbors no doubt lacked the manual dexterity to attempt.

By the chair of the African guest stood a huge black servant with a long-handled fan such as is used in tropical countries to wave away the flies. A captain of waiters, too proper to criticize the table manners of a guest, could stand it only so long before he vented his frustration on the servant:

"There are no flies at The Plaza, and we are air-conditioned. You don't need to use that thing."

Naturally, the servant ignored him. He knew the formalities due a chieftain better than The Plaza staff did.

Some stories of eccentricities grow in the telling, such as the news that the millionaire Percival Kuhne, a Plaza first tenant, had installed in his living room a marble fountain brought from Versailles, France, reported to have been a favorite fountain of Marie Antoinette. The marble lobby buzzed with the story, newspapers picked it up, and an avid public read that the fountain filled a room twenty-six by eighteen feet. Mr. Kuhne indignantly explained that the fountain with the cupid riding a swan was just about the size of a water pitcher.

Stranger stories flourished. A man wearing a gold stickpin with the number 13 in his tie checked into the hotel with a unique request, for room number 13. Since there was no such number, he settled for a room on the thirteenth floor. The guest explained that he was a member of the Thirteen Club. He always began his business negotiations on the thirteenth day of the month, and signed the contracts on the following thirteenth. He always had thirteen people at his dinner table.

"Mr. Thirteen" occupied his rooms on the thirteenth floor for exactly thirteen days; he died on the thirteenth of the month.

The Plaza prides itself on providing an interpreter service for foreign guests who do not speak English. But when 180 German-speaking visitors descended upon the hotel before the First World War, pandemonium reigned in the lobby as desk clerks and bellmen tried to overcome the language barrier. This was the Academic Singing Society of Vienna, hailed as the second-best male vocalists in the world, an irrefutable statement in the absence of any judgment on who was better. As they arrived at The Plaza they attracted a crowd, not of later Beatle proportions, but of size enough for the police to take over. Though they wore no long haircuts, they were a colorful sight in wine-colored student caps and sporting canes and with opera glasses slung by straps about their necks.

The singers were here to give a concert at Carnegie Hall, and they celebrated their success by visiting Coney Island. In true European style, the 180 guests left their keys at the desk every time they left their rooms and demanded them back, in German, as many as five times in a day. Never before, and never since, has The Plaza been so frustrated.

Incidents which seldom made news have survived in Plaza legend. Every Sunday, at seven o'clock, a well-dressed woman, tall and graceful, used to come and stand on the corner near the entrance to the hotel, and carry on a brief happy conversation with a man who was not there. Successive doormen have passed along the story that as a young girl she had an engagement with a man she loved, to meet by The Plaza at seven o'clock. The man never came, and the girl never saw him again, but for years she kept a rendezvous with her imaginary lover.

To Enrico Caruso goes the honor of being the hotel's most temperamental guest. When the great Italian tenor first came to The Plaza the electric clock was still a noisy novelty not to be silenced by anything so simple as pulling a plug. To Caruso's sensitive ears, it was an abomination.

Practicing in his room one day, he found himself competing with the electric buzz of the clock, and in a burst of operatic temperament, he lunged at it with a knife, putting the whole works out of business.

Soon the phones on the manager's desk began ringing with maddening persistency from all directions. What time was it? Why had the clocks stopped? With his little hatchet Caruso had succeeded in stopping all the clocks in the hotel, which were controlled by a master magnetic clock, the first of its kind in a hotel.

The engineer and a host of men began knocking on doors, examining all clocks to find out what had caused the breakdown. When they finally came to Caruso's room, he refused to open the door. Manager Sterry was called, and his pleading prevailed. Struggling for the English to convey his indignation, Caruso flailed the workmen removing the clock until one of them exploded: "I don't give a darn!"

"Darn? How do you say that—darn?" This new word for his vocabulary of invective appealed to the singer's musical ear, and he was repeating it with quiet delight as the workers escaped.

Instead of sending Caruso a bill for damages, the management wrote a letter of apology for the intrusion and delivered it with a magnum of champagne.

That's The Plaza for you.

One of The Plaza's richest tenants in recent years was also one of the most eccentric. The Duchess de Talleyrand, née Anna Gould, daughter of Jay Gould, the Wall Street buccaneer who left some hundred million when he died at the age of fifty-seven, occupied a large and elegant ninth-floor suite during and after World War Two. Few outside of the executive personnel and those who served her were aware that the rather shy, little old lady who came and went so unobtrusively was an heiress who for over sixty years had made sensational international headlines, and had been the subject of hundreds of magazine articles.

Anna Gould was one of the first great American heiresses to capture, if that is the word, a European title. In the nineties she was married at the Gould home on upper Fifth Avenue to the profligate French Count Boni de Castellane, who managed, in the first ten years of their marriage, to squander some ten million Gould dollars, and gave truth to rumor by writing a book about his sensational spendings. The union was dissolved by divorce, and a second title was bestowed upon the onetime Miss Gould when she became the bride of the count's cousin Duc de Talleyrand-Périgord, a happier marriage than her first.

Since her first marriage Anna de Talleyrand had resided in Paris, where her home, a great pink marble mansion, was regarded as one of the most beautiful baroque houses in the world. The outbreak of the Second World War drove her back to her native shores while her magnificent home was taken over as general headquarters for Nazi officers during the days of the German occupation.

Returning to New York, the Duchess, a widow since 1937, took up residence at The Plaza which had always been favored by Goulds from the first day when Anna's brother, George Jay Gould, and his family moved in. Another brother, Howard, was also living there when he died in 1959, leaving an estate estimated at sixty million dollars.

Never pretty even as a girl, and by now a short, dumpy woman who nevertheless dressed expensively and had an air of French chic about her, the Duchess de Talleyrand was possessed of a deep-rooted persecution complex, a fear that she would be poisoned. Like the kings of old, she required that all her food had to be tasted before she would eat it, and she was always accompanied by two bodyguards, one of whom was her chauffeur, and by one or two nurses. Her therapist came to her every morning.

Several times a week she would drive up to Lyndhurst, the great monstrous Gothic estate at Tarrytown-on-Hudson, which she inherited from her father and where she did most of her entertaining; but so great was her fear of being murdered that she hired Ray Schindler, the private detective who had investigated the Oakes murder case in Nassau, to protect her. Schindler and his family moved up to Tarrytown, where she needed more protection than at a hotel.

Unlike other very rich people, Anna Gould de Talleyrand was one of the most generous of women, and one of the most extravagant. She had her own private plane, her jewels were magnificent, she spared no expense to get what she wanted, and she shared her wealth with those she liked. She tipped most lavishly the chambermaids, housekeepers and all others who served her. Harold, a veteran Plaza doorman, declared that she used to tip him five dollars when he helped her into her car, until, he added ruefully, her bodyguard prevailed upon her to stop.

The Duchess continued to maintain her apartment at the hotel even after the war was over. She died in Paris in 1961, in her late eighties. When movie queen Brigitte Bardot made her widely publicized trip to New York in 1965, one of the grandest suites at The Plaza was set aside for her—the suite which had been the haven in New York of kindly, eccentric, fear-ridden Anna Gould de Talleyrand.

While few Plaza guests, or newspaper columnists, were aware of the Duchess de Talleyrand's residence at the hotel, it remained for an even wealthier woman, Hetty Green, "the Witch of Wall Street," to land The Plaza on the front pages of the nation's newspapers by the mere act of taking a suite there for a single month!

Hetty Green was hailed as the richest woman in the world, but so widespread was her reputation as a miser who lived in a cheap broken-down tenement in Hoboken and for years wore the same shabby black frock that had turned green with age that it was headline news when she moved out of her flat, stored whatever furniture she had and, on May 2, 1908, moved into "the world's most elegant hotel." It was mentioned at the time that she had rented a suite that cost fifteen dollars a day, but as in all financial matters, Hetty managed to get herself a better arrangement; when she moved out after a month it was reported that she paid three hundred dollars for the month, or ten dollars per day.

Accompanying Hetty was her daughter Sylvia, who had been christened with the impressive name of Hetty Sylvia Ann Howland Robinson Green. At thirty-seven, Sylvia was still unmarried; and if this did not trouble Hetty it apparently did trouble one of her few close friends, Annie Leary, a socially secure spinster who was to receive the papal title of Countess for her many Catholic charities. For all her charitable interests Miss Leary also liked the social game; her entertainments were large and lavish, and one of the outstanding parties in Newport in the summer of 1897 was the reception she gave in honor of Sylvia Green.

In their book, *Hetty Green,* Boyden Sparks and Samuel Taylor Moore wrote that Miss Leary, "who was both friend and social mentor to Miss Green, believed in miracles and the final effect of her constant and subtle maneuverings was a miracle." It was she who arranged for Hetty Green to give one of the most sumptuous dinners ever held in that center of sumptuous entertaining, The Plaza. She even managed to get Hetty into Mme. LeClair's Fifth Avenue beauty parlor for a thorough beauty treatment.

The dinner was held in the suite occupied by mother and daughter, and according to authors Sparks and Moore "it was served from gold plate loaned for the occasion by Miss Leary. The food was as expensive as The Plaza chef could contrive in ten courses. There were three wine glasses beside each of twenty plates." There were flowers, music and favors, and Hetty wore a gown of black satin trimmed with old-rose-point lace which bulged over her roundness, since she would not wear a corset.

Among the guests, who included Mr. and Mrs. Howland Pell and Mr. and Mrs. Amory S. Carhart, was a kindly, aging bachelor in his sixties, Mathew Astor Wilks, whose middle name was derived from his grandfather, John Jacob Astor. There is little doubt that the affair, plus Wilks's presence as a guest, was engineered by the romantic-minded Miss Leary. Less than a year later, in February 1909, Sylvia and Wilks were married in St. Peter's Protestant Episcopal Church in Morristown, New Jersey.

Crank letters were nothing new in Hetty's life, but after receiving a threatening letter while at the hotel she was always joined by a house detective when she stepped into the lobby, to see that she was not molested.

Her duty to her daughter done, Hetty moved out of the hotel, put aside her new finery, and soon was again to be seen trudging down to Wall Street, wearing a battered old hat and her worn-out old alpaca dress.

She did deign to explain her unprecedented extravagance: "I'm merely paying off Sylvia's social debts," commented the woman whose miserliness was legend.

CHAPTER TEN

Much Ado About Something

As a place of proper reserve and dignity, the very correct Plaza has few equals, but now and then in its history events beyond its control have evoked painful consternation among management and conservative guests.

Mrs. Patrick Campbell lit a cigarette at The Plaza.

And holy smoke, what a conflagration! Headlines flared and antismoking ordinances were passed.

Scarcely six weeks after The Plaza opened, the famed English actress entered the tearoom and, by drawing on a Russian cigarette, created a hullabaloo which rocked the nation. Jewel robberies, fires, fights, divorces—little that happened since caused such a furore as the incident of November 15, 1907.

"It is a scandal." The headwaiter came running to Lucius Boomer, then an assistant manager, later to become president of the Waldorf-Astoria. "A lady, she smokes in the tearoom."

"Tell her to desist."

"I do. She only laugh."

Boomer rushed to talk reason, only to lose the battle of words. For his contestant was the woman whose lively correspondence with playwright George Bernard Shaw contained drama enough to revive recitation on Broadway more than half a century later.

"I have been given to understand this is a free country. I propose to do nothing to alter its status." Mrs. Campbell was unmovable until the cigarette went out of its own accord, as Russian cigarettes will.

The newspapers got wind of the story and played it for all it was worth. The reaction was of bombshell effect.

"Smoking by women is indecent," shouted the *New York Journal.*

"Smoking by women is definitely un-American," said Mrs. Clinton B. Fisk, president of the Home Mission Society.

Reporters spread the story across the country, and even in later years it served crusading clergymen, reform groups and women's clubs as proof of the decadence of New York.

In Manhattan, Dr. Charles G. Pease of the Non-Smokers Protective League seized upon the excitement Mrs. Campbell caused to line up a majority of the New York Board of Aldermen in favor of an ordinance barring women from smoking in public. This idealist then threw his own monkey wrench into the works by proposing a provision making it illegal for men to smoke in the presence of women. That was going too far. The measure was defeated on both counts.

Dr. Pease did succeed in getting an ordinance passed which is still in effect—barring smoking in the subway.

Manager Sterry observed that Americans abroad did not object to the sight of a woman smoking in the smart restaurants of London and Paris. But, "to try it here is another matter. The Plaza does not want to be the first to permit the custom."

On the other side of the fence, James Martin, proprietor of the elite Café Martin, made news by announcing that women would be permitted to smoke in his luxurious supper rooms.

Ethel Lloyd Patterson, a woman columnist and a novelty in her day, wryly commented, "Are we really going to permit women as wide latitude with their foibles as we allow them with their morals? . . . When the novelty wears off, will women lapse into lethargy, or push on to cigars?"

Her question was answered only a few years later when Mrs. Frederic Neilson, a doughty dowager whose daughter Cathleen was the first Mrs. Reginald C. Vanderbilt, adopted a black cigar as her trademark. It created more smoke than fire—by then not even the waiters at The Plaza, where she had long maintained an apartment, dared to interfere.

It took a blast of gunfire about a year after the hotel's opening to shatter not only one of the great windows of the dining room facing Central Park but the nerves of the usually imperturbable guests lunching there. A bullet fired by a would-be assassin from a vantage point behind some Park foliage just narrowly missed its target, Harry N. "Taxicab" Allen, conspicuously observed lunching at one of the window tables. Fortunately, the shattered glass was the only casualty.

The shot brought into sharp focus a battle raging between the union of hansom cab drivers in New York and the man who introduced the rival taxicab (a word he coined) to New York simultaneously with the opening of The Plaza on October 1, 1907.

While the public marveled at the fleet of snappy bright-red motor-metered Darracqs lined up at the Fifth Avenue side of the hotel, the hansom cab drivers, at the time, scoffed and predicted they would never replace horse-drawn hansoms and broughams. The laughter of the fiacre fleet soon turned to worry. By the summer of 1908 the country had begun to learn what the automobile could do, and by that time Harry Allen not only had over seven hundred cabs in operation, but the rights to place them at hotels, railroad stations, steamship lines and ferries. The meters of the cabs, visibly recording the exact price of transportation, were the big selling point to the public, too often subject to large overcharges by hansom cab drivers.

On Christmas night 1908, following a party he gave for his employees, Harry Allen came home full of good cheer to be told what no one would reveal at the party—that he had a strike on his hands, with a demand that he permit his people to organize a union local. The next seven weeks, before the strike was settled, were marked by the violence of shootings and bombings. Allen decided he had had his fill when the dead hand of the past lashed out at him through the drivers' union, dominated by the horse hackmen. The attempt on his life was largely instrumental in his decision to sell out soon after the strike was settled.

WIN DRIBBEN

Mrs. Kingman Douglas (Adele Astaire) with Tom Clifford, The Plaza's first doorman.

Mrs. James Fosburgh with her sister, Mrs. William Paley.

General and Mrs. Eisenhower and Floyd and Jacqueline Cochran Odlum.

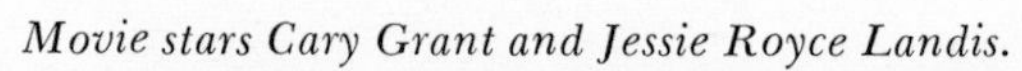

Movie stars Cary Grant and Jessie Royce Landis.

D'ARLENE STUDIO

One of the Beatles is hurried through the lobby.

Crowds swarm outside The Plaza during the Beatles' first visit.

EDWARD OZERN

Alfred E. Smith and Mrs. Daniel Mooney in the Persian Room.

Adlai Stevenson and Mrs. Charles Engelhard at the 1965 Diamond Ball.

D'ARLENE STU

Mrs. Guy Martin standing before a portrait of her grandmother, Mrs. George J. Gould.

Sculptor Carl Milles dines with Mrs. Clark Williams.

D'ARLENE STUDIO

D'ARLENE STUDIO

The author greets the King of Morocco at his reception in 1963.

Frank Lloyd Wright with a model of the Guggenheim Museum.

IRWIN DRIBBEN

IRWIN DRIBBEN

The Duke and Duchess of Windsor dance at the Rendez-Vous.

D'ARLENE STUDIO

Senator John F. Kennedy and Mrs. Kennedy at a benefit, 1959.

Eloise's portrait delights teen-agers Orianne Rodman and Tamar Head.

D'ARLENE STUDIO

Ironically, the small remaining remnant of the great fleet of horse-drawn carriages and high-hatted cabbies, a last link to the preautomobile past, is to be encountered in New York only at the sunny southeast corner of Central Park, at Fifty-ninth Street—directly across the street from the hotel where "Taxicab" Allen first introduced motor-metered cabs sixty years ago.

A dispute between the two orchestra leaders who alternately provided soft music under the soft lights of the Tea Court and amid the flickering candles of the Café Restaurant early in Plaza life struck a discordant note loud enough to be heard the length of West Fifty-ninth Street. Nahan Franko and Goetz-Hocky, beneath their smiling countenances, were each jealous of the other's prerogative. Goetz-Hocky had a longer hair-do than the Beatles, and Franko not only teased him; repeatedly he mussed it up. Franko went too far the night he suggested: "Why don't you do it up with hairpins?"

"My wife fixes it and combs it every day just so, and just so I let it stay," *The New York Times* quoted Goetz-Hocky. "Now lay your hands on me again and I will fight you."

Goetz-Hocky threatened to kick Franko, and Franko threatened to "finish" Goetz-Hocky. Happily one of the orchestras began to play loudly and drowned out the war of words. Gleefully the gossip columnists of the day reported the quarrel and tried to keep it alive by egging on the musical conductors with constant references to the incident, but Manager Sterry controlled the situation under threat of dismissal.

One time he could not control a situation was when two men, while dining with a lady, got into a war of words, and rose to fight it out to the accompaniment of crashing glass and china. Henry N. T. Beekman, a prominent attorney living at the hotel, and his dinner guest, Samuel S. Ellis, took their dispute up to Beekman's room. A few minutes later Beekman called, not the management but the police, to report that he was locked in his room and unable to get out. Guests watched appalled as the gendarmes arrived. They found Ellis and the hotel physician in the corridor outside the room, while Beekman pounded on the door, roaring to be let out.

The police trundled the men off to the station house, where the lieutenant in charge found no reason to hold Ellis despite Beekman's demand for his arrest and incarceration. The lady had escaped without identifying herself. The cause of the dispute was never known, but the case is unique in that it is one occasion when The Plaza failed to abide by the rule that the customer is always right.

Add a title and a pair of brass knuckles to an argument about money, and you have an international sensation. In 1911 Baron Richard von Arkovy was arrested in the lobby of the hotel on a charge by one Julio S. Jarrin that he had stolen two platinum crucibles valued at nine hundred dollars. The Hungarian baron made matters worse by resisting arrest, whereupon detectives searched him and found spiked brass knuckles in his pocket. His story that brass knuckles were *de rigueur* accessories to a baron's attire cut no ice, and the detectives whisked him away. They did allow him to stop off at his bank, where he drew out three thousand dollars, the sum just covering his bail. In addition to brass knuckles, von Arkovy affected a gold-headed walking stick, astrakhan overcoat, silk top hat and a monocle.

Jarrin said the Baron had taken the crucibles to sell for him, but pawned them instead. The Baron's story was that the crucibles were given to him in payment of a gambling debt of $280.

The news of the brass knuckles hit New York society hard and made press headlines—for the Baron, who had married an American brewery heiress, Elsie Schroeder, was a member of a party of titled foreigners who had come over for the wedding of British Lord Decies and heiress Vivien Gould, the George Jay Gould daughter. It didn't hurt the sensational reporting of the juicy story that a pal of the Baron was Lord Camoys, an important member of the British peerage, who was to be best man at the wedding. While here Lord Camoys met, and later wed, a prominent Newport heiress, Mildred Sherman.

A love triangle, in 1949, produced another noisy and unpleasant incident at The Plaza. Involved were Aleta Arlen, former wife of Karl Lowenthal, Wall Street banker, and Claudia Campbell, heiress to a soup fortune and frequently referred to as Lowenthal's date. The two ladies were friends and were cocktailing in harmony at the hotel when they decided it would be fun to call on Lowenthal, who was registered there. Miss Campbell located him in Room 1438—with him was his bride of a few hours, dark-eyed Alynne Fisher. What happened next is recorded in a memo from Mr. Reick, an assistant manager, to John Klugherz, resident manager.

> On receiving various complaints from guests on the Fifth Avenue side of the fourteenth floor, Mr. Sabello, the house officer, found that quite a commotion was going on in 1438, occupied by Mr. Karl Lowenthal. It appears that Mr. Lowenthal got married this afternoon and while in his room with his bride a lady came to visit him, and upon hearing the news became hysterical and started a fight. Police were called. The lady finally left at 11:30 P.M.

With a display of honesty rather rare in such situations, Miss Campbell admitted, "I created a scene. Karl tried to quiet me and put me out of the room. I hit him. He tried to drag me out of the room. I have a black eye. The police came and I left."

Some fascinating incidents besides occasional fights and fits of temperament on the part of guests have occurred at the hotel.

Sir Henry Stanley found Dr. Livingstone in darkest Africa. A woman claiming direct descent from Stanley, identifying herself as Lady Eve Stanley, found the man who robbed her in Paris in the Palm Court of The Plaza.

Mrs. Stanley, who was then living on Park Avenue, was having tea one afternoon with a friend, Clive Webster of Dallas, Texas, when she happened to glance at the next table and gasped. "That's the man," she whispered to Webster, who knew what she was referring to.

As she later told it, a man using the name of Albert Navarro, posing as a wealthy exporter and always riding in a chauffeured Rolls-Royce, squired her around Paris in 1958. She gave him $10,000 in francs, which he was to deliver to her in Spain—why was not specified. He never did arrive, and when she returned to

Paris she found her apartment looted of $500,000 in jewelry, furs and other valuables. Navarro had disappeared without trace until he turned up at The Plaza.

To avoid a public scene, Mrs. Stanley shied from approaching the man she saw in the Palm Court with a classic "Mr. Navarro, I presume." Webster, however, decided to do some quiet sleuthing, and when Navarro left, trailed him to the New York Hilton Hotel, where the arrest was made. The man was booked as Raoul Matalon, forty-two, of Mexico City. He said he was Elias Bayer, a German, but the police contended he had at least six aliases. Matalon-Bayer insisted that Navarro was not one of them. However, he was held on fifty thousand dollars' bail pending word from France. But, having reported the incident and the arrest, the New York newspapers somehow never did get around to recording what happened next.

A veritable treasure trove of plots for a novel or television thriller could be found in stories about Plaza guests. One for *Secret Agent* is the tale of a debonair and elegant Frenchman, Antoine Riniere, who checked into the hotel sometime in 1962. Riniere, under indictment in France for selling a forged Matisse painting, was suspected by Interpol, the international police organization, of trafficking in gold and narcotics. Customs officials at Idlewild, examining his baggage without finding anything significant, permitted him to go about his business—ostensibly free of suspicion.

At the restaurant "21," where he lunched, Riniere paid in francs, explaining he had no American money. From there he went straight to The Plaza, where, upon departing for Chicago, he paid in dollars, a fact which was not immediately considered odd—until checked by Interpol. Riniere was safely, he thought, flying nonstop from Chicago to Paris when his Swissair jetliner made an unscheduled stop in New York. Three customs officials apprehended him and found he was carrying $247,400 in cash. For refusing to divulge the source of the money Riniere was sentenced to six months in jail on a charge of contempt of court. How he came into such wealth, still nobody knows.

Where the rich congregate, it is almost impossible to control robberies. Jewel robberies are a constant source of worry to all hotel managers, and their greatest headaches are guests who will not put their valuables in the safes provided for that purpose.

Few hotels in the country could outdo The Plaza in the wealth of jewels the first tenants and subsequent guests brought to the hotel. Security measures were rigid; in addition to a huge safe for the valuables, the hotel employed a large corps of house detectives and carefully investigated the personal lives as well as the past employment record of all personnel before hiring them.

In the early days guests took advantage of the protection of the safe, and an old-timer on the staff recalls the scenes each evening when personal maids lined up to pick up the jewels their mistresses chose to wear that evening. When Milady was ready to retire, the process was reversed as the maids were returning the jewels to the safe.

A new generation has grown careless with its well-insured jewels; many find it too much trouble to play a game of "put and take" with safe and gems. Several years ago, when a wave of robberies swept through Manhattan's most fashionable hotels, the police department had crack detectives on day and night duty in a number of hotels, suspecting a cat burglar who could scale walls like a cat and was as slippery as an eel. A hilarious scene took place one day when an agitated guest called down to the front desk from his twelfth-floor apartment swearing he had seen a man peering into his window. That was the signal for the cops to get busy, and in and out they scurried, on roof and sidewalks. They actually spotted the man clinging to a ledge; but by the time they reached the ledge window he was gone—off into the wide, blue yonder, never to be seen again.

One of the most noted hotel security officers in the country was William F. Hartery, who for years was in charge of a force of twenty-five detectives on twenty-four-hour duty at The Plaza. Bill Hartery's reputation as a relentless sleuth was well earned. He thought nothing of working forty-eight hours at a stretch without a wink of sleep when it was necessary to catch a thief. His diligence was once dramatically illustrated, before he came to the hotel, when he was on the trail of a man who had absconded with $200,-

000 from one of the country's largest business houses. Bill had the man he suspected under constant personal surveillance, without relaxing, from one Saturday morning at eleven o'clock until nine o'clock the following Monday. When he finally nabbed the man, it was discovered the suitcase he was carrying contained a cool $185,000 in cash and a ticket to Bolivia on a boat leaving that morning!

Boston-born Bill Hartery looked like anything but the popular concept of a hotel "dick." In his "uniform" of knife-creased striped trousers, snappy tie and well-cut jacket, he was often mistaken for a distinguished guest. He had an amazing faculty for never forgetting a face, and it was said of him that he could scent a phony through "shaving lotion or perfume."

He also had a genius for finding gems hidden by their owners in the oddest places and then forgetting where they had "carefully" put them. Once a woman stuck a diamond ring in a cold cream jar for safekeeping but forgot she had put it there. The alarm she raised was a real humdinger—but Bill, wise to such feminine habits, promptly found the gem.

The legends are legion of valuables lost and found at The Plaza. A Mrs. Robert P. Watson, years ago, lost a hundred thousand dollars in jewels, and four newspapers headlined the news of their loss and amazing recovery. Mrs. Watson had taken her valuables from the hotel safe, paused at the Western Union desk to send a telegram, and departed for her suite. Not until she was dressing for dinner did she notice that her jewels were gone. She had absolutely no notion where to look. All she remembered was that she *had* taken them with her from the safe and that she had not left the hotel.

The security staff began a careful search through the lobby, the elevators, the corridors, etc. Questioning Mrs. Watson on where she had stopped en route from safe to suite, they narrowed it down to the telegraph desk. There they found the jewels, still in the little sack where Mrs. Watson had put them. Thirty persons had stopped to send telegrams, and hundreds had passed within easy reach of an innocent-looking little cloth bag containing a fortune in gems during the several hours that had passed.

A strand of priceless oriental pearls belonging to Mrs. J. B. McDonald was found in a Plaza vacuum cleaner when it was being emptied, and Harry Golden, the syndicated columnist, once found a diamond bracelet in a Plaza elevator, early in his career.

As Golden related it in a recent column about The Plaza, he was earning $17.50 per week as a reporter at the time. A scheduled interview with a VIP was to take place in the latter's suite at the hotel, and as Golden was being sped up in the elevator he saw a diamond bracelet sparkling in a corner. He told the operator the number of the suite he would be in, and to notify the manager.

Golden had just finished telling his host the story of the find when the manager arrived accompanied by a gentleman whom he introduced as Mr. Franklyn B. Hutton. The father of Woolworth heiress Barbara Hutton looked, as Golden wrote, like a fellow whose wife not only wore, but occasionally lost, diamond bracelets. Golden wasn't too proud to explain to Mr. Hutton that he was a poor reporter, just getting started. Hutton reached in his pocket and gave him a hundred-dollar bill.

"The Plaza," wrote Golden, "is probably the only place where wives lost diamond bracelets in the elevator and husbands retrieved them with $100 bills."

One of New York's most mysterious jewel robberies (and equally mysterious recovery) involved Mr. Hutton's sister-in-law, Jessie Woolworth Donahue, who together with Mr. Hutton's first wife had inherited millions amassed by their father, founder of the Woolworth stores.

The disappearance from the Donahues' Plaza apartment of gems valued at $683,000 occurred in September 1925, while Mrs. Donahue was in her bathroom. Neither James Donahue, her husband, or the maid and valet, who were all in the apartment, had seen or heard anything out of the ordinary. Mrs. Donahue recalled that when she came out of the bathroom, she noticed the door of her bedroom was ajar; she remembered having shut it.

The Donahues immediately informed the hotel management of the disappearance of the jewels, but to avoid publicity did not notify the police until two days later, with the urgent request that they withhold the news. Both insisted that their servants were absolutely above suspicion.

Despite the efforts of all concerned, the news leaked out, and the newspapers had a field day. All the elements of a front-page story were there, and the newspapers gave it the full treatment.

Among the gems was a magnificent necklace of rose pearls valued at $450,000. A reward of $65,000 was offered by the insurance company. Just as mysteriously as they disappeared, the jewels were returned a few days later by Noel C. Scaffa, a private investigator, on a "no questions asked" basis.

Scaffa later came up for trial on charge of compounding a felony. The jury disagreed, and he was acquitted, but to this day the identity of the thief and the circumstances surrounding the return of the loot remain an unsolved mystery.

CHAPTER ELEVEN

To Set Before a King

IN a glass museum display case off the kitchens of The Plaza are two prize-winning fighting cocks, brilliant-colored, ferocious-looking little beasts going for each other's jugular vein. They won their honors not in the fight ring, but in a spun-sugar fairyland at the National Hotel Exposition in New York's Coliseum.

Not so tough as ordinary fighting cocks, they would be delicious to eat. But who would dare? The culinary art at its zenith rises above taste sensation in sheer delight in the look of them. Temperature and chemicals combine to keep the cocks from melting away. For these are works of art by André René, the chef of The Plaza, at thirty-nine the youngest chef in its history.

Chef André has the distinction of having won the greatest number of culinary awards for one so young, including the highest of all, the Medal of the French Government, presented by the Société Culinaire Philanthropique. His office is papered with citations; for want of space there are countless more at home. A singular honor came to him in January 1964, when he was one of two American chefs selected by the United States Department of Agriculture to represent our country at the annual International Hotel and Catering exhibit in London. The other man was also a Hotel Corporation of America man, Chef Stefano of the Charter House in Euclid, Ohio.

It was the first time United States agricultural commodities participated in the Olympia Hall exhibit, the biggest of its kind in the United Kingdom. In the United States demonstration area of five thousand square feet, the largest in the show, Chef André prepared American dishes using nine national commodities, while hundreds watched the procedure. Again honors were heaped on the young Plaza chef.

Neither those who see nor those who taste lament the passing of the "good old days" of ten-course dinners, when emperors and rajas had all the time in the world to feast on epicurean delights from the Plaza kitchens. As a matter of fact, thanks to revolutions, ex-royalty has more time than ever to develop simple tastes, while all sorts of plebeians have acquired the wherewithal to enjoy a banquet fit for a king.

While modern food processing and the jet freight age have brought greater variety to the American family table, they have wrought no revolution at The Plaza. Its restaurants have featured exotic foods from the start, when live lobsters and turtles arrived by ship, and canvasback duck, grouse, partridge, plover and hothouse grapes were daily items on the menu.

There are secrets galore below ground level in the gleaming kitchens of the hotel. Like chefs before him, Chef André has invented recipes he refuses to divulge, not because he doesn't want to share, but because he alone can achieve the right subtlety of taste as he goes from pot to pan in his *chapeau blanc* performing the daily ritual of seasoning.

He seasons literally to taste, but instead of a pinch of salt here, a dash of Worcestershire there, his taste buds tell him when to use a pound of salt or a bottle of sauce. For he is dealing not with family-size pans but with twenty-gallon pots.

From the very beginning all Plaza chefs have been award-winning Europeans, and each has been a hard act to follow. To start his hotel off with the right seasoning in 1907, Manager Sterry brought seventy-year-old Eugène Laperruque back from retirement in France. He had been chef to the Rothschilds, the banking family of Europe, but more important to gourmets in this country was the fact that he had been chef at the old Fourteenth Street Delmonico's in 1875 and had opened the "new" Delmonico's when it moved to Twenty-sixth Street. For years, too, he was chef at the Hoffman House, New York's famous bygone hostelry.

Not one, but two Laperruques held forth in the Plaza kitchen. His *sous* chef was Chef Laperruque's nephew Charles, who had been trained in his father's hotel in Le Havre.

The art of sculpture is a *sine qua non* for worldwide fame as a chef, and Laperruque set the style at The Plaza. When the Société Culinaire Philanthropique held its exhibition in the Plaza's Summer Garden restaurant that first year, Laperruque contributed a lion springing for its prey. He sculpted *en graisse* (in fat), and only a small portion of the exhibit, a bit of lobster in jelly was edible. Another entry was entirely edible, a portrait of President Theodore Roosevelt done in dark-brown truffles on a ham. But no one dared consume any part of the President.

Neither the art nor the method of culinary sculpture has died, but both have been refined. Thirty-nine-year-old Chef André, as gifted an artist as seventy-year-old Laperruque, won kudos in a recent culinary exhibit with a "wicker" hamper, literally woven out of potatoes, covered with edible roses and filled with potato-inspired goodies. For the same exhibition he reproduced an "etching" of a Japanese tea ceremony, using tan and brown sugar and chocolate. As in an art gallery, the observer had to step back to get the proper perspective to appreciate the picture.

Albert Leopold Lattard, Laperruque's successor, won as much fame for his clay figures as for his food sculptures. A bust he did of Laperruque was exhibited at the National Academy, where it received high praise. While the public was admiring it, M. Lattard was devising means of cooking oysters, which were then coming under indictment as causing typhoid fever when eaten raw.

An autocrat in the kitchen, Chef Lattard was also something of a scholar. Between stirrings of soup and testing of roasts he would discuss in four languages matters of ancient history, philosophy and art. He maintained a studio on upper Broadway, where on his days off he would indulge his love for painting.

As much for his genius as a chef Lattard won fame for the dishes he named after celebrity guests, a practice which did as much to perpetuate the fame of the honored as inclusion in the history books.

Mme. Melba arrived at The Plaza one year fresh from the triumph of having Pêche Melba named for her in London, to discover that Lattard had named an egg dish after her manager. Far from being pleased, the famed diva was so annoyed she hid the menu, and the name of the manager has been lost to history. Then she insisted that Lattard invent an egg dish in her name. Thus was born Eggs Melba, a concoction of poached eggs on artichoke bottoms and broiled mushrooms, covered with hollandaise sauce and *foie gras*.

Lattard's most famed creation, still a specialty of The Plaza, is Crab Meat Remick, named for William H. Remick, president of the New York Stock Exchange from 1919 to 1923. Giving the recipe here is not divulging a Plaza secret; too many guests asked for, and received, the following instructions:

Crab Meat Remick

Take:
1 pint chili sauce
1 pint mayonnaise
1 dash Tabasco sauce
1 dash Worcestershire sauce
1 teaspoon English mustard
½ teaspoon paprika
1 pinch celery salt.

Mix all well with a small quantity of tarragon vinegar and season to taste. Select large crab flakes, place in empty clam shells and heat in oven. When the crab flakes are warm, coat with Remick sauce and sprinkle with Parmesan cheese. Place under broiler to brown.

It was M. Lattard's published conviction that progress was as apparent in cookery as in any other line of invention. "Every time a new electric light, a new phonograph, or any patent mechanical device is invented, an equally great discovery is made in the culinary world," said he. He proceeded to defend "modern" cookery vs. the traditional with the observation that "a few years ago guinea hens were never used, fruit salads were unheard of, radishes for flavoring instead of onions were unknown, carrots were used merely in braises." Radishes for flavoring never gained popularity, but Lattard's recipes are still the pride of The Plaza.

Many a Plaza specialty has been declared "the best," and you could start an argument with some habitués as heated as any political hassle on the relative merits of the Plaza's famed cream of chicken soup vs. the equally popular finnan haddie in cream. Colonel Ed Bradley, whose now-defunct gambling casino in Palm Beach was as renowned as Saratoga's Canfield, or Monte Carlo, wouldn't flick an eyelash if the "house" went broke—but just try to compare his favorite chicken soup with any other and he'd as lief bar you from the casino. He was a Sunday noon fixture in the Edwardian Room when in residence at the hotel, spooning away at a big bowl of soup. Those who have sampled it once come back for more, and as with the Crab Meat Remick, the chef could not for long keep the recipe a secret—from men as well as women who pleaded for it. Here it is:

Chicken Soup à la Plaza

6 ounces leeks
½ stalk diced celery
2 onions
4 ounces butter
4 tablespoons flour
3 quarts chicken broth
1 fowl, ready for cooking
1 cup cooked rice
2 cups heavy cream
salt and pepper

Place the diced leeks, celery and onions in a casserole and add the butter and smother, cooking slowly. (Do not allow to brown.) Sprinkle the flour over this and stir until blended. Add chicken broth and chicken and cook slowly for two hours. Remove the fowl and cut the breast meat in squares (rest of the meat used for other purposes). Skim off fat from soup, add the cream, the cooked rice and breast meat. Season to taste.

Spaghetti is not a Plaza specialty, but the country's best-known and most widely sold spaghetti-and-meat sauce dinner originated with three brothers who worked at the Plaza. Chef-Boy-Ar-Dee products, today the biggest-selling Italian packaged product in the United States, are due to be expanded to Europe. There they will be distributed as Boiardi products—under the proper name of the originators. The colossal sales growth was due to the help and encouragement of a prominent Plaza tenant. Influence, not money, was his investment.

It might be said to have started many years ago in Italy. Breakfast in his room had been perfect that morning, and a great man beamed on the handsome young hotel waiter who served him. "You know your job, my boy."

"Thank you, *signor,*" replied the waiter. "Soon I hope to go to Berlin. I have a friend at the Hotel Adlon."

"Why not America?" asked the guest.

"America, *signor*—ah, that is a distant dream. I have no friends there."

"You have now," said the gentleman, giving the waiter a card. "Come to see me if you go there." The card read: "Enrico Caruso."

A year later, in 1911, Paul Boiardi was a waiter at the well-known Knickerbocker Hotel in New York, where Manager Regan, at the request of Caruso, gave him a job. Other and better ones followed, and in 1917 Paul joined the staff of the Plaza Hotel. Tall and handsome, with just the right touch of continental deference, Paul soon became one of the most popular waiters, and when the Persian Room opened in 1934 he was appointed maître d'hôtel there.

From the money he earned Paul saved enough to send for his young brother Hector, and obtained for him a job in the hotel kitchen. Some years later a third brother, Mario, was brought over and became a waiter under Paul.

Hector yearned to go into business for himself and after a few years at The Plaza left for Cleveland to open a small restaurant specializing in Italian food. The restaurant was an instantaneous success; Hector was a chef de luxe at his native foods, and as the fame of his cuisine spread and the place became the haunt of gourmets who relished Italian food, customers were soon asking to buy and take home some of the delicious Italian meat sauce. Hector obliged by bottling the sauce; and then packaging a spaghetti-and-meat sauce dinner on demand. Sales grew, and before long proprietor Hector was in an expanded business. Salesmen went out on the road, selling the products, but they couldn't crack the supermarkets springing up all over the country.

Brother Paul was still in charge of the Persian Room, where among the regular customers were Mr. and Mrs. John Hartford, who occupied one of the hotel's largest suites. Looking over a menu of such delicacies as pheasant *en casserole* and soufflé Rothschild one night, Mr. Hartford murmured that what he really would like was a dish of real Italian spaghetti.

"I'll make you some," said Paul, "from my brother's recipe." Soon he was telling Mr. Hartford about the Cleveland restaurant, its success and the difficulty getting the products into supermarkets. After sampling spaghetti and meat sauce as prepared by Paul shortly afterward, Mr. Hartford said, "I'll help you. I'll see that the products get into all A & P stores."

This was no idle boast. John Hartford and his brother George headed the Great Atlantic and Pacific Tea Company, which was founded by their father, George Huntington Hartford, with a single store in New York's downtown Vesey Street. The chain became one of the greatest in the country; by 1951, the year of John's death, there were outlets in 3,100 cities in the United States and Canada.

John Hartford was as good as his word—and his word proved to be a bonanza for the Boiardis. Before long A & P shoppers were buying "Chef-Boy-Ar-Dee"-labeled foods up in the millions. The Boiardi boys thought up the phonetic spelling to simplify its pronunciation.

Business boomed, and in 1941 Paul resigned from The Plaza to help out with the expanding factory established by the brothers in Milton, Pennsylvania, where they now had a large farm to grow their own vegetables. They ran the business until 1964, when American Home Products bought it at a reported price of six million dollars.

Brothers Paul and Hector divide their time between Cleveland, New York and Milton; Mario has died, but his son Manuel, in 1966, was still upholding Boiardi tradition at The Plaza—as a waiter in the Persian Room.

Of exotic foods served at The Plaza perhaps the most exotic was kangaroo meat. Three Australians staying at the hotel interested the chef sufficiently to try it out, and arranged to have saddle of young kangaroo and tender chops imported. For a while the menu featured kangaroo chops at $1.50 each, but the demand was small and the item was dropped.

One of the waiters who served such delicacies turned out to be as titled as some who ate them. When he left, the management confirmed that this was Count Ernesto di Conosia of Italy, a former officer of the Italian Army. The count had run short of funds while touring America, and at The Plaza he earned his fare home.

Another waiter of an early Plaza era, Max Christen, revealed when he departed that he was the senior member of the respected firm of Christen Brothers, hotel proprietors and caterers of Genoa, Italy. He knew that one way to ferret out the secrets of The Plaza's successful operation was to observe it from the bottom up.

The standards Fred Sterry set in the kitchen did not decline when Conrad Hilton took over the hotel. François Gouron, who joined the staff in 1923, was named executive chef in 1944. It was a test of his ingenuity to defeat wartime ration-stamp shortages. He shed no tears about the lack of gum sugar for creating centerpieces, but it did make things difficult when there was a shortage of sugar for desserts, and a rationing of meats which limited orders for tournedos of beef with Bernaise sauce.

Chef Gouron directed a training program for chefs after the Second World War under the GI Bill of Rights and the auspices of the Veterans Administration. At the 1946 National Hotel Exposition five of his student veterans took the top prizes in their category. An idea of how far The Plaza's very own veterans went to see that the boys won is contained in the fact that M. Gouron personally caught, or "killed," as fishermen say, the salmon which took first prize. Gouron brought the salmon back from a fishing trip in Canada, and student Ernest J. Fritza prepared the prize-winning "Cold Salmon Parisienne."

Gouron supervised the preparation of the first postwar banquet of Les Amis d'Escoffier at The Plaza in 1946; it was such a success that this *ne plus ultra* of culinary experiences has become an annual event at the hotel.

Humbert Gatti succeeded Gouron as chef in 1953, and he was determined to top Gouron. The menu he served in 1954 at a dinner dance of the Chefs de Cuisine Association of America, Inc., suggests that he succeeded. The wonder of it is that any of the guests could dance after consuming a six-course dinner which included four wines.

Like Chef André after him, Gatti won the Medal of the French Government. And like chefs before him he invented new dishes that became Plaza specialties. His Supreme of Chicken, Plaza—a slice of ham, topped with breast of chicken and firmed in tomato aspic—is the *pièce de résistance* of many a buffet menu to this day.

Kitchens and banquets go hand in hand. Charity balls, wedding receptions, bar mitzvahs, fashion-show luncheons, large organization dinners, and special holiday functions are among the most important sources of revenue in a large hotel. A hotel geared to such business loses money when banquet business is down, and banquet figures were in the red when Clyde Harris came to The Plaza as banquet manager from the famed Ritz-Carlton Hotel, just before it was razed to be replaced by an office building. With him he brought many of the great annual functions that had been held there, some of which are still making social history as well as money for The Plaza. In 1950 the gross for food and beverage in his department was $625,000 for the year; when he left in 1959 to join Hilton's Waldorf-Astoria, the gross was over $2,000,000. The figures continued to rise with impetus under the new banquet manager, Pierre Birie. In 1965 the department grossed almost $3,000,000.

Harris brought a new concept of food and service to the banquet department. "Out with chicken patty" . . . and he revived the oyster bar, where guests could get freshly opened crustaceans as an adjunct to cocktails before sitting down to dinner. To Chef Gatti

Harris gives full credit for a great part of the Plaza banquets which, from 1952 on, became "grander and grander."

Harris' single near catastrophe came when a wedding reception was booked in the Terrace Room, where through some booking error a radio exhibition was also scheduled for that and the following day. There, at five o'clock, were those hundreds of Emerson radio sets and placards—what to do, what to do? Harris wrung his hands twice, but in a thrice had an inspiration. Before the wedding guests were due to arrive he had camouflaged everything with screens and flowers and was settling back in a glow of relief. But he reckoned not with an irate mother of the bride, who came early to check and discovered the trick. The enraged mother insisted all radios and assorted paraphernalia be removed; immediately an emergency crew of men was called in, out went the stuff, in came a fresh mass of flowers just in time, and the wedding reception proceeded as planned. At 1 A.M. back went the radios for the next day's exhibit. Harris still shudders at the memory of an angry female racing after him with a hammer.

Pierre Birie, Harris' successor, has his share of headaches, too, when it comes to overbooking, especially in the romantic merry month of June. There was the day when no less than five weddings were booked. The first, at 11:30 A.M., was a ceremony in the Terrace Room, after which guests went on to a wedding breakfast in the Persian Room, to make way for the second ceremony at 12:30. Guests at wedding No. 2 then went through the receiving line at a reception in the ballroom, while the Terrace Room was being made ready for wedding No. 3. Five o'clock brought wedding No. 4, followed by dinner in the ballroom. The last wedding took place at 8 P.M. in the Terrace Room.

All told, nine hundred meals were served, and the income for the one day netted over $25,000. If some of the assistant banquet managers developed ulcers later, at least it was justified in the accounting department.

No one event is like another. The special requests are legion when functions run from meetings of corporate directors to gargantuan cocktail parties given for anything from launching a new bra to floating a loan in Cambodia.

Thousands were spent for a comparatively small dinner to honor a retiring officer of the Standard Oil Company of New Jersey. Forty guests graced the outside rim of a large oval table, encompassing a miniature African jungle of exotic foliage and flowers especially imported for the occasion. In the midst of this simulated jungle a life-sized (not real) tiger bared his teeth, and monkeys (synthetic) swung from the ceiling and branches of the jungle trees. It can be guessed from this that the retiring executive had served his time in Standard Oil's African offices.

Some families will spend a small fortune on decorations for a wedding, yet one bride wanted only a single rose on her table. Another, who was married on St. Valentine's Day, had an all-red wedding. Thousands upon thousands of pink roses were used for the twenty-fifth wedding anniversary of Mr. and Mrs. Edward M. M. Warburg in the Terrace Room in 1964. Their florist even outdid Frederick Townsend Martin to create the setting of a rose garden in full bloom. Each table centerpiece was a high-rising rose bush spreading its fragrance over the guests; to simulated branches were tied hundreds of fresh roses. The room itself was also decorated with masses of roses, as was the Terrace Room foyer, where mounds of caviar on ice, at eighty dollars per pound, predominated at a long table among hot and cold cocktail canapés of insatiable variety. Arriving guests walked through a corridor banked with fragrant rose "trees."

The Plaza wins so many prizes for its wedding cakes, it scarcely pays a chef elsewhere to compete. Chef André's many-tiered fantasies of sculpted sugar cupids have delighted thousands of brides. To each bride, management presents a gold charm in the shape of a miniature Plaza.

A wedding cake was, of course, one of the items Gert Ries, assistant banquet manager, discussed with slender Lynn Steuer, daughter of Appellate Justice Aron Steuer for her wedding reception in the Persian Room.

"Oh, never mind about that," said Miss Steuer.

"Never mind about a wedding cake?" said Mr. Ries, shocked.

"Just forget it," said Miss Steuer.

"Forget it!" cried Mr. Ries. "You mean there'll be *no* wedding cake?"

"Oh, sure, there'll be a wedding cake," said Miss Steuer, "and I'm going to make it."

This was the first time in the long history of Plaza weddings that a bride baked her own wedding cake, and a staff trained to maintain a poker face could only wait and watch. To the astonishment of the banquet department, the cake was exquisite and delicious and decorative enough to impress even Chef André. What Mr. Ries and the others did not know, but which the wedding guests were gleefully aware of, was that the bride was an amateur cook of professional excellence. She had won culinary contests galore, the prize awarded in one having been a hundred thousand S. & H. Green Stamps. Although the Plaza kitchens remain a male preserve, she could have had a job there baking wedding cakes had she not preferred a family-sized kitchen.

While The Plaza, like all hotels, maintains a permanent staff of trained waiters, there are times when so many functions are going on at one and the same time that the regular staff has to be augmented by outside waiters supplied by the Union. At the height of the season parties may be booked in every function room. Often as many as three large fashion-show luncheons are in progress in a single day—in the Persian Room, the Terrace Room and the Ballroom—as blond and petite Mary Alice Rice, a former Follies girl in charge of the shows, sprints from one to the other.

If guests sometimes wonder about the laxity of service at some of these events it is because they are unaware that the waiter is not meticulously Plaza-trained, but Union-sent. The waiter at one fashion-show luncheon in the Terrace Room addressed a dignified matron with a cheery, "What will it be, dearie?" Only a pained wince on the face of the headwaiter indicated his distress.

Nobody goes hungry at The Plaza. Guests have a choice of five public restaurants for meals and a sixth for a snack and entertainment. Each has its special manners as well as its special clientele, each caters to a different taste in atmosphere, and there is something for everyone's palate, if not quite every pocketbook.

While tourists from afar have on occasion expressed shock at the price of a Plaza meal, suburban housewives shopping in Manhattan have expressed equal astonishment that they can lunch among its luxurious surroundings for no more than they spend in less atmospheric chain restaurants.

The Palm Court caters to them with a menu of many salads and few calories. Seven, including the Plaza's famed Chef's Salad, and a seafood salad, are priced at $2.95. Of course coffee costs an additional fifty-five cents. But after all, this is The Plaza.

Acclaimed the most elegant of Plaza dining rooms is the Edwardian Room, with its tall windows draped in ruby-colored velvet, its mahogany walls polished to a mirrorlike sheen. A window table overlooking the Park is a sign of prestige eternal; a table by a Fifth Avenue window is a mark of celebrity status. Imperious dowagers of old held a priority on these tables, and headwaiters dared not assign them to others, even though the ladies might be an hour late. It took Hilton to introduce some democracy and the rule that choice tables would not be held indefinitely for tardy dowagers. Before this policy was made to stick, one expendable headwaiter had to be fired for infuriating a doughty matron arriving an hour late on a busy day to find her table given away. He was quietly rehired, and dowagers learned to be prompt if they wanted more than the Renaissance ceilings to look at.

For the romantics, dining by candlelight in the Edwardian Room is the ultimate—not the candlelight of Greenwich Village wine bottles, but of tall silver candelabra in the manner of a formal home dinner party. Those who choose to can find on the menu Belugia caviar at $5.00 a portion. But a young couple on their honeymoon or a middle-income husband and wife celebrating an anniversary can also enjoy a banquet if not a ball for $6.95, feasting on cherry-stone clams, half chicken, Poêlée Hindustani, with rice and raisin pilaf; roast tomato, chiffonade salad and Plaza parfait. No extra charge here for the demitasse, and if the headwaiter senses it's a birthday, or anniversary, there's a surprise cake and candles.

Breakfast in the Edwardian Room is rarely the leisurely gargantuan repast it used to be but neither is it the gulp-and-run sacrilege of fruit juice and coolie fodder out of a patent package. Such robust dishes as steamed lamb hash with Madeira sauce, planked shad in season, campanile of hot cakes, and of course the famed creamed finnan haddie have lost none of their popularity as breakfast dishes here. The late Lucius Beebe, gourmet of the cafés, declared that breakfast at The Plaza was a fine reproach to foreigners who claim that the craziest of American insanities is the habit of having nothing but black coffee for breakfast.

If any public restaurant in the country can be compared to a man's club, it's the Oak Room at lunchtime, when it caters only to the male palate and to the same palates day after day. The Oak Room and the adjacent Oak Bar are in happy harmony and perfectly agreed that while they love the ladies, they love them from 3 P.M. on—except Saturdays and Sundays, when their affection for the fair sex is an all-day and -night affair.

Here the luncheon hour is a prolonged one as patrons linger on from noon to three, discussing business matters with colleagues and prospects. The hum of conversation can range from talks relative to deals in which an option on Mars is considered a legitimate transaction to the latest TV Nielsen ratings or indignation over a President's move to hold the line on steel prices. Brokers, bankers and brewers were familiar faces in the olden days; today the most steady customers are movie, radio and TV executives and merchants from the fashionable shops in the area.

Frequently the headwaiter gets a warning call from the secretary of a businessman entertaining at lunch. The message? When he orders a Bloody Mary, bring him a Bloody Shame—no vodka. When the check comes, nobody is the wiser except the shrewd, clearheaded host—who wanted it that way.

The Persian Room offers both entertainment and the most lavish of Plaza menus—and none of it is cheap. Crab Meat Remick is a fine dish to make at home, for in the Persian Room it is priced at $4.45. *Homard à la américaine,* a lobster cooked in the style of Brittany, not Maine, costs $7.10, and for dessert there is an *omelette norvégienne* with Cherries Jubilee at $6.00 for two. But one can also settle for half a broiled chicken at $3.75 before the lights are dimmed and an Ethel Merman or a Dinah Shore takes over the spotlight.

The most exotic menu is offered by The Plaza's newest restaurant, Trader Vic's, the only single restaurant which has its own kitchens, including Chinese smoke ovens. Its rare rum drinks and Samoan fish are for the gourmet who has tried everything and wants more. Its soft, dim lights beckon, "Hello, young lovers." The fortune cookies are for everyone.

In the intimate surroundings of "Plaza 9"—the little scarlet Edwardian *boîte* below lobby level, adjoining Trader Vic's, no hot meals are served. But hors d'oeuvres and sandwiches, in addition to drinks, are available for those who would catch the latest political parody staged by Julius Monk.

People eat less than they did fifty years ago. Where once a five- or six-course meal was the rule, diners today tend to settle for an appetizer, main course and dessert. They also drink less. Except when a special celebration is in order, a single wine will accompany a meal where in the early days two and three wines and champagne with dessert were proper accompaniments to a proper dinner.

None of this has served to reduce the load on bartenders and chefs, however. In 1907 the Plaza had eight hundred rooms; the building of an addition of some three hundred rooms in 1921, the subsequent breaking up of large suites into bedrooms and small suites, to accommodate an increase in guests, and public functions have combined to increase food consumption enormously.

The Plaza regularly serves up to some two thousand meals a day in its various restaurants and room service. When banquets and other functions are scheduled, the number of meals to be prepared can run up to four thousand. The recipe for chicken consommé would begin with, "Take one hundred five-pound chickens, . . ." and with the vegetables to be prepared the chickens can be left to simmer in a fifty-gallon vat.

Yet The Plaza has never had to expand its kitchen. To add certain new timesaving items, replace certain equipment, yes. But successive managers after Sterry have examined the great original kitchen without finding any major changes necessary to improve it. Even today it remains a model for hotels offering an à la carte menu. Not so long ago the State Department requested permission for several hotelmen from India, who were contemplating the building of a new hotel in their country, to be taken on a kitchen tour of inspection. Even to a visitor who has seen American hotel kitchens before, these are still a fascinating spectacle.

Much of the original equipment remains the best available, and no structural changes have been made to the gleaming white-tiled walls. Equipment additions have included such items as a rotating broiler capable of cooking twenty turkeys at a time. Only copper pots and pans are used for top-of-the-stove cooking, for they retain heat best; the great gleaming ones hanging from the ceiling are not the originals, but they look the same.

They still cook with gas at The Plaza—and this was a saving grace during the great blackout of 1965. Guests marooned at The Plaza were able, in the Edwardian Room, to order a complete meal of soup, roast beef, green beans and baked potato as well as dessert and coffee. And since dinner in the Edwardian Room is always by candlelight, it looked like "business as usual" that night—but plenty more of it.

Faithful to its original concept of providing only the finest of fresh foods, The Plaza, unlike some other hotels, uses almost no frozen foods save for an occasional out-of-season item. This means the food buyers must stay on the alert to price trends on all commodities, and service staff and headwaiters are kept informed of this via weekly meetings of the food and beverage staff. The meetings are also concerned with discussions and instructions on all the little niceties of service that have always characterized Plaza operation.

Overlord of this most important department is forty-one-year-old Beda Havelka, who remains true to the meticulous policies of his predecessor, retired Semy Ernest, and the traditions of The Plaza whose history he has carefully studied.

"Mr. Beda" as he is known to all, was a natural to follow the "Grand Old Man" of the business. Born in Prague, where his father owned a hotel and restaurant, he was exposed to the hotel and food business from early childhood. It was to be expected that when he was planning his career, his father entered him in the Hotel Management School in Lausanne, Switzerland, which has turned out some of the world's greatest hotelmen.

He finished school in 1948. Because of the political situation in Czechoslovakia, he never went back but journeyed to France. In 1955 he decided to come to America, and exactly one week after landing in the United States he had a job at The Plaza.

He takes pride in the fact that the first flag of the Republic of Czechoslovakia to be flown anywhere in the world fluttered from the Plaza flagpole. Thomáš G. Masaryk, first President of the Republic, was in the United States for a series of meetings with President Woodrow Wilson when the republic was declared on October 30, 1918.

A good chef must also be a keen executive. Cooking isn't all. How do you get one person's dinner together, to say nothing of two thousand dinners, without confusion? The trick is to delegate proper authority, but also to keep an eye on everything, check every cost, every item. Chef André has four *sous* chefs and some 125 assistants, but they do not spoil the broth, because he's overseeing things every minute. If someone were to forget to turn down the heat on the chicken consommé, the consequence would be a flood of alarming depth. Those fourteen hundred loaves of bread must not bake a minute overtime; roast beef for five hundred or more must be watched carefully for the right ratio of rare, medium and well done.

It is an exacting profession, and a first-rate chef can earn up to $35,000 a year. If he has won the Medal of the French Government, he can write his own ticket.

An early Plaza pastry chef who was rich enough to buy out many of the wealthy guests found romance in the kitchen. New Yorkers heard about the wealthy French chef when they read of the elopement of sixty-three-year-old François Beraudier and Miss Gertrude Lathrop, the twenty-year-old blond secretary of the chief steward. Tall and distinguished-looking and of an old French family, Beraudier could afford to do as he pleased, and it pleased him to make pastry. Before coming to the Plaza he was chief pastry cook for the Duke of Westminster, as well as for one of the Barons Rothschild.

THE PLAZA

It was his poems more than his pastry that won the girl's heart.

I work for you, I dream of you
You are my inspiration.
And whene'er a new dish I discover,
'Tis all because I am your lover.

The verse which really won her Yes contained this promise:

Your lover I will always be,
And live and serve none other;
But if you'll have me for a mate
I'll cook for you and bless my fate.

She did, and he did, and they honeymooned at the bridegroom's ancestral château in southern France.

CHAPTER TWELVE

In Marble Halls They Dwelt

THE late Joseph E. Widener, Philadelphia millionaire and turf tycoon, twitted about the great price he paid for a not-too-great painting, is credited with having made the classic remark: "I may not know much about art, but I know what I like."

Two Plaza tenants, Chester Dale and S. R. Guggenheim, not only knew what they liked but also knew a great deal about art, and they assembled collections that today are among the greatest art collections in the country. While they lived at The Plaza, works of art worth millions were housed there. The masterpieces they hung on their walls now hang in the most famous museums in the United States.

Chester Dale, a wealthy retired investment broker, was hailed as one of the world's great collectors of French Impressionist and Post-Impressionist paintings. Art connoisseurs from all over the world came to the Dale apartment at the hotel to feast their eyes on the treasures. Sir John Lavery, famous English painter, raved: "I have never in my life seen such magnificent hanging." M. George Salles, for years director of the Louvre, declared the collection to be one of the greatest examples of French art of the nineteenth and twentieth centuries that "I know of in the world."

Mr. Dale and his first wife, Maude, were living in a six-story mansion on East Seventy-ninth Street when World War Two broke out. What with servants leaving for war plants, oil for heating a large house difficult to get and other wartime problems making the upkeep of a town house a headache, the Dales moved to a suite at The Plaza, bringing with them a considerable art collection.

Mrs. Dale was an artist in her own right, and she encouraged her husband in his absorbing hobby of collecting. A year after Maude Dale's death, Mr. Dale married Mary Ball, who had worked with the first Mrs. Dale on the collection both at the town house and at The Plaza. She, too, continued to encourage and aid Mr. Dale in the acquisition of great paintings. Before long the hotel suite became too small to house all the masterpieces Mr. Dale acquired, and more and more adjoining rooms were added. By then every square inch of apartment walls was covered with priceless works.

Among the paintings which adorned the apartment were Picasso's "Le Gourmet" and "Pedro Manachi"; van Gogh's "Girl in White" (one of the last three done before the artist's suicide); Renoir's "Susanne Valadon" (the mother of Utrillo); Monet's "Cathedral"; Degas' "Mademoiselle Mal"; Renoir's "Girl with a Hoop"; Toulouse-Lautrec's "Corner of Moulin de la Galette." There were also a number of Modiglianis; Mr. Dale was the first to bring Modigliani to this country.

The Dales loved and lived with their treasures. Mr. Dale's personal enthusiasm for each purchase knew no bounds. When he bought Édouard Vuillard's "The Visit," he said to an interviewer, "It's terrific. When a picture does something to you, you don't hesitate. But where will I put it?" He sighed as he looked at the picture-laden walls. "But I've got to have it here. I look at my pictures every night before I go to bed." Gesturing at the paintings, he declared, "Every picture in this apartment will go to the public. I consider myself the custodian."

Hundreds of friends were invited from time to time to view the collection at The Plaza, but thousands more who were anxious to see it had to be disappointed. The Dales could afford to set aside only a certain amount of time for public viewing. They protected their private life.

Americans came into a priceless art legacy after Mr. Dale's death in 1962, when he willed the greater part of his collection to the National Art Gallery in Washington, of which he was president from 1955 until his death. Eighty-eight paintings, works never seen by the public, which hung in the apartment, joined over 150 masterworks already loaned to the National. All, along with sculptures and several dozen examples of graphic art, are now the property of the Museum. The Metropolitan in New York and the Philadelphia Museum of Modern Art also came heir to a fine legacy through the generosity of Mr. Dale.

When asked about the safety of paintings of such enormous value being in a public hotel, Mrs. Dale replied: "Nothing was ever disturbed. When we left for a visit or a vacation, the doors were double-locked by a master key which was kept in a safe." In fact, she felt the hotel was safer for the Dale treasures than a private home.

Mrs. Dale moved to an East Side apartment a year after Mr. Dale's death. By the terms of Mr. Dale's will she could retain what paintings she wanted for her lifetime, and after that they would be added to the collection in the National Art Gallery. She did not, however, keep a single one; as she said, it would be like pulling a finger from a hand to break up the collection. Among her own personal art possessions is a portrait of Mr. Dale, and among her memories are happy days lived at The Plaza.

Like the Chester Dales, Mr. and Mrs. Philip Gossler closed their fine town house on East Sixty-fifth Street in the early forties because of wartime hardships in maintaining a large house, and moved to The Plaza for the duration. They brought with them a number of cherished paintings and furniture which represented the finest work of bygone master craftsmen and world-famed artists.

The multimillionaire president of the vast Columbia Gas and Electric Corporation (and director of some fifty other companies), Mr. Gossler owned a collection of paintings which included a portrait of the Earl of Grosvenor, done by John Hoppner toward the end of the eighteenth century; a portrait of Francis Horner painted by Sir Henry Raeburn in 1815; George Romney's famous painting of Lady Parkhurst; Sir Joshua Reynolds' "Lady Frances Sondes" and John Hoppner's "Master Mercier." The Plaza apartment was a fittingly elegant setting for these and many other equally distinguished paintings, which hung there until Gossler's death in 1945. He left an estate of ten million dollars, and his art treasures were divided among wife, son and daughter.

S. R. Guggenheim, metals multimillionaire and art collector, and his wife occupied one of the most magnificent, fabled apartments at The Plaza, a series of rooms taking up almost one half of the first floor of the hotel. Known as the Guggenheim Suite for years, even after the Guggenheims departed, it included two beautifully appointed rooms which are now the famed State Suite, a jewel-like setting for countless small private parties.

The exquisite Louis XIV rooms, with handsome marble fireplaces, paneled walls, delicately decorated ceilings and crystal chandeliers, would have been ideal backdrops for Gainsboroughs, Romneys, Reynoldses, Watteaus, Fragonards, Bouchers, and others of the romantic school. Mr. Guggenheim knew what he liked, and he liked Matisse, Seurat, Léger, Chagall, Klee, Bonnard, and it was paintings by such artists as these that hung on those elegant nineteenth-century-period walls.

It was said of Mr. Guggenheim that he would spend as much as ten thousand dollars for a single canvas by a totally unknown artist. That such works survived to be acclaimed in the modern art world is a tribute to Mr. Guggenheim's *avant-garde* eye and art-pioneering courage. Many of the paintings were placed in storage after his death in November 1949, later to be hung in the Guggenheim Museum, that unique, startling-looking structure on upper Fifth Avenue designed by the late Frank Lloyd Wright.

Wright had chosen to live at The Plaza because it was not far from the site of his Guggenheim Museum, and each morning he would take the walk up Fifth Avenue to oversee the construction.

A footnote to Plaza history is contained in a book of family reminiscences, *The Valley of the God-Almighty Joneses,* authored by Wright's sister, the late Maginel Wright Barney.

She wrote that he loved the "opulent old hotel," even though he had completely altered his own suite, one of the former Celebrity Suites. As Mrs. Barney describes it, the walls and cornices were golden, the curtains a rich wine color, and the functional furniture which he designed was covered in shades of maroon and plum and purple.

A hilarious prologue in the book describes a wet winter night in the 1950's when Wright's sister entered the hotel carrying a paper grocery bag in which there were three baked potatoes and part of a cooked ham. Her brother had said, "Come to dinner, Sis. . . . Come *with* dinner. . . . Plain food. . . . We've had enough of caviar and sauces."

"Into the lobby of one of the world's great hotels I came," she writes, ". . . into a place filled with light and music, with beautifully dressed women and men and the aura of luxury, with the romantic illusion of entering another era. Under the gold arches, past the palms, I threaded my way among all those expensive-looking people, and from the warm paper bag I carried came a humble but enticing odor."

Her brother, she reported, loved the hotel. Even though the nineteenth-century architecture of Henry Hardenbergh was so entirely different from his own style, he enjoyed the place and was thoroughly at home there. While he assailed other architects, for Hardenbergh's work he had a great respect, and of The Plaza he said, "It's genuine. I like it almost as much as if I'd built it myself." Maginel Wright Barney could remember his saying that only one other time—about her old house in Nantucket.

The renowned in New York's art world made The Plaza a meeting place since the very beginning. In the early years, almost any day in the week would see such outstanding figures as Mitchell Kennerly, Costikyan, Jo Davidson, Sir Joseph Duveen, William Randolph Hearst and Jules Bache gathered around the little center fountain in the Oak Room. The Plaza flowered as a gathering place for gallery owners and collectors in the twenties, as established art galleries and newly opened ones moved uptown in the fashionable East Side area around Fifty-seventh Street, and the Grand Ballroom and Rose Room figured as a setting for some of Manhattan's most exciting art auctions.

The most famous art dealer of them all lived at The Plaza. Sir

Joseph and Lady Duveen, whose Duveen Brothers Gallery was close by, lived in the suite originally occupied by Mr. and Mrs. George J. Gould. Their daughter Dorothy made her debut in 1923 in the ballroom that was to be the arena of a bidding duel, in which her father figured, which was to make art-auction history.

The old American Art Association–Anderson Galleries, founded in 1885, from which emerged Hiram H. Parke and Otto Bernet in 1937 to start the now internationally known Parke-Bernet Galleries, held many of its important sales at The Plaza. It was quite the most exciting thing for socialites and art enthusiasts of every school of painting to attend these auctions, where Corots, Renoirs, Hoppners, Gainsboroughs, Boudins, Tissots and Reynoldses exchanged hands to the swift intonation of the *going, going, gone* theme and the thud of the auctioneer's hammer. The thrill of the swift-rising bids was intense.

The duel which made history in art circles on two continents was a contest between Joseph Duveen and Howard Young. Young did not become famous because he is Elizabeth Taylor's uncle. He was a well-known gallery owner and art dealer for years, and his gallery at 1 East Fifty-seventh Street still stands. Liz Taylor wasn't even a twinkle in her father's eye in 1928 when the great auction contest took place in the large new ballroom.

The painting that started the battle heard around the art world was Thomas Gainsborough's "The Harvest Wagon." It was among thirty-nine paintings put up for auction by the American Art Gallery for the estate of Judge Elbert H. Gary, Board Chairman of U.S. Steel. The total rung up for the entire sale was a hitherto-unheard figure of $1,184,640 in hard, 1928-purchase-value dollars.

Duveen had originally sold the painting to Gary for $165,000. He was a dealer who maintained his position in the art world by making sure that no picture of his ever declined in price and was, therefore, constantly buying back, or having his clients buy, pictures from the estates of his customers in order to keep the market up.

For that reason Howard Young was certain Duveen would go a long way to get the Gainsborough. A rival of Duveen's, he had been gently feuding with him, and the rumor at the time was that he wanted to create some fun and excitement, and at the same time make Duveen pay plenty, by bidding the price up—although he had no client in mind for it and didn't want the painting for himself.

The auctioneer was Hiram Parke, and the opening bidder was Carmen Messmore of the art firm of Knoedler and Company, who started his bid with $200,000 and wasn't heard from for the rest of the evening. The bidding took a slow crawl to $260,000, and it looked as if Joe Duveen was going to get the picture at that price.

Howard Young signaled to the auctioneer, bidding $10,000 more; Duveen upped it another $10,000; Young bid $290,000; Duveen bid $300,000. The ballroom, crowded with society, international art collectors, dealers and the press, was tense and hushed with subdued excitement as the silent battle of the art giants continued.

Young, smilingly but by this time with fingers crossed, quietly signaled a bid of $350,000. Duveen, who, it was now apparent to all, was determined to have the Gainsborough at any price, bid another $10,000, bringing the price up to $360,000, and Young let it rest at that. Duveen got the Gainsborough by paying $200,000 more for it than he had originally sold it for to Judge Gary, and $100,000 more than he expected to pay at the auction's start.

Before the stock market crashed, this was the highest price ever paid for a single painting in the United States, and it set a record for any price paid at a public sale in the world. It remained a record for years, until later auctions in the Parke-Bernet Galleries were to bring even more fabulous prices.

"The Harvest Wagon" was later sold to Frank Woods, Canadian oil magnate, who presented it to the Toronto Museum. What he paid for it was Duveen's secret.

Many other exciting art auctions were held in the Plaza ballroom, and while none were as spectacular as the Duveen-Young contest, a number of pictures also brought record prices. A Corot from the George Crocker estate, which cost but $14,000, brought $85,000 at an auction in the twenties.

It is an axiom that "names make news," and Liz Taylor, Howard Young's niece, made some kind of history at The Plaza. As the first wife of Nicky Hilton, Conrad Hilton's son, it was her home for a while, and glamour was the ingredient she added to the social scene.

Her divorce from Nicky did not deter the beauteous Miss Taylor from returning to The Plaza from time to time. In a brief autobiographical story she wrote for a magazine, she related with obvious humorous relish an embarrassing experience she had there.

To celebrate a movie success, she came to New York for "the first spree I'd ever had in my life." She moved into The Plaza and was assigned a sumptuous suite. When she asked the daily rates ("I was on my own expense"), she was told, "It's with the compliments of the house." "Oh, really, how nice," she answered. She stayed six weeks, but the day came when she thought she had better get her bill—"for food and stuff." It was for $2,500. The "complimentary stay" had been for four days.

Montgomery Clift and Roddy McDowell helped her pack. Someone had sent her six dozen double long-stemmed chrysanthemums, and the stars got to dueling with them. A carafe of martinis arrived, and soon petals were all over the suite. When Liz unpacked at another hotel, in a less expensive room, she found a Plaza bath nozzle, Plaza towels, bath mats, even the martini carafe in her suitcases.

"That was the work of my dear old friend Monty," Liz recalled. "I called the head housekeeper, apologized like mad and sent flowers and candy."

Men, it has been said, reveal themselves by the hotels they choose to frequent—even Presidents. And Presidents galore, during, before and after they served, made news at The Plaza. President William Howard Taft and Mrs. Taft came often—and Mr. and Mrs. Charles Taft made it their home from time to time. Harry Truman lunched there often with daughter Margaret, and Dwight D. Eisenhower, as General and as President, was honored at numerous functions at the hotel. His presence there, shortly after the end of World War Two, was the occasion of a bomb scare. The General was attending a dinner in the Baroque Room given for the Air Force by the country's leading aviatrix, Jacqueline Cochran Odlum. The photographers were out in force; they had just departed when a waiter picked up a strange-looking object from the floor and someone murmured, "It looks like a bomb."

That was all that was necessary. Within minutes fire engines and bomb squad, sirens screaming, roared up to the hotel. The suspicious-looking object was rushed out to the fountain in front of The Plaza and dipped in a bucket of water. Nothing happened but a flash of light; it was a photographer's range finder.

The day he conceded the Presidential election to John F. Kennedy, Richard Nixon arrived at the Edwardian Room for luncheon with his wife. The moment he made his appearance, guests, ignoring political loyalties, rose as one to greet him with a burst of applause. There was a suspicion of moisture in Dick Nixon's eyes.

Kennedy people have long been "Plaza people." While the Carlyle Hotel was his New York home when John Kennedy was President, his parents usually favored The Plaza. Two of his sisters had their wedding receptions at the hotel—Pat when she married Peter Lawford and Jean when she married Stephen Smith. Joseph Kennedy, the father of the brides, personally handled every detail of the arrangements—according to banquet managers who worked with him—decorations, food, wine and music. Mrs. Rose Kennedy hardly got into the act, generally a ritual for the mother of the bride.

Eunice Kennedy, who married Sargent Shriver, almost missed a wedding at The Plaza, but fortunately it was not her own. She was to have been a bridesmaid at the marriage of Harriet Boynton Wells to Fellowes Davis on December 1, 1946. Storms delayed the first postwar voyage from England of the liner *America,* but she docked in time for Eunice to have a piece of the wedding cake.

A future President was an outstanding guest at a hilarious Wild West fancy-dress dance at The Plaza in 1959. Senator John F. Kennedy had a gun belt under his sleek black dinner coat, worn with a string tie; Jacqueline Kennedy was a demure dance-hall girl in rose-pink taffeta with a pink rose in her hair; Bob Kennedy sported a long-tailed black coat; his wife was an Indian squaw complete with papoose (not real). Mrs. Joseph P. Kennedy and Jean Kennedy Smith also upheld family tradition and support for the event, a benefit for the Kennedy Child Study Center for Retarded Children.

It came as a mild shock to Bruce Kirby, headwaiter in the "Plaza 9," when Senator Robert Kennedy strolled in one night with a small group to see the midnight show of Julius Monk's revue, *Pick a Number*. The Senator was wearing a sports jacket and slacks, but no tie. It is a hotel ruling that men must wear ties; but what was a headwaiter to do in such a dilemma? Turn away the brother of the late President? He was damned if he did, damned if he didn't. The Senator was permitted to remain, but the question raised by columnist Louis Sobol, whether anyone else would have, remained unresolved.

The Plaza has from the very beginning been a source of news and anecdotes rich in abundance for the press—colorful, glamorous, sometimes hilarious, but always intriguing. The activities of the illustrious tenants, the flow of national and international "greats," the celebrities of the theater, literature, and the arts, the colorful pageantry unfolded almost nightly in the ballroom and other function rooms, was the stuff of which detailed stories and interesting column items were made.

There was the brief item involving Cary Grant. The story behind the story is an insight into Grant's reputation for wanting to know just what he gets for his money.

Cary Grant had ordered tea and muffins in his room. But when his order arrived, Grant noticed only three muffin halves. He was baffled and asked the waiter where the fourth was. The waiter expressed ignorance; the assistant manager, who was next questioned, was equally uninformed; room service was contacted, but no one there knew the answer. By this time, just for the hell of it, Grant was determined to find out why three halves of two muffins were served instead of four, even if he had to go down to the kitchen himself and see the chef. And he did.

"What do you do with the fourth half?" he asked.

"We use it for the base of eggs Benedict," replied the chef.

At this point Grant saw the futility and the humor of it. But he must have chuckled to himself when, at his next order, he was served four muffin halves. Tea drinkers and muffin eaters, ordering from Room Service, can be grateful to Grant. The Plaza now serves four half muffins.

Ferenc Molnár, the Hungarian playwright, agreed with Oscar Wilde that "an address inspires confidence." As he often told friends, it was his lifelong custom to take the smallest room in the finest of hotels and eat in the least expensive restaurant. The Plaza was his New York home from 1940 to 1952, and he lived in one room and ate most of his meals in a delicatessen on Sixth Avenue.

Paul Sonnabend once said, "Do you notice that nobody ever says, 'We like' the Plaza; they say, 'We love the Plaza.' "

Ferenc Molnár loved The Plaza, and paid tribute to all its endearing charms in an article he wrote in June 1950, for *Park East,* headed simply, "The Plaza." He described it as "a citadel, a fortress for all of us who live here. After two decades of wandering, during which I have stayed in those good but noisy hotels with cardboard walls, any time I come home to this mighty edifice with the wide open free space about it, I have a sense of quiet security, solidity and steadiness. . . . Perhaps the nuclear scientists will smile at this, but in this house I am not even afraid of the atom bomb."

Molnár expressed surprise that "one of the greatest of Europe's greatest, the late Maurice Maeterlinck, lived here under the same roof with me for eight years—but it took me three years to find that out." And he added, "How the management of The Plaza can achieve this is a mystery." It is left for others to wonder why nobody thought to introduce the Hungarian dramatist to the Belgian dramatist. A possible explanation is that both yearned for solitude. Maeterlinck, famed for his fantasy *The Blue Bird,* described tragedy in the theater as "the expression of those profound emotions that exist in solitude and silence."

There was no solitude and silence in the life of Clara Bell Walsh at The Plaza. Hers was an abundant, fullsome existence from that first day in 1907 when she and her husband, Julius Walsh, took up their residence at the hotel. She had a lust for life matched by few anywhere and by none at The Plaza, and a passion for people regardless of their station in life. The only requisite was that they had to be "interesting." A Southerner by birth, she was proud of her friendship with Bill Robinson, at whose funeral she was asked to be an honorary pallbearer.

Big, blond and buxom, she was Society, Broadway and the Turf all rolled into one. At Belmont Park, Saratoga, the Kentucky Derby, wherever the horses were running she was a familiar figure until she decided it was more comfortable to watch the races on television. Lexington, Kentucky, was her birthplace, and she liked to say she was "born on a horse." She certainly was a great horsewoman, and in the early years in New York she had her own saddle horses and a matched team of harness horses, when that was the fashionable thing. When younger and slimmer she would take a canter in Central Park every morning, sometimes accompanied by Fred Sterry, who was an old friend and himself a lover of horseflesh. For years she exhibited, and would take prizes, at Madison Square Garden horse shows.

But Mrs. Walsh was happiest when entertaining in her seventh-floor suite at the Plaza, whose decor she never changed. There was still the original overstuffed furniture of 1907, and a vast collection of china dolls, Victorian and Edwardian bric-a-brac and hunting prints everywhere.

From 5 P.M. on, the door was open to her friends, and here any day one could encounter celebrities of stage, screen, and Tin Pan Alley, a mélange she mixed with café society. A little sad, Jimmy Savo would sing, "River, Keep Away from My Door"; Vincent Lopez would play "Kitten on the Keys," and Amos 'n' Andy, Ed Wynn and Mae West would listen.

Clara Bell had lived at The Plaza for fifty years when the hotel reached the age of fifty, in 1957. Her own birthday was in March of that year, and she wanted to have an official golden anniversary celebration. But the hotel was planning to have a big bash of its own in October, and Hilton wasn't for letting Clara Bell take the edge off it. So she settled by having Mary Martin and her husband, Richard Halliday, as guests of honor because "Mary is a very good friend of mine." The guest list must have made Elsa Maxwell green with envy.

Clara Bell Walsh did not live to attend The Plaza's Golden Jubilee. She died in August 1957, just a few months short of rounding out a half century of joyful living there. She was "the First Lady of The Plaza," a legend in her time, and there was nobody else quite like her anywhere.

In quiet, conservative contrast were Mr. and Mrs. T. Suffern Tailer of Newport. During winters spent at The Plaza they entertained in a manner that was the *ne plus ultra* of correctness. Each month during their tenure they would give a series of three dinners on three consecutive evenings, and there was a reason for this procedure. Since their own apartment was too small for seated dinners of forty and fifty, and yet, since they wished them to be as much as possible like a dinner in their own home, Mr. and Mrs. Tailer would re-create the atmosphere of a private apartment in the White and Gold Suite. They had their own linens, china and glass, silver, proper accessories, personal pictures and even certain pieces of their own furniture brought down from their suite to give the feeling of a soiree "at home." The setting remained intact for three evenings, after which everything was transported back to their apartment until the time came for their next series of dinners.

Emily Post would have put her seal of approval on every phase of the parties, which started off with a reception in one room, dinner in the adjoining room, and a finale of bridge, Mah-Jongg (then the rage) or a musicale in the third adjoining room.

The surprising fact about Plaza dowagers is not that they grow old, but that they remain so young. In 1957 Mrs. Frank Stanley Freeman, a resident for thirty years, celebrated with champagne both the hotel's fiftieth anniversary and her own one hundredth birthday. She lived to be 103 years young— and was The Plaza's proudest guest.

Mrs. Freeman, née Ella Peterson Tuttle, owed her wealth to a forward-thinking father, one of the country's first manufacturers of radiators. Born in Brooklyn before the Civil War, she wore hoopskirts and attended a fashionable school which saw no reason to teach young ladies fractions.

Mrs. Freeman's husband, a Brooklyn banker, died on their honeymoon in Atlantic City in 1887, and she never remarried. Nor did she lose her enthusiasm for the male sex. When being interviewed, male reporters found her a delightful conversationalist;

she did not waste her time talking to the women. Always a lady of fashion to the last of her life, Mrs. Freeman dressed elegantly, but never did she lapse into the habit of so many elderly ladies of dressing "too young." She chose her wardrobe in the latest style, with taste and dignity; her silver hair was always carefully coiffed, but she liked wearing hats and always had a large variety of them.

For her one hundredth birthday reception she wore an ankle-length white gown and orchids. Eugene Voit, the manager then, gave her a special champagne party and invited all The Plaza's veteran employees, as well as friends and relatives of the guest of honor. Of course he included Bertha Meyers, the chambermaid who kept Mrs. Freeman's room filled with flowers daily.

Mrs. Freeman survived her immediate kin, and her fourteen-month-old great-grandnephew was her special delight as a guest. President Dwight D. Eisenhower sent "Happy Birthday" greetings to add to the hundreds of others she received. Mrs. Freeman was ninety-nine years old when she voted for the first time, to reelect Eisenhower.

That it takes a lot of living to make a home is an undeniable truism, and a hotel, like a home, breathes with the life of its "family."

Much of the magic of the Plaza was in its family of permanent tenants.

CHAPTER THIRTEEN

Eloise and Her Friends

FROM an oil portrait on the wall of the lobby floor at The Plaza a little girl grins impishly at passersby. A man who might be hard put to it to identify the Queen of England without her crown would know, if he wandered into the lobby: This is Eloise. She is six.

People who have never been to New York have poked into every nook and cranny of the Plaza with the incorrigible child created by Kay Thompson in her best seller, *Eloise*. Before and after Eloise, her real-life counterparts have been matching such antics of hers as crossing up elevator operators, pouring water down the mail chute, commanding Room Service to send up a raisin and seven spoons, hunting for Skippordee the turtle, and Weenie, the dog who looks like a cat and likes to have its back scratched with a wire coat-hanger.

After the book was published in 1955, several women who spent their childhood at the Plaza wrote the hotel to claim the dubious honor of having been the original Eloise. One was aware enough to write, "I know you have heard this before . . . but Eloise *is* me." A middle-aged gentleman living in New York, who was once employed as a musician at the Plaza, insists he was the model for Eloise.

As everyone who can read must know by this time, Eloise is the terrible little hoyden whose sophisticated mother boards her in a Plaza suite with her English nanny, while she skips from Miami to Paris to Palm Springs. While the adorable little monster didn't actually take over the management of the hotel, she was into everything else "... half the time I'm lost, but mostly I am on the first floor, because that's where catering is...."

Eloise's mischievous behavior could be attributed to the fact that she was born not at the Plaza, but in a Las Vegas nightclub, the brain child of an irrepressible singer–comedienne Kay Thompson.

Tall, lanky, blond Miss Thompson was one of the country's outstanding entertainers. Her singing had brought her early success as a vocalist with Fred Waring and other orchestra leaders; during the great musical film era of the forties, she was a vocal coach at MGM. A dancer and choreographer, she also had a genius for mimicry and pantomime, and when she teamed up with the Four Williams Brothers in a nightclub act, the critics hailed it as the peak of sophistication.

In the summer of 1948 the act was booked into a Las Vegas nightclub. It was a hundred degrees in the shade, and rehearsal time found everyone tired and tense. Miss Thompson arrived late. Quickly sensing the tension, she became a timid little child, announcing in a small-girl voice, "I am Eloise. I am six." Her meek, helpless air brought a burst of laughter instead of an outburst of reprimand.

And so Eloise was born. Everyone loved Eloise. The Williams boys and others refused to speak to Miss Thompson; they'd talk only to Eloise. Whenever Miss Thompson appeared at a party, Eloise had to do her stuff. People took to calling the actress and asking to speak to Eloise. When she checked into the Plaza for a Persian Room engagement with her musical pals, the staff wanted to "talk Eloise" with her. She lived at the Plaza for five years—and soon everybody was doing it, "talking Eloise."

As Eloise grew in popularity, it was inevitable that Miss Thompson would put her in a book. She was brilliantly abetted by artist Hilary Knight, who sketched an Eloise now quite as famous as Lewis Carroll's Alice.

They took the child down to a publisher, who ran her through the presses almost as fast as Eloise could run through the Plaza lobby. The book was an instant best seller; in no time over a hundred thousand copies were sold. Not only children, but even those who considered themselves the intelligentsia were fascinated with the hilarious tale of the spoiled brat of The Plaza. Kay Thompson had struck not a gold mine, but a uranium mine. Even she could never have dreamed that her baby would become a national industry.

Soon Eloise was absolutely everywhere—in the nation's bookshops, in department stores and toy shops, in children's apparel stores and record shops. All over the country appeared Eloise dolls, Eloise dresses and Easter bonnets (designed by none other than Mr. John) for little Eloises everywhere; Eloise emergency kits in a child-sized model's hatbox contained such Eloisiana as turtle food, bubble gum, crayons, note pads and "Please-Do-Not-Disturb" signs from the Plaza. All products were from "Eloise, Ltd.," the wildfire industry of which Kay Thompson was president.

A special Eloise room was set up by The Plaza which small-fry from all over the country visited when Mummy and Daddy brought them to New York; they could order from a special Eloise menu, with a cover illustration of Eloise on her tricycle and her pet turtle and the dog that looked like a cat, and featuring such delights as Skipperdee Sandwich (peanut butter and jelly), Supersonic Sherbet, and "Milk, Milk, Milk!"

Fact and fancy merged, and soon the Plaza was entertaining a real-live Eloise, seven-year-old Evelyn Rudie, who had been chosen to play the part of the *enfant terrible* on a nationwide television show. For weeks children all over the country were on the *qui vive* waiting for the program, while the TV columnists built up interest. Little Evelyn was a joy as the naughty, incorrigible child, even if she had lost two front teeth eating meringue glacé.

But the show turned out to be a real dud, even with a cast that included Mildred Natwick, Monty Woolley, Charles Ruggles, Slapsy Maxey Rosenbloom, Ethel Barrymore, and Conrad Hilton and Kay Thompson, the latter two playing themselves. According to *San Francisco Chronicle* reviewer Terrence O'Flaherty, Hilton muffed his only line, "Oh, my poor hotel is falling apart."

Eloise's popularity, however, continued to soar—and so did the mountain of publicity for The Plaza. Never before had any hotel received such national, nay, international, publicity, and the amount of mail was surpassed only by that to be received by the Beatles less than ten years later.

From Dublin, Ireland, came a letter on American Embassy stationery. Mrs. Grant Stockdale, whose husband was United States Ambassador to Ireland, wrote, "Eloise has come to Ireland. At least she capers about the walls of Suzie Stockdale's classroom in the American Embassy residence. . . . We converted Suzie's room, where she was to be tutored, into a classroom of sunny yellow. Sally, our oldest daughter, and I painted our favorite little character sitting primly on the door, lounging in the cupboard, hanging from the blackboard, cavorting over the globe. People who tour the residence are amused by our attempts. . . . Maybe The Plaza ought to paint *their* Eloise on the wall."

The Plaza didn't paint Eloise on the wall, but did the next best thing. A brand-new portrait by Hilary Knight (to take the place of the original, which had mysteriously disappeared from the lobby wall the night of a roistering fraternity dance, never to be found) was not hung, but permanently attached, to the same wall.

Princess Grace of Monaco was unwittingly responsible for this second Eloise portrait. The former Grace Kelly, on one of her trips to the United States, brought her children to The Plaza especially to see the Eloise she herself remembered. What a disappointment to discover the little girl gone! Semy Ernest, beloved, venerable Plaza executive, was strolling through the lobby at the time and noted the children's disappointment. He promised, "The next time you come, Your Grace, Eloise will be here again." And she was.

Eloise, who had been cavorting in Paris, Rome and Moscow, returned to the Plaza for the New York World's Fair in 1964. Fifty youngsters, including children of United Nations diplomats, attended a party to welcome her, and Senator Javits' teen-age daughter Stephanie had the honor of unveiling the new portrait. The youngsters gorged themselves on ice cream and cake, and each received a photograph of the new portrait, signed by Eloise, "With

Love." *McCall's* magazine, with a full-page color picture, hailed Eloise's return: "Look who's back at the Plaza!" And the Beatles, only recently departed from the hotel, sent a telegram, "We want to hold your hand, yeah, yeah, yeah."

Two young chums, Orianne Rodman and Tamar Head, aged twelve and thirteen, asked by their parents what they wanted for Christmas, said they wanted to be "Eloise at The Plaza." Not too far away, the Heads in Greenwich Village, and the Rodmans across the river in New Jersey, booked their daughters into the hotel for a weekend, gave them twenty-five dollars spending money, OK'd a charge account with the Credit Department, and left them to enjoy themselves in an Eloise way.

The girls brought along Tamar's pug dog, a dead ringer for Weenie, and like Eloise they kept Room Service hopping. ("Oooooo, I *love* Room Service.") Because Eloise had a turtle, they ordered turtle soup. Orianne didn't like it. But both loved the caviar and champagne they ordered one night; steaks for breakfast made a New England breakfast look like a spare snack, and they gorged themselves on pastries. They raced up the stairways and slid down the banisters and found so much to explore that they never left the hotel for three days. For a souvenir, the manager presented them with snapshots of themselves taken in front of the Eloise portrait.

But the conservative Plaza kept what would normally have made a news story of their escapade from the press. It just sounded too pat to be true.

Eloise, 'twas written, played with the staff for want of playmates her own age, but in truth there never has been a shortage of children at The Plaza. Youngsters abound—at Easter, at spring school vacations, at Christmas, at all holiday times. The first tenants brought their children with them, Mrs. Young Heyworth of Chicago, whose name was the fourth to grace the opening-day registry, signed for a five-room suite with "Master Otto" and "Miss Gwendolyn." The fifth family to register was another Chicago couple, Mr. and Mrs. Alexander H. Revell, who brought "Master Alexander, Jr.," and daughter "Miss Margaret" with them. Looking farther down that first page, one found that Master Lyman

H. Treadway, Jr., accompanied his mother, Mrs. Lyman Treadway and sister Elizabeth from Cleveland.

In an era when accouchement occurred in the home, rather than in hospitals, countless babies were born in The Plaza, which was home to many an expectant mother. The hotel welcomed its first baby in time to celebrate its first Christmas, in 1907. The stork must have felt a strange sensation when business called him to the elegant new Plaza, where in mid-December he left a baby girl in the seventh-floor apartment of Mr. and Mrs. Reginald Ronalds. Society editors noted that the beautiful mother, the former Miss Thora Scott Strong, was as popular in London society as she was at home.

More visits from the stork followed. On July 19, 1911, the *Herald,* with a lapse of editorial memory, gave a sixteen-line head to a story announcing, "The First Birth at The Plaza," eighteen days after the event. Reduced to the truth, the story still would have made news, for with the birth of baby Henry A. Alker, Jr., Andrew W. Rose, financier, yachtsman and socialite, then cruising on his oceangoing steam yacht, the *Emrose,* had gained a grandson.

Once reporters started watching, there was no end to the stories of babies at The Plaza. Within a month the papers reported the birth there of a granddaughter for railroad mogul James J. Hill, president of the Northern Securities Company and builder of the Great Northern Railway. The parents, Mr. and Mrs. Anson M. Beard, received second billing. The same year Pierre Cartier, who founded the New York house of Cartier, the Paris jewelers, and his wife, the former Elma Rumsey of St. Louis, became the parents of a baby girl born at The Plaza.

Home is where you hang your childhood, and to thousands, as years and children multiplied, The Plaza supplied the proof that you can go home again.

To celebrate his wife's fiftieth birthday in 1964, Jackson Martindell, publisher of *Who's Who in America,* naturally chose The Plaza. For she was born there. Mrs. Martindell, the former Anne Clark, first saw the light of day in 1914 in an eighth-floor suite where her parents, Mr. and Mrs. William Clark, made their home while young Mr. Clark was attending law school in New York. As a Federal District Court Judge, Clark lived to serve at the Allied War Crimes trials in Nuremberg, Germany, after World War Two.

For her birthday, Manager Alphonse Salomone presented Anne Clark Martindell with a gold charm replica of The Plaza. In a thank-you note, Mrs. Martindell wrote, "I feel very sentimental about my birthplace. . . . It is one of the few places left with atmosphere and elegance."

Mrs. John G. McCarthy, the former Lily Lambert and wife of the president of the Television Program Export Association, was born at The Plaza within weeks of Anne Clark Martindell—and she was born there because of her. Lily's parents, Mr. and Mrs. Gerald Lambert, were living in Princeton, New Jersey. Dr. Edward Cragin, who was treating Mrs. Clark in New York and Mrs. Lambert in Princeton, finally protested, "I can't keep running back and forth all the time," and advised the Lamberts to come to New York. They checked into The Plaza—and there Lily Lambert was born.

In one way or another, The Plaza has continued to figure in Mrs. McCarthy's life. Her two daughters made their debuts there at the exclusive Grosvenor Debutante Ball. And she was one of the guiding lights on the arrangements committee for the great Golden Anniversary Ball in the Grand Ballroom in October, 1965, commemorating the fiftieth anniversary of the founding of Grosvenor Neighborhood House and honoring six of the original founding members.

Mrs. McCarthy is fond of telling an episode of the time when she was living in Washington during the war. Her husband, who was stationed there with the Navy, had to make a hurried trip to New York. There was no time to telephone for a hotel reservation, and when the McCarthys arrived at The Plaza in the late afternoon, a polite, though harassed, desk clerk expressed regret that he could not take care of them in the wartime room shortage.

"Young man," said Mrs. McCarthy, in her best Social Register manner, "I'll have you know I was born right here in this hotel."

"Not really!" exclaimed the clerk. "Yes, really," replied Mrs. McCarthy—then, making the bravest of feminine admissions, she added, "on September 3, 1914."

A sense of drama inherent in the young man sent him into the rooms managers' office in a hurry. He came back with the word, "We've been able to find a small suite for you. Compliments of the management."

Babies came, grew up at The Plaza, made their debuts in the Ballroom, held their wedding receptions there, brought their children to dancing class, celebrated anniversaries there, and met their grandchildren for tea in the Palm Court.

On the occasion of The Plaza's fiftieth birthday in October, 1957, Andrew Shiland, Jr., an official of Avianca, the Colombian International Airline, expressed the feelings of many in a letter. "As one who learned to take his hat off in your hydraulic elevators, learned to dance in your ballroom and learned to call on elderly ladies at tea time, please accept my heartiest congratulations."

While three generations of New Yorkers worried about the rising tide of juvenile delinquency, three generations of very little teen-agers were learning to curtsy and bow as well as dance at Plaza dance classes. Of course, there was the time the boys let loose a crate of live lobsters on the dance floor, and several boys-will-be-boys, etc., scandals have resulted from introductions made on the dance floor. But whatever happened to them later, thousands of men and women remember with nostalgia the annual spring parties given at The Plaza for more than twenty-five years by Claire Holcomb Bloss (Mrs. Douglas Halsted) for her dancing classes; the annual Holiday Dances for sub-debutantes and sub-sub-debs, dances still being held there annually; Miss Clementine Miller's dances for the teen-age elite, and others.

It was fun to be young at The Plaza. And if you had an uncle or a cousin or any other relative connected with the hotel, as did George A. Fuller, Jr., it could be thrillingly exciting. Even at the age of ten George was already making headlines a year or two after The Plaza opened.

Little George was the nephew of Harry Black, and Uncle Harry outdid Santa Claus the year George was ten. For Christmas he gave

George a miniature custom-built automobile, a replica of the new motorcars competing with carriages on the streets of New York. Painted black and red, it boasted a one-horsepower motor driven by a 200-volt storage battery. But that wasn't the half of it; Uncle Harry also arranged for the construction of a speedway one seventh of a mile long, winding around in the sub-basement of The Plaza. New York gasped at the news that Georgie raced his car beneath the hotel at speeds as high as twelve miles an hour.

The "speedway" is still there; its once exciting function has been reduced to acting as a runway for hand trucks conveying a variety of supplies from one part of the basement to another.

If you were very young in the forties and had a tricycle, you could garage it in the Plaza's tricycle garage, located at a corner of the service entrance and all done up in the darlingest peppermint stripes. For fifteen cents a day, or three dollars a month, you could park your tricycle in a red rack with chains for protection. The Plaza issued blue-and-white license plates to the pint-sized vehicle owners, and in a display of favoritism not unknown in the state, saved the low numbers for permanent guests. This evoked a picture of small-fry boasting at birthday parties of having License Plate No. "Plaza—1, New York."

The tricycle garage came about when Robert J. Caverly, a vice president of the Hilton chain, then owners of the hotel, happened to mention to general manager Eugene Voit how expensive it was to carry his daughter's tricycle to Central Park by cab. Buses did not allow the three-wheelers, and it was hard on mothers and nurses to pilot them back and forth to the park.

"Now, there's an idea," thought Voit. "Why not a tricycle garage?" And *voilà,* in no time there was one. For several seasons garaging at The Plaza was the "in" thing to do in the small-fry set. The Plaza added a mural showing tricycle routes to such favorite spots as the lake and the zoo, and featuring such contradictory slogans as "Curb your tricycle," and "Look Ma, no hands."

Not only the elegant offspring of socialites collected happy memories at The Plaza. For Christmas one year, a little boy named Eddie Murphy got a pair of pot-metal ice skates and could not resist trying them out on the not-too-frozen lake in Central Park.

Eddie went under, his companions ran shouting out of the park, and chauffeurs stationed in front of The Plaza rescued the child from drowning. At the solicitation of a lady who ran out of the hotel to watch, Eddie was carried into the luxurious Turkish baths, then a Plaza service. Stripped of his scant and soaking clothing, he was treated to a steam bath and later to an electric bath, whatever that was. There is no doubt he enjoyed the tea and cakes which followed. As for the baths, the *Herald* commented: "It will probably take some time for him to live them down with his companions."

In 1923, a Cinderella's wish was granted to a crippled shut-in, Helen Collins, a young girl from Amsterdam, New York. George McManus, famous Hearst ("Jiggs and Maggie") cartoonist, and his wife read of her desire for a trip to New York, published in a letter to the *New York American*. They invited her down to the big city and put her up at The Plaza. She went to the Metropolitan Opera, shopped for souvenirs for her family, enjoyed the luxury of breakfast in bed, and had her hair coiffed in the beauty shop. The redoubtable Mrs. Frederic Neilson—she of the big, black cigar and crony of Freddy Townsend Martin—sent her a huge box of goodies, together with a bouquet of carnations and a note, "I have been ill, or I certainly would have called on you before."

It might be stated here that Mrs. Neilson was not so charitable to celebrities of the stage. Sydney Jones Colford, who succeeded Reginald C. Vanderbilt as her son-in-law, told of the time he was in the Palm Court with Mrs. Neilson and her daughter Cathleen when Lily Langtry passed by. "She was, to me," said Sydney, "the most beautiful woman in the world." When Mrs. Neilson spied "the Jersey Lily," she exclaimed, "Sydney, don't you dare notice that infamous woman if she should have the audacity to speak to us. She was the mistress of my brother, Freddie Gebhard, and of King Edward of England."

"On leaving," Colford said, "she glided up to our table, addressing my fiancée, 'Cathleen, darling, is this charming gentleman your new man?' She utterly disarmed me with her beauty and charm and gracious manner."

A small boy named Bobby Wagner made his first public appearance at a Plaza theatrical in the role of Portia, the heroine of Shakespeare's *Merchant of Venice.* At eleven he won his first oratory contest in the Plaza ballroom. Forty years later Robert F. Wagner stood on the same stage to speak his own lines as Mayor of New York.

Another small boy, whose parents were stopping at the hotel, discovered one day he had overspent his allowance and asked the doorman for the loan of a quarter. Ralph Davenport was the veteran doorman who loaned twenty-five cents to the boy destined to be future President of the United States, John F. Kennedy.

The special magic of The Plaza for the young was demonstrated in 1963. "Why is Deirdre dancing in her dreams?" was the caption of an ad which appeared in the *New Yorker,* accompanying a filmy scene of a slender young girl doing pirouettes in front of the hotel. Why? "This summer on the week of her fourteenth birthday her parents will take her to The Plaza." The name Deirdre was no more than a copy writer's dream, so one can imagine the management's surprise when a letter arrived from John J. Godfrey, Jr., assistant manager of the Connecticut General Life Insurance Company, in Hartford, Connecticut, who wrote, "Your advertisement had my daughter really dancing in her dreams because she *is* Deirdre and she *will* be fourteen in July, and we *shall* take her to The Plaza. So please reserve rooms for her and my wife and me for July 23, her birthday."

Plaza executives couldn't believe it. To make sure this really was a coincidence, they cross-examined the copy writer, called Mr. Godfrey and checked on Deirdre. Deirdre was for real, and it *was* a coincidence. The Plaza gave Deirdre a birthday celebration with a big cake and candles but did not invite the press to the party, for fear those cynics wouldn't believe it wasn't a publicity stunt.

Deirdre, as a proper young lady, sent a note of thanks for the suite, the birthday cake, the music and "the magic. It is hard coming back to reality," she wrote.

The children at the Plaza have had a way of capturing the hearts of the staff. Chambermaids have cooed over Eartha Kitt's little girl, and Margaret Alford, a ninth-floor maid, was so enchanted with five-year-old Danny, son of actress Celeste Holm, she dedicated a poem to him which was more distinguished for its note of affection than its meter:

> Early in the morning, at the Plaza near the park,
> I hear little childish chatter, happy as a lark.
> Little gentle footsteps, running across the floor.
> Then I hear a squeaking, someone at the door.
> It's Danny with his teddy bear, and he wants to play.
> Though I am very busy, I run out to see.
> We both laugh and laugh, we're happy as can be.

Like children, dogs have always been welcome at the hotel. Unlike many another hotel, The Plaza has accepted dogs from the very start, and the canine stories are amusing and endless. To this day dogs have a lovely time at The Plaza once they learn that the Palm Court was not put into the Plaza for their use.

When it opened in 1907, the hotel boasted a room for dogs in the basement. Although some cynics whispered that the dogs were treated better than the servants, the accommodations failed to satisfy Edward Ellsworth, wealthy real estate broker. For his French poodle Nana he engaged a private room and bath. There a maid baby-sat with him, a tutor taught him tricks, and the valet groomed him.

Soon the dogs begged their way into more and more suites, and the Plaza chef prepared special meals for them. This was before the era of canned dog food. The mistress of a French bulldog ordered three meals a day for him and insisted upon supervising the menus herself, to make certain his dishes were as varied as her own. For this, in 1911, she paid $21 a week, service extra.

One of the most famous canine guests at The Plaza was a Boston bull owned by Mrs. Benjamin B. Kirkland of Philadelphia. Instead of fetching newspapers, as some dogs were trained to do, Sir Kirkland fetched jewels. Each evening he accompanied a maid to the office, to collect a Russian leather case containing the jewels his mistress planned to wear that evening. The gems were worth thousands, and the dog seemed to have known it. He would carry nothing else but the jewel case.

Memorable dogs of all breeds have stayed at The Plaza, their one common ground being their pedigrees. A wirehaired terrier owned by Mrs. Robert Bacon for years lorded it over other dogs as the oldest canine inhabitant of the hotel. Pelleas was a chic Pekingese owned by Maurice Maeterlinck. Cliffort Columnist was the kennel name of Timothy, an English springer spaniel brought to The Plaza by columnist E. V. Durling. Sandy, a twelve-year-old English-born Sealyham owned by Mr. and Mrs. H. J. Levee, was provided with white cotton socks when taken for a walk, since the sidewalks hurt his feet.

Ed and Pegeen Fitzgerald, of radio fame, arrived in New York from California, via a South American cruise, on a snowy day in 1935, with their tiny Maltese terrier, Mopsy. Because Mopsy had left the boat for a while in South America with the Fitzgeralds, they had to put up a bond when docking in New York, that Mopsy would not herd sheep, and this was stamped on his entry blank. The Fitzgeralds stayed at The Plaza all that year, and to The Plaza the authorities came regularly to check up—apparently to make sure he wasn't herding sheep in Central Park.

Fashions in dogs change, just as fashions in costumes change. For years the Pekingese was in high favor. The Pekingese pet of the Duchess de Talleyrand was long the leading socialite canine at The Plaza. The Plaza ballroom was the setting for several years for an annual Pekingese show, one of the most memorable being an exhibit the year after the hotel opened, when the Dowager Empress of Japan donated a Peking vase.

The most popular dog to live at The Plaza was Coco, the pet French poodle of Mr. and Mrs. Chester Dale, who maintained a large apartment at the hotel until Mr. Dale's death in 1962. After the famous art collector died, his widow moved to an apartment at Sixty-sixth Street and Fifth Avenue.

In the spring of 1964, Mrs. Dale was getting ready to go to the opening-day ceremonies of the New York World's Fair as a guest of Robert Moses, and the maid took Coco to Central Park for his walk. Somehow Coco got away, and nobody could find him. Mrs. Dale postponed her departure for the fair to go through the park calling "Coco, Coco,"—to no avail.

In the meantime, a small but distinguished poodle, very certain he belonged, entered the revolving door at the Fifty-eighth Street entrance of the Plaza, waited at the elevator, and entered the lift when the door opened. He knew where to get off and where he wanted to go. At the sixth floor, when the elevator door was opened, he trotted down the corridor, tail wagging, to the apartment formerly occupied by the Dales.

The floor maid recognized him. "Why, it's Coco. We must get him back to Mrs. Dale. She'll be worried." Frantic was more the word for it. Coco's loss would be more than a personal tragedy; it touched the memory of her husband, who had loved the dog. The sigh of relief Mrs. Dale breathed when she received the message that her pet was safe at the hotel was followed by her appreciation of Coco's homing instinct. "I guess I'll just have to move back to The Plaza," said she.

More exotic guests have come and gone—rapidly. Romeo Giannini recalled the day a woman guest decided she'd like a monkey for a pet. "Get one right away," she phoned. A boy was dispatched to buy a monkey. "But get him on approval," Romeo said. He knew his dowagers well enough. The monkey cavorted for a day in a Plaza suite before the lady called again, "Get that damned thing out of here."

The strangest guest the Plaza unknowingly accommodated was a rare pink snake, which in 1923 created a sensation and a still unsolved mystery by disappearing from a room in the Hotel Commodore; six months later it turned up at the Plaza. Lawrence Klauber had checked into the Commodore at Forty-second Street and Lexington Avenue bearing gifts from the San Diego, California, zoo to the Central Park Zoo. While he was at dinner, the snake, an albino gopher with coral markings, disappeared.

Months later, seventeen blocks uptown, a guest at the Plaza telephoned the desk frantically to report there was a pink snake loose in his room. Whatever the manager thought of this tale, the gentleman obviously was sober, and staff members rushed to his room, to find that indeed he had cornered a snake. The visitor donated the reptile to the Central Park Zoo. It was recognized by Professor Raymond L. Ditmars, the curator of reptiles, and Dr. Harry M. Wegeforth of the San Diego Zoological Society confirmed the identification. The mystery still persists as to how it found its way to The Plaza.

"Tidy Coon," mascot of Maine's antilitter campaign, came to New York in 1965 to attend a "Keep America Beautiful" awards luncheon at The Plaza. Tidy arrived too late of an evening to get a suite in a pet shop, and The Plaza was so tightly booked that even humans couldn't get a room there. So Gert Ries, assistant banquet manager, took him to his suburban home for the night. Where but at The Plaza would even a coon get such personal service?

A room at The Plaza was, however, found for Ella, a fifty-pound cheetah which arrived with Mrs. Jomo Kenyatta, wife of the President of Kenya, on Pan American Airway's inaugural flight of service to and from Nairobi, in November 1965.

Ella, who caused more excitement than the host of celebrities on the flight, was accompanied by her own butler, Kenya animal trainer David Roberts. Roberts, who runs the Fish Eagle Safari Club in Lake Baringo, Kenya, found her as a cub and raised her at home with his six children.

When she went sightseeing on a leash, Ella behaved like a native, and at The Plaza, where she slept in a cage, the fourteen-month-old cat was as tame as a kitten.

As everyone knows, because Eloise told them, "The Plaza is the only hotel in New York where you can keep a turtle." To say nothing of lion cubs and cheetahs. And she wasn't telling the half of it.

CHAPTER FOURTEEN

Hands Across the Sea

PREMIER Nikita Khrushchev of the Soviet Union attended a reception at The Plaza given by the Togo delegation to the United Nations in 1960. Two well-dressed old ladies in the lobby said "Boo!" and Khrushchev said "Boo!" right back.

The world was going to miss him yet, after its fashion. But that was the year Khrushchev was pounding his shoe on the table at the General Assembly, and nobody knew but that he might use the atom bomb for a noisemaker next.

The customers might boo, but The Plaza, citadel of conservative elegance and a symbol of die-hard capitalism, has a reputation to uphold for doing the correct thing, making the correct gesture, even comes the revolution.

From the five huge flagpoles jutting from the balcony of the Fifth Avenue entrance, four foreign flags are frequently flying along with the Stars and Stripes, in recognition of the heads of as many countries currently at the hotel. The flags had just been lowered and brought in as usual, at 4:30 P.M., on the day of Khrushchev's visit when Neal Lang, then manager, realized that the Soviet Premier was due any minute. He quickly ordered the flags rehoisted—and the leader of world communism walked under the American flag as well as the Hammer and Sickle. To some alarmed telephone callers, asking the wherefore of the Soviet flag, the phone operators calmly explained the facts of international protocol.

When Khrushchev reached the elevators, he expressed annoyance that a car was not waiting to whisk him to the reception. Here a sizable group of people reacted with disapproval. Khrushchev turned quickly and stuck out his tongue at them. Security forces literally took over the lobby. Happily no more untoward incidents occurred.

Khrushchev's visit was but one presenting countless problems of security with which The Plaza has to cope during the visits of international heads of state, whether they are to stay there or merely arrive to attend some diplomatic function.

During his visit to the United States in 1965, the Shah of Iran expressed a desire to see the Persian Room and its show. Arrangements were carefully timed for his arrival with his retinue; the Plaza staff worked with official security officers to escort the Shah in and out of the hotel with the least possible commotion and the maximum protection.

The arrival was calm; the party was so quickly and quietly seated that many in the room were not even aware of the Shah's presence. At a nearby table a couple watched amusedly as several members of the large party picked up one of the large service plates of Persian design, looking on the reverse side to see if they were products of Iran. (The name was a "made in America" one.) A waiter even heard the *verboten* word "Persian" mentioned.

In the meantime the word had gotten around, as word so mysteriously does, and a crowd with that ominous look indicating "demonstration" had gathered at the Fifth Avenue entrance. Just as the Shah emerged, an incredible blast of noise erupted—but it was not the roar of the crowd. At a prearranged signal of split-second timing, the engines of the motorcycle escort were revved up at high, so loud and blasting they drowned out the shouts. Away roared the motorcade, with the Shah unaware that New Yorkers had a thing against him except possibly his habit of divorcing pretty queens who fail to bear him heirs.

With proper protocol and equally proper recognition of native customs, the Plaza has played host to kings and queens, maharajas and sultans, prime ministers and presidents, generations of foreign dignitaries from everywhere, since the day it opened.

The creation of the United Nations brought to New York a huge new deluge of foreign notables, heads of states and diplomatic representatives from almost every country around the globe, many newly created. The Plaza received those who sought its elegance and luxury with the ease and grace born of years of experience.

It was easier, of course, in the earlier days, when life was grand and gay, and many of the titled foreigners flocking to these shores sought merely social diversion or a rich American bride. Heiress-hunting was a popular sport in the early Edwardian era for European gentlemen with impressive titles but of impecunious status, and The Plaza was a happy hunting ground. If society did not exactly bend the knee, hostesses vied with one another to pay social homage to the visiting nobility.

All, of course, were not fortune hunters. There were many genuine love matches. Count Lazlo Szechenyi wooed Gladys Vanderbilt in the Tea Court, and theirs was an international match that endured. Lord Decies came to take Vivien Gould, the George J. Gould daughter, as his bride. His best man, Lord Camoys, fell in love with Mildred Sherman, a Newport heiress. Theirs, too, was a happy marriage; years later their daughter Nadine was courted by Philadelphian John R. Drexel, 3rd, in the Palm Court. The Earl and Countess of Castlestewart often came from England to visit her parents, the S. R. Guggenheims, at their elegant Plaza apartment.

Society writers did their best to inform their readers of the status of the titled guests. The Viscount and Viscountess Bertie of Thame were identified as relatives by marriage of Lady Randolph Churchill, the American-born mother of Winston Churchill. Living at The Plaza at the time were the American cousins of the former Jennie Jerome, Williams S. Fanshawe and his wife, née Jerome, who moved in the year the hotel opened. Years later, when the world was mourning the death of Winston Churchill, the aged Jessie Jerome Fanshawe, their daughter, proudly reminisced with the author about "Cousin Jennie."

The Princess di Stigliano Colonna returned to The Plaza from Italy with her mother, Mrs. John W. Mackay, whose husband had "struck it rich" as one of the gold-rush Forty-niners. The Princess was a sister of the telegraph tycoon, Clarence Mackay, and an aunt of Ellin Mackay who married Irving Berlin.

Titles lost a little of their luster when Russian Princess Dmitri Galitzine, the American-born Frances Stevens, struggled home to The Plaza with the news that the actions of the Bolsheviks were the behavior of "a people nearly gone mad." Her father-in-law, the last Prime Minister of Russia under Czar Nicholas, was made to work as a cobbler in what was then Petrograd. Her husband was learning carpentry in Paris, at the school for White Russian refugees established by Mrs. William K. Vanderbilt.

The Maharaja Gaekwar of Baroda, possessor of twenty million dollars in jewels and recipient of an annual income of twelve million dollars, found an unpleasant surprise on his arrival at the Plaza in 1910 for a reunion with his son, the Hindu Prince Jaisingiae, a student at Harvard. Lying in wait behind the palms in the Tea Court were two marshals, prepared to impound the Maharaja's fifty trunks unless the Prince paid a bill of $89.95 he owed the Hotel Lenox in Boston. The prince had forty dollars on his person—Daddy paid the rest. The Maharani, wearing a pearl collar and a huge diamond necklace, found the time to inform the press that Indian ladies neither wore stays nor did they dance.

Before World War One, no member of European nobility could create the excitement caused by the arrival of a Chinese prince, exotic in skullcap, pigtail, and satin robes, or a kimonoed Japanese. Prince Tsai-Tao, uncle of the Chinese Emperor, was a colorful figure at The Plaza in the spring of 1910. New York's Mayor Gaynor and J. P. Morgan entertained him, and the press grumbled that the Steel Trust monopolized him. The Prince reportedly placed an order for fifty million dollars' worth of arms. His brother, Prince Tsai-Suun, who came for a visit a few years later, used the private automobile of steel mogul Charles M. Schwab to cross the country by slow stages.

The press accorded due recognition to the visit of Prince

Tokugawa Iyesato, head of the Japanese House of Peers. His was one of the first of many missions to come seeking money, a loan of a hundred million dollars, for the Government of Japan. Prince Tokugawa hobnobbed with Kuhn, Loeb and Company.

Three thousand American beauty roses and two thousand orchids decorated the scene at a Plaza dinner for Admiral Count Togo and a mere forty-five guests during his stay in 1911. The Plaza's gold service, worth fifty thousand dollars, was used, and guests dined on breast of Guinea hen, Japanese style. Tragedy touched another Japanese dignitary while a guest at the Plaza. The Japanese Ambassador to the United States, Manarso Hanihara, was ensconced at the hotel on September 1, 1923, when he received word of a terrible earthquake in Japan, and rushed back to Washington to try to reach Tokyo through the Imperial Wireless stations. The toll in that catastrophe: 143,000 dead.

A queen was one of The Plaza's most popular royal guests, the beautiful Marie of Rumania. Chambermaids sighed over her, bellmen fought for the opportunity of carrying her royal luggage. Her regal bearing was humanized by a grace of manner and a dazzling smile.

The international polo matches at Meadowbrook, Long Island, lured the polo-playing Prince of Wales to these shores in the early twenties, years before Fate, in the person of Wallis Warfield Simpson, changed the course of his life, and that of the British crown. "He looked like any young Englishman, not a prince," said an old-timer bellman. "So democratic, and he'd shake hands with you."

More and more internationalists kept coming to The Plaza as the years and the means of swift travel multiplied. Latin Americans particularly favored the hotel. Of these, one of the most popular was pipe-smoking President Betancourt of Venezuela, who shares a birthday with the first President of the United States. He was a guest at The Plaza on Washington's Birthday, 1963, and they gave him a party with a large cake, one half decorated with the crossed flags of Venezuela and the United States, the other half with a frosted pipe. Present at the party were the President's wife and daughter, armed with birthday presents. The packages when opened confirmed the fact that women are the same the world over when buying gifts for their men. Ties, that's what the President got for his birthday, six ties from Sulka.

It was keen-witted syndicated columnist Inez Robb who declared that the pixies and the gremlins must have been at work when Soviet Ambassador Andrei A. Gromyko and the Russian delegation to the United Nations decided on The Plaza to house them before moving to a Park Avenue mansion. Two key men in management at the time were White Russians who had fled the Bolshevist revolution for their very lives. Colonel Serge Obolensky, a former Russian prince who became an American citizen, was a Plaza vice president, and Vasilli Adlerberg, a former count, was an assistant manager.

Gromyko and his retinue were politely, if unenthusiastically, received and escorted to their quarters by the two former czarist army officers, who recognized their obligation to all Plaza guests.

The Grand Duchess Marie of Russia, who wrote books about Czarist Russia with authenticity, lived at The Plaza in the thirties. She was spared a confrontation with the Communists, having moved to South America before World War Two. It was her brother, the Grand Duke Dmitri, who had assisted in ridding Russia of the sinister monk Rasputin.

Gromyko, a handsome man in a rather deadpan way, and a quiet contrast to the ebullient Khrushchev, declined a suite with a balcony as too dangerous. He kept a force of twelve security men on constant alert, and demanded that a list of all guests in the hotel submitted to him for his personal security assurance. He insisted that the law demanded this. Management disagreed and declined. For once he bowed.

But the management could do nothing about the eating habits of the Russians. They had three cooks on their staff and insisted on cooking all meals in their rooms. Into the last outpost of gracious living the Communists brought huge bags of groceries and vegetables. In such a citadel of elegance this was regarded as equivalent to bringing a box lunch to the opera. One hundred pounds of caviar were delivered and consumed monthly, and the heady stench of boiling cabbage pervaded the fifteenth-floor corridors.

The air wasn't cleared until the departure of the delegation to their new Park Avenue headquarters.

The smell of burning incense was everywhere on the Plaza's fourteenth floor when Hassan II of Morocco was in residence for ten days in April 1963. Like the Russians, the Moroccans had brought their own cooks—but unlike the Russians they did not cook in their rooms.

Because of their religious beliefs and taboos of certain foods, the handling of meals for the Muslims was left entirely to them. In respect for their native customs, The Plaza turned over a large section of its kitchens to the Moroccan cooks. Plaza chefs had no part of food arrangements, but the steward would find out beforehand what was required for the meals served the party in their rooms and purchase it.

A memorandum to the Plaza food and beverage staff, just before the arrival of the King and his entourage, directed that the "entire catering department, especially Room Service, must be ready to give special service." Dates, figs, goats' milk, goat cheese and mint tea were especially ordered for them. Since alcoholic beverages are denied Muslims, they consumed gallons of orange juice, soft drinks and coffee, and pounds of bonbons and other candies to satisfy the well-known Moroccan sweet tooth. Pork and beef were taboo, but chicken and lamb permitted. Many a Plaza kitchen helper learned the method of roasting a whole lamb. Five whole roasted baby lambs graced the buffet at a party for the King in the ballroom.

It took this proud young king to behave like a potentate, in contrast to his father, King Mohammed V, whom the Plaza entertained in 1957. After paying a quiet call on President Eisenhower, Mohammed returned to The Plaza just as quietly, with little press fanfare. The visit in 1963 of his thirty-four-year-old son and successor was another story.

King Hassan came to the United States for economic assistance, yet he went on a shopping spree which left the State Department speechless and the columnists gleeful. Reporters trailed the young man around Manhattan reporting every fabulous purchase: five Cadillacs, a fleet of Fords, enough linens to re-equip The Plaza,

150 blankets, sterno cans by the hundreds. Several department stores opened on a Sunday especially to accommodate His Majesty. As truck after truck delivered his purchases, boxes and cartons piled up in the hotel receiving room and littered the fourteenth floor. When the King departed, a special plane was required to transport the voluminous stuff home.

The unconfirmed report that the King's party was spending four thousand dollars a day at The Plaza and that members of his retinue ordered caviar by the pound in the Persian Room did not sit well with the New York *Daily News,* ever eager to tell American taxpayers how Washington is wasting their money. What the *News* did not tell its readers is that our government pays for only a limited number of foreigners on state visits. Everything in excess of this official budget is paid for by the foreign visitors or their own government.

The King of Morocco was followed, a few months later, by the Emperor of Ethiopia. They provided a dramatic study in contrast for Plaza staff and guests—in behavior and habits as well as appearance.

Like Hassan II, Emperor Haile Selassie had made a state visit to President Kennedy, and paused at The Plaza for a few days, en route to Ethiopia, to confer with U Thant, Secretary General of the United Nations. The conquering Lion of Judah was accompanied by his granddaughter, the apple of his eye, Princess Ruth. In the absence of his royal lions, he proved to be a wonderfully gentle little man, with smiling eyes and exquisite politeness, plus a healthy appetite. His visit caused no food crises at The Plaza. As a Coptic, he had no food prohibitions; a preference for high-protein foods probably was the secret of his slimness and energy.

Despite his age, the Emperor had tremendous stamina. At a reception in his honor in the Grand Ballroom, he stood in the receiving line for hours, shaking hands and acknowledging the bows of something like a thousand guests. If it taxed the energy of this elderly man, he never showed it. Though slight of frame, he seemed to tower over people; one had an inexplicable feeling of "tallness" in him, a sense of power and authority in spite of his gentle manner.

He was most considerate of the Plaza staff, never demanding, always charmingly polite. Yet a simple request somehow became an order. In a popularity contest among personnel, the little Emperor and his always exquisitely dressed granddaughter—a Nefertiti in profile—would have ranked above all royal guests.

With the establishment of the United Nations and the emergence of many new nations, a curious problem beset The Plaza and other fashionable hotels—the problem of simple pronunciation. Telephone operators had to cope with such strange cognomens as Kodjo Botsio of Ghana; Wadjiri Yaya, of Cameroon; Antoine Maboungou from Congo-Brazzaville; Obame Ntoutoume, of Gabon; Maitourare Gadjo of Niger; Abdulatif Al-Hamad of the State of Kuwait; Vassilios Papathanassopoulos of Greece, Daouda Diawara of Guinea, Seye Maissa Tall of Senegal; Samuel Agereburu of Togo; N. Agathocleous of Cyprus.

All of these foreign dignitaries—and thousands with names equally difficult to pronounce—have been registered at The Plaza. The wonder of it is how comparatively few are the mix-ups, with so many language barriers to be surmounted, so many national customs to be recognized. The answer is The Plaza's International Department.

Early in the life of the hotel, so many importantly placed Europeans were journeying to these shores, that shrewd, foresighted Sterry inaugurated the custom of meeting luxury liners from England, France and Germany down the bay. A wireless reservation service was already in effect between various steamships and the hotel, one of the first in the city to have its own wireless station. Passenger lists printed an announcement that rooms and suites at The Plaza could be reserved via wireless at the expense of the hotel.

Now those with reservations were to be met by a "marine runner," so called. With typical Sterry persuasion, arrangements were made with the proper authorities for a hotel representative to board the revenue cutters going out to meet arriving steamships, and upon docking to assist Plaza guests through customs with the least possible delay. Limousines were on hand to transport them to the hotel; baggage wagons to transport their luggage.

This service was but one of many designed to give aid and comfort to Plaza clientele. But it was a limited service. Recognizing the need for more comprehensive attention to the constant flow of foreign guests in a jet age of international travel, Paul Sonnabend, when he took over Plaza management several years ago, established a separate International Department devoted entirely to business of an international nature.

Leading hotels in world capitals have of late years established such international departments. But The Plaza's alone also boasts a highly experienced chief of protocol.

This diplomat is a lady, Yugoslav-born Ivanka Nina Lytle, tall, handsome and titian-haired. She came to the hotel from Venezuela, where she worked with the government on protocol for international conferences and where she met and married an American with business interests there, Glenn Lytle.

A sable stole and long white gloves are her working clothes; a fluency in six languages, a knowledge of international politics, and a familiarity with the national customs of many countries are her working tools. She knows that white flowers are not to be placed in the suite of a guest from Rabat; white flowers are for funerals in Morocco. She greets dignitaries as they step from official limousines; her curtsy before a king reflects her European background. When distinguished VIP's and their entourage are to be in residence for any length of time, she moves from her own home to a Plaza suite for the duration. Before their arrival she inspects every nook and cranny of their quarters. Everything must be just so to satisfy this perfectionist; no housekeeper is more meticulous. If a group needs laundry service, drycleaning or such, Mrs. Lytle advises the proper department. If an Ambassador's wife, speaking no English, asks where to shop for a certain article, Mrs. Lytle offers herself as a companion guide.

Under Mrs. Lytle's guidance The Plaza has avoided mistakes made by some other hotels. A Park Avenue luxury hotel years ago created a "Spanish Floor" with the notion it would be cozy for Spanish-speaking guests. Former Prime Minister Medina of Venezuela, a guest at that hotel in 1946, moved to The Plaza when he discovered that his next-door neighbor was the colonel who had jailed him in the revolution that overthrew him. The very foundation of American diplomacy rests on the awareness that Latins hate each other more than they can conspire to hate the United States.

More than 70 percent of the thousand employees at The Plaza are bilingual, and some are multilingual. A card placed with mints on all pillows each evening says "Good Night" to guests in nine languages.

A particularly specialized job at the hotel is that of Victor DiBella, the flag attendant. His collection of more than one hundred flags is worth some thirty thousand dollars, and it costs thirty dollars to clean one. On a brief vacation DiBella took one year to visit his family in Palermo, Sicily, The Plaza panicked. No one could find the flag required to honor the President of Austria. An SOS to DiBella produced the intelligence that he had loaned it to the Waldorf. The flag was retrieved and the day saved.

The delicate diplomacy of which foreign flag to fly first has been resolved by policy: hang them in alphabetical order. This, alas, was no solution to the problem the flagman faced on December 16, 1963, when The Plaza found itself housing the foreign ministers of thirteen countries.

Happily, diplomats chat and even joke at The Plaza with a nonchalance one would scarcely expect from the manner in which they snap at each other in United Nations debates. But the hotel often has its tense moments; one was in 1964 when the Prime Ministers of Israel and Jordan both were in residence during a crisis between the two states. Life is calmer when chiefs of state come one at a time.

One wholesome junket from abroad afforded lively gay diversion. The inauguration of Nigerian Airways, with an initial flight to this country in 1964, brought not only four Cabinet ministers to The Plaza but four dancers, numerous trumpeters and miscellaneous entertainers. A cocktail party in the Terrace Room during which they entertained in native fashion was literally a howling success.

If someone in management does not recognize a titled identity, one or another executive on the staff is certain to.

Said a memo of January 18, 1965, from the Publicity Department to Manager Salomone: "Noticed on the list of arrivals the name of Beatrice, Lady Granard. She is an elderly lady, the former Beatrice Mills, daughter of the late Ogden Mills, and one of the few Americans married to British titles who became close friends of the late King George and Queen Mary. Suggest VIP attention." And out again rolled Plaza red-carpet treatment.

An article in the weekly magazine section of one of New York's Sunday newspapers suggested that "a good place to start a round-the-world-without-leaving-the-city trip is the lobby of The Plaza. Under its lofty, ornate ceiling you can eavesdrop in several languages."

And that's from Russian to Arabic to Portuguese to Japanese—any morning, afternoon or evening.

CHAPTER FIFTEEN

Bold Boniface

As any Plaza dowager still alive can recall, something cataclysmic happened in 1943. The Plaza was sold.

After thirty-six years under one continuous, original management, the hotel was passing into other hands. The world-acclaimed hostelry which cost twelve million dollars to build in 1907 and which could not be duplicated for forty million dollars in the twenties or re-created at any price during World War Two, went, at the height of that war, to Conrad Hilton for $7,400,000.

Consternation swept through the corridors. For Plaza tenants the name Hilton Hotel meant only one thing—a commercial hotel. Little old ladies with large pocketbooks whispered, "It can't happen here," and as it turned out, it didn't. Even Hilton, the bold boniface, was cognizant of the very special aura which surrounded The Plaza—cognizant and impressed and determined to keep it so. But he had to win his battle for popularity and the admiration of his tenants.

The sale of The Plaza created headlines even in the midst of wartime news; with incredulity financiers read that for a penny-ante $600,000 down, Hilton and Floyd Odlum's Atlas Corporation had taken control of the hotel. How could this happen; how did it happen? The basic truth was more shocking than the headlines. Behind it was a familiar story, the overexpansion of United

States Realty Company, undermined by a series of misfortunes that first began with the Wall Street crash and the deaths of three hotel bulwarks.

The overexpansion was typical of the early and midtwenties, and United States Realty did its share in a building boom that produced hundreds of hotels from New York to New Mexico, from Pottsville to Pittsburgh. Too often it was not because of a real need but as an expression of the booming spirit of the times. When the country's economic structure toppled in 1929, hotels and their builders were among the hardest hit.

The Savoy-Plaza Hotel, a 1927 arrival on the New York hotel scene, was but one of United States Realty's projects of the decade. The company had put up many buildings, guaranteeing the second mortgage bonds. Among the first to come due during the depression were those of the Savoy-Plaza, and United States Realty paid them. But the empire was crumbling, even as Harry Black was beginning to foresee. Many years later, Frederick Beinecke, son of one of the founding fathers, observed that the empire could have been saved were it not, paradoxically, for the upright morality of the men in whose hands the company was left—saved by renegotiating and by postponing paying of bonds. But they were men of honor, whose word was their bond, and they continued paying off when no cash was coming in. This they could do only by liquidating property and, in the thirties, at great loss.

By 1943 the situation was so critical that The Plaza had to be put up for sale. Edwin Beinecke was then serving as deputy commissioner of the American Red Cross in London, and he and his brother Frederick conferred by transatlantic phone. They wanted to save the fine hotel, wanted it for themselves, for it had been their father's most precious dream fulfilled. The market price of $7,400,000 presented no difficulty, for they had the money, thanks to the conservatism of Ben Beinecke in a boomtime era when everyone else was going speculation mad. But ethics would not permit. Were they, the insiders, to buy the hotel for themselves at that shockingly low price, it might be viewed as less than an arm's length transaction; it might cause those who would lose plenty, the bondholders, to wonder and suspect.

To avoid criticism The Plaza was sold to outsiders.

Floyd Odlum's Atlas Corporation grew out of the depression on the principle: "Buy when they have to sell." By the time United States Realty was forced to sell The Plaza, Atlas had grown into a hundred-million-dollar investment trust. For the paltry $600,000 cash they put down, Atlas and Hilton purchased the stock and bought up the notes of the company. These had a paper value of $4,992,500. The rest of the purchase price was represented by a first mortgage of $6,800,000 held by the Metropolitan Life Insurance Company. Hilton secured an extension of the mortgage at the lowered interest rate.

If Conrad Hilton is not the greatest hotelman in the world, he is without doubt the most famous. He is to hotels what Rhodes was to diamonds, Carnegie to steel, Heinz to pickles. The chain of towering hotels bearing his name stretches clear around the globe, one in almost every capital of the world. A wag in the business remarked that after the first man lands on the moon, a Hilton hotel will soon spring up—to be known, no doubt, as the Lunar Hilton.

By the time he gained control of The Plaza, Hilton was a courtly gentleman, aged fifty-five, hard of hearing but hard to fool. He had come a long way, and legends were springing up about him. If he did not encourage them, neither did he discourage them. No one has ever accused "Connie" Hilton of modesty; publicity was like the breath of life to his hotel empire, and Hilton executives, like the boss, have always been quick on the draw when any opportunity for publicity reared its welcome head.

"From bellboy to owner of The Plaza." Publications everywhere told of Hilton's rise in the manner of Horatio Alger. However factual in some respects, the theme was misleading. Hilton was anything but the "hick from the cow country," as he was sometimes described in magazine articles. His father was a well-to-do businessman who was caught in the panic of 1907. He managed to hold on to a store he owned and to his home, a rambling adobe house in San Antonio, New Mexico, the birthplace of Conrad Nicholson Hilton. Gus Hilton was well on his way to recovering the family fortune before the son left college to join him in running a small bank and a "hotel" of sorts. The latter was the Hilton home, part of which had been converted into a seven-room hotel.

The rise of Conrad Hilton from small beginnings to worldwide fame as the "biggest hotel man in the world" made magical material for the newspaper and magazine writers. Out of the legends of his Midas touch came the conviction that he never lost, and rumors that he would make The Plaza pay by taking the jewel out of the case and substituting dime-store glitter troubled many a Plaza guest.

It also troubled the Gardiner School heads. After Edwin Beinecke gave up the penthouse which Harry Black had built atop the hotel for himself, the seventeen-room mansion-on-the-roof became the home of the John Barry Ryans of the wealthy Thomas Fortune Ryan clan. Later, during the first two years of World War Two, it housed the fashionable Gardiner School for Girls when its first home became inadequate. Among the girls who "went to school at The Plaza" were Barbara Cavanagh, who was to become the second wife of Mayor Robert F. Wagner of New York, and Longine watch heiress and artist Zita Davisson, who later married lawyer Frank Delaney. Miss Elizabeth Masland, principal of the school, wrote in the classbook the first year that the Gardiner School had "found a wonderful answer to all the uncertainties and difficulties of the war years in the beautiful penthouse."

Shortly after Hilton acquired the hotel, Miss Masland moved the school, declaring that "the plan of 'modernization' . . . did not augur well for the conservative atmosphere demanded by a girls' school."

As to that "plan for modernization," Hilton did not wait for the war to end before beginning a renovation program that would involve several millions. Because hotels were so essential to the winning of the war, he had little difficulty in getting priorities. Old-time tenants and guests quaked at the prospect, and dowagers shook their lorgnettes in emphasis of their disapproval. Any violation of Plaza tradition, any change in its elegantly entrenched pattern, was unthinkable.

Hilton found time to write personal letters to every permanent guest, assuring all of his intent not to disturb, but in fact to restore, the hotel's original grandeur, in all truth now somewhat faded. The fact that in the midst of war, even with priorities, it would take time to change very much, helped to reassure the disturbed dowagers.

"Make the space pay" was a Hilton credo, and he applied it wherever possible. When he learned that E. F. Hutton and Company were still paying the minuscule rent of $416 a month for its brokerage office on the Fifty-ninth Street side, Hilton moved Hutton upstairs to a mezzanine office. He then proceeded to transform the space into the Oak Bar and in doing so created what is today one of The Plaza's most famed, as well as most profitable, rooms. In a relatively short time the bar was to yield a gross of $225,000.

An outstanding artist of the period was Everett Shinn, and following the example of Henry Rost for the Persian Room, Hilton engaged the artist to do a series of murals for the Oak Bar. Shinn restored a nostalgic mood with three murals depicting the New York of the Edwardian era. In one, The Plaza is seen in mistlike silhouette through the trees and rain of Central Park. Another is a painting of the Pulitzer Fountain in the square. Most impressive of the trio is a painting, in Shinn's soft, misty tones, of the old Cornelius Vanderbilt château, which occupied the Fifth Avenue and 58th Street corner, across from The Plaza, where now Bergdorf Goodman stands in all its fashion glory.

Hilton executives, like the great man himself, were infected with his make-the-space-pay virus. Bob Williford, one of his top men, saw a chance to make $18,000 a year by renting a small showcase, a "vitrine," so called, in the lobby corridor. He wired Hilton for his OK. Hilton wired back: "I don't know what a vitrine is, but if it will bring in eighteen thousand dollars, install it immediately."

For a quarter of a century impeccable but impecunious young men had mounted the marble staircases to sit at the desks on the mezzanine and use, for free, crested Plaza stationery to answer their invitations. Hilton eliminated the desks, closed in the space and converted the mezzanine to offices. In the process, it involved the major operation of also eliminating the beautiful huge Tiffany glass dome reflecting dancing lights over the Palm Court and substituting a modern ceiling. This caused many to weep at the time; today there are few who can remember it.

Far from bringing the Wild West in the sacrosanct precincts, as some direly predicted, Hilton added tone with titles. The fringes of New York society were fretted with refugees using titles as genuine as their costume jewelry. To The Plaza Hilton brought two White Russians of fourteen-karat gold, Prince Serge Obolensky and his aide-de-camp, Count Vasilli Adlerberg.

Oxford-educated Obolensky's first marriage had been to a member of the ruling family of Russia, the Romanovs, and he had fought the Bolsheviks in 1917. His second wife was Alice Astor, daughter of John Jacob Astor and sister of the late Vincent Astor. Although later divorced from Alice, Obolensky remained a favorite with his brother-in-law, who brought him into the hotel business as an executive of the Astor-owned St. Regis.

Prince Obolensky, by now an American citizen, earned his colonelcy as a paratrooper in World War Two. In 1944, when in his late fifties, he parachuted into Italy behind the German lines, a courageous feat at his age. Placed on inactive status after the liberation of Paris, he joined the Hilton hotel family in March 1945 as promotion and public relations director at The Plaza. The following year he was named a vice president.

Although his former wife remarried, Obolensky never did. Tall, aristocratic-looking, with a natural and rare charm enhanced by Old World manner, he has long been one of New York's most popular bachelors; but though sought after by women, he commanded the respect and admiration of even the toughest of businessmen. A bequest of ten thousand dollars "for his friendship and in admiration of his courage" was left to Obolensky by the late Viscount Astor.

Obolensky worked hard at what he knew best, which was in the area of society and entertainment promotion, and his efforts brought results.

Like Frederick Townsend Martin before him, Obolensky in his capacity as public relations director entertained generously and for society's most prominent, but never on the same lavish scale. Highlights of each season were the parties he arranged on the

Russian Orthodox Christmas every January 6, and the colorful Russian Easter parties. A superb dancer, he executed the flaming-sword dance, in traditional Russian costume, as no man in his sixties has done before or since.

Unlike Martin, Obolensky was a business executive with responsibilities in every area of hotel operation which touched on entertainment, and this also meant creating new settings when possible. One of the triumphs of Obolensky and Adlerberg was the enchanting Rendez-Vous, which opened in October 1947 in the old Grill of tea-dance fame which was used for storage during the depression. The transformation from storeroom to a setting reflecting the grandeur of czarist Russia was a dramatic coup. Trellised ceilings, murals of bewigged pages, apricot and gold walls, crystal sidelights and rose-hued banquettes set a dreamy mood for dinner and supper dancing.

It was a gourmet's heaven. Even the food literally sparkled. Flaming swords of shashlik were brought in aloft, while lights were dimmed; frozen desserts had lighting effects; diners watched as crêpes suzette and marrons flambés flamed before them. The hotel's ice-carver was responsible for a triumph of his art, an ice-sculptured tree laden with frozen oranges. Gypsy musicians alternating with a modern dance orchestra supplied just the right additional romantic touch.

The Rendez-Vous found immediate favor with the smart younger crowd as well as exerting a nostalgic lure for their parents, who had furiously toddled and Charlestoned to Joe Smith's music a generation earlier. Evening clothes predominated every night; the elegant background demanded it, even if the management did not.

By the end of the second year, with air-conditioning installed to make the room a twelve-month operation, the Rendez-Vous grossed more than a half-million dollars, a sizable sum in anybody's business for space that had been lying fallow for years.

Obolensky and Adlerberg were inspired to have a number of suites transformed into "Celebrities Suites," and persuaded the internationally known socialite decorator, Lady Mendl, to do several of them. The one she herself occupied was known as the "Lady

Mendl Suite." Elsie deWolfe Mendl admitted to the age of seventy-five and was probably older when she undertook this, her last big project. Often she would direct workers while lying on her bed, which had belonged to the Duchess of Sutherland: "... a little more green here, a touch of white there." The results were as breathtaking as her own famed home in Versailles, the Villa Trianon. Green was the predominating color she chose for her own suite; mirrors added depth, and she designed her own chairs, small but not clumsy, and comfortable enough for the average man. A Regency mantel, a crystal chandelier and a huge antique clock gave a touch of opulence to her drawing room.

Many later guests no doubt were impressed with the aura of being in the Lady Mendl Suite. Not so actress Marlene Dietrich, who occupied it for several years. La Dietrich couldn't abide that bright scarlet-and-gold clock which Elsie Mendl had installed as her pride and joy and declared she couldn't live with it. "Too much gingerbread," she said, and Lady Mendl's fifteen-hundred-dollar clock was banished.

Other suites, decorated by celebrities, bore their names. The Cecil Beaton Suite was dramatically Victorian, as only the English artist-photographer who designed the beautiful costumes for *My Fair Lady* could do. Fashion designer Christian Dior created a suite in the grand continental manner. It was later occupied by Frank Lloyd Wright, who had his own ideas of decor and redecorated it in a fashion described by some of the staff as looking like a circus—"a hodgepodge of reds, golds and purples."

Rosie Warburton, daughter of the late Mrs. William K. Vanderbilt, was given a chance by her good friend "Vava" Adlerberg to try her hand at a suite for Somerset Maugham while he was ensconced in the south of France. It made for good publicity—for society and the public if not for the literati.

Those suites, as such, are no more. It is axiomatic that when new decorators come into a hotel to redecorate, they pick the finest rooms to show off their talents, and at The Plaza the celebrity suites were the ones subsequent decorators chose. In every case it was a complete change-over. David Williams was to do some quite lovely rooms later; heiress Ellen Lehman, who decorates for love of her work, not money, but gets plenty, applied her special talents for luxurious backgrounds to several rooms, as did Melanie Kahane. A considerable amount of later redecorating was done by Henry End, still an adviser to the hotel.

Hilton did not touch the lofty, impressive baronial Oak Room, nor was anything done to change the restaurant known simply as the Fifth Avenue Café, except for some mild refurbishing. In 1955 the Café acquired a name of its own, harking back to the age of magnificence during which the hotel was built. Fittingly enough, it was christened the Edwardian Room.

Obolensky and Adlerberg supervised a slight change in the Terrace Room and enhanced its original beauty. Their particular pride were five stunning new chandeliers, copies of the chandeliers which hung in the Palace of Versailles and which were bought by Emperor Paul of Russia for the Palace of Pavlovsky in czarist St. Petersburg. Obolensky, by some great good fortune, had photographs of these originals, and the magnificent copies, which are now such an elegant feature of the Terrace Room, were made in New York by Charles Winston, brother of jeweler Harry Winston.

The two friends left The Plaza in 1949, to become associated with the Sherry-Netherland Hotel. Eventually Serge Obolensky returned to the scene of his first hotel experience, the St. Regis, as head of promotion and publicity; Vava Adlerberg became associated with jeweler Winston.

The face-lifting job at The Plaza continued. Hilton decided to do over the Persian Room, and Henry Dreyfuss, famed for his interiors on the liner *Independence,* produced an almost entirely new room with but a mere reminder of the Persian motif. A decor of bronze figures inset with colored stones was created by Ruth Vollmer to blend with the window fabrics especially designed by Dorothy Liebes. In the process of renovation, three different sets of walls were removed—the layer put up when the room served as an automobile showroom; underneath it, the exquisite Persian murals, and beneath those, the gilt walls of the original Rose Room.

Guests and staff members recently have been lobbying for a

genuine restoration and return of the original Persian murals—which happily have been preserved and carefully stored.

The penthouse also soon had a very proper new tenant. *Gourmet* magazine moved in when the Gardiner School moved out, establishing stunning, impressive offices. It was a perfect setting, for *Gourmet* saw itself as The Plaza of the culinary-magazine field, bringing to its readers the same pleasure in fine-food literature that the Plaza chef brought to diners in epicurean cuisine. In the mid-sixties *Gourmet* had so expanded that it had to move to larger offices on Third Avenue. The penthouse was subdivided to provide several new offices and an apartment for the manager.

Hilton dared to introduce modern furniture to many Plaza rooms, striking an incongruous note in the large, high-ceilinged rooms with paneled walls, carved marble fireplace mantels, and the fine details of an earlier generation of building.

If anyone was disgruntled by this modernization, he could find solace in the State Suite, restored to its original grandeur and opened for public functions after the departure of Mrs. Charles O. Maas. The decorators studied pictures of the rooms taken when it was part of the Guggenheim apartment. George Lange, Plaza upholsterer, hunted down original divans, chairs and tables in storage and scattered throughout the hotel, and restored them with loving care. Golden silk-damask curtains were hung on the tall windows, but no architectural changes had to be made. The basic beauty was still there, and the suite was transformed into one of the handsomest of settings for gala small parties.

The fortieth anniversary of The Plaza in 1947 brought a spurt of gay activity equally as glamorous as the opening twoscore years earlier and considerable Plaza history-making. The celebrations started off with a dinner given by Hilton in the Baroque Suite, patterned after the first dinner given by Fred Sterry—down to every detail of the menu, and with the gold service in use. Again there was only a limited group of especially selected guests—about one hundred in all. Lucius Boomer, of Sterry's original staff, returned to dine on roast pheasant with Grover Whalen, New York's official greeter, and Floyd Odlum, Hilton's backer. Chief speakers were Connie Hilton and Edwin Beinecke, son of the hotel's first president.

Festivities wound up with an anniversary ball on October 3, a benefit in the Terrace Room for the Soldiers' and Sailors' Club of New York, by now something of a Plaza party tradition. Frank Crowninshield, the eminent editor, was entertainment chairman, and a nostalgic history of The Plaza was composed for the souvenir program by the late Lucius Beebe, who left his heart in the Oak Room when he moved to San Francisco.

Hilton did not forget the staff in observing the anniversary. Whatever the mixed opinions of Hilton management by the guests, there was never any disagreement among the employees: they thought him a great guy, a generous, considerate boss, and the *esprit de corps* was always high during the Hilton regime. Other managements have been generous with special-occasion parties for the staff, but where they gave dinners and cocktail parties, Hilton gave banquets with dancing, functions probably born of his own love of Terpsichore. He was an excellent dancer, and liked to show it off.

Committee members for a Travelers Aid Society benefit opening in the Persian Room one year still recall that evening with chuckles.

Mrs. John C. Wood, who was in charge of the benefit, had just finished overseeing the arragements of tables when Hilton came in and requested a certain table for ten at ringside. He had made no previous reservation, but he was "The Plaza," and Frances Kelley Wood, a daughter of Cornelius Kelley, onetime chairman of the board of Anaconda Copper, could do nothing but oblige, even if it meant last-minute reshuffling of tables.

A special entertainment program was a feature of the evening. In a burst of impulsiveness Hilton announced that he would perform an exhibition dance, and proceeded to the floor to do the Varsoviana, a dance having its origins in Hilton's Southwest, around Santa Fe and Albuquerque. What the committee thought about this unscheduled addition to the program is known only to themselves, but the audience was intrigued. Columnist Frank Farrell was there, and since Hilton had voluntarily become part of the show, Farrell included him in his next day's review, and it was not entirely complimentary. If certain dark looks were cast in his direction later by the management, only Farrell knew the reason why.

The wives Odlum and Hilton brought into The Plaza picture were also attracting much attention. Mrs. Odlum, better known as Jacqueline Cochran, was the nation's leading aviatrix and, sex aside, one of the greatest solo pilots in aviation history. She organized the Women's Air Force, which did as much as men would let them do in World War Two—flying transport planes across the country. Indignantly she argued that the women she recruited were better pilots than many the Army Air Force had time to train. During the war, when scores of wealthy refugees from abroad were comfortably, even luxuriously, ensconced at The Plaza, Jacqueline Cochran Odlum was sleeping in a cot in a Maryland camp and running her show from a desk in a drafty hangar. She became the gracious Plaza hostess only after the war.

The first decoration with which Hilton adorned The Plaza was his wife Sari, who later, as Zsa Zsa Gabor, actress and television personality, came in for as much personal publicity as did Hilton. The marriage, Hilton's second, lasted a mere four years, but while it lasted, Plaza rhymed with Zsa Zsa. She could brighten the darkest day with her bubbling spirits and her irrepressible chatter—invariably about herself. In her first interview at the hotel, she told a story which then was as fresh as it later became familiar, of her escape from Hungary and her travels through seven countries at war to reach the United States.

Hilton also introduced to the hotel a long succession of managers such as The Plaza has never before, or since, seen. He changed managers almost as frequently as some Plaza patrons changed their wardrobes. It was said his reason for this was to give top executives in his chain the experience of observing how things were done at a splendiferous hotel. It might have made for well-trained executives elsewhere, but at The Plaza it created confusion and uncertainty among the staff.

Where United States Realty had but three managers in thirty-six years of ownership, Hilton, in seventeen years of operation, had nine, and of these one served at three different periods. Arthur Benaglia was briefly in command the first year of operation, and upon his death that year Hilton brought in Frank G. Wangeman, who remained until 1945. He brought him in again from 1947 to 1949, and again from 1953 to 1954.

James B. Herndon, who switched from banking to the hotel business when Hilton discovered him in 1929, was manager between 1945 and 1947; in rapid succession followed Joseph Binns, who was in command for the by now two-year period, from 1949 to 1951; Dean Carpenter, Hilton's brother-in-law, who married his sister Rosemary (their daughter was named Connie Ann), had a 1951–52 tenure; he was followed by John A. Klugherz, who met a tragic death in a fall from the fourteenth floor in 1953. Frank Wangeman stepped in again until Porter Parris, a native of the Lone Star State who had started as a room clerk with the Hilton hotels in 1935, took over in 1954; Eugene Voit, whom Lucius Boomer discovered in Europe and gave his first job in this country as busboy in the old Waldorf-Astoria, succeeded Parris in 1955. Two years later he moved across the street as manager of the Savoy-Plaza, whose name had been changed to the Hilton-Plaza when acquired by Hilton. His successor, John G. Horsman, held the record for managers under Hilton. He served from 1957 until Hilton and The Plaza parted company in 1960.

Hilton had sold the hotel in 1953, but continued to operate the hotel under lease from the new owner, Boston industrialist A. M. Sonnabend. He was, therefore, on hand to cut the cake on the Plaza's fiftieth birthday in 1957.

Always known as a man who spared no expense when the occasion called for it, Hilton produced for the golden jubilee a spectacular to equal any in The Plaza's history. He called the hotel a "fine old lady" who needed a lot of pampering, and to celebrate the "fine lady's" birthday on October 1, 1957, a grand Golden Ball was held for the benefit of the Recreation Service for the Children of Bellevue. By now no large subscription dance in New York society had a chance unless it bore the label, "for Sweet Charity."

All that glittered in the ballroom that night was golden. The great stage was banked with yellow- and gold-hued chrysanthemums behind miniature white fences to simulate a garden in full bloom; gilded smilax was entwined around the columns of the room and outlined the boxes; the souvenir programs were printed in gold, and the champagne, of course, was effervescent gold. Two orchestras played for continuous dancing, and the menu was the same as at the fortieth-anniversary ball. Mrs. William B. Harding presided as chairman, "Connie" Hilton cut the cake and blew out the candles, Mayor Wagner sent a letter of congratulations to "one of our great landmarks," and Dame Margot Fonteyn, famed British ballerina, represented the arts among the social gathering.

The party was Hilton's last great gesture at The Plaza. He was already losing interest in his "fine old lady," and was more concerned with a younger lady, the Waldorf-Astoria, which he acquired in 1949. With that purchase he almost outdistanced his biographer. It all happened so fast, so unheralded, that 7,500 copies of a book to be called "The Man Who Bought The Plaza," by Thomas Ewing Dabney, were already printed, and the publishers, Duell, Sloan and Pearce, had to wait for Dabney to catch up with the man, with a new last chapter and a new title: *The Man Who Bought the Waldorf.*

By 1957 Hilton, already nearly seventy years of age, had a chain of twenty-six hotels in the United States and was globe-trotting constantly to oversee the building of countless more around the world. His apparent disinterest in The Plaza spread to others, and a management which had begun by spending millions to renovate, redecorate and improve, began letting rooms run down, service to lapse. At a time when other hotels were thriving and Hilton himself was the recognized genius of the business, The Plaza began losing money; occupancy rate fell even while the city's average hotel occupancy rate was rising. There was an unmistakable laissez-faire attitude in every department.

Many attributed the sad conditions to the fact that Hilton's lease would be expiring in 1960. Why care when you were giving up the game? Conditions worsened, and financial conditions were desperate. Indeed the day came when The Plaza was threatened with extinction.

When, on April 1, 1960, Hotel Corporation of American took over the operation of the hotel, The Plaza was at the most critical time in its history. It took A. M. Sonnabend to breathe life back into it. He was custodian of the "fine lady," and he did not intend to let her die.

CHAPTER SIXTEEN

Captain Courageous

THE Shakers, a little-known religious sect now practically extinct but which flourished in the United States during the eighteenth, nineteenth and early twentieth centuries, lived by a strict credo: "Hands to work, hearts to God."

Abraham M. Sonnabend probably never heard of that motto, if indeed he knew anything about the austere, hard-working Shakers, whose inventiveness produced many of the country's industrial "firsts." But it could be said of him, too, that he was devoted to work and devoted to his God.

In September 1954, when Sonnabend was nominated for the office of chairman of Botany Mills at a time when that company was in failing health, his nominator, Washington lawyer Alfons Landa, said: "If he is saddled with the responsibility he will work like a dog." And work like a dog he did, bringing Botany Mills up from huge losses to huge profits in a few years. *Fortune* magazine, in 1957, listed Botany as having the highest ratio of profit to net worth of any in a list of five hundred large United States corporations.

In his private life, Sonnabend was a modest family man, conservative and unpretentious despite his millions, delighting in his twelve grandchildren. His philanthropies were endless, diversified and little publicized. He liked people and had the rare ability to understand the other person's point of view, and, if not entirely in agreement, could coordinate it with his own. An informal, outgoing man, he liked to join Chef Gatti down in the kitchen for lunch of his favorite "Chef's Pâté" and prosciutto ham. For all his seemingly simple tastes A. M. Sonnabend was a man of culture, an art collector and omnivorous reader.

Conrad Hilton from New Mexico and A. M. Sonnabend from Boston first engaged in friendly competition in 1949, when each tried to acquire the Waldorf-Astoria. Sonnabend, owner of several successful hotels, wanted the Waldorf as the keystone of his expanding chain. The price required the purchaser to produce three million dollars in cash. Sonnabend was able to raise the money and was all set—only to discover that Hilton had just beat him to it by one day, and had won the Waldorf.

"My heart was broken," said Sonnabend. "But I did even the score a year later."

Shortly afterward Hilton and Sonnabend were competing for the purchase of the Chesapeake and Ohio Van Sweringen properties in Cleveland, which included the thousand-room Hotel Cleveland, the fifty-two-story Terminal Tower and three other big office buildings. In an eight-million-dollar cash deal the buyer had to produce one million down by Saturday night, September 30, 1950. Sonnabend had only heard of the offer and the terms on the preceding Thursday and went into action immediately. This time he won: he persuaded a known third contender for the properties to team up with him, and together they came up with the down payment just under the deadline. The contract, for some reason, had to be signed in the State of New Jersey, and never did a legal document have such a fantastic wrap-up. It was signed under a New Jersey street light, just before midnight.

Sonnabend next turned his attention to Manhattan's famed Plaza, which Hilton had added to his chain in 1943. In 1953 he went to Hilton and said, "OK, Connie, you got the Waldorf away from me. Why don't you sell me The Plaza?" Hilton was planning, at the time, to build the Beverly Hilton in Beverly Hills, California, but had come up against some resistance from his Board, which was concerned with an overemphasis on Hilton luxury properties. When Sonnabend offered to buy The Plaza, it solved Hilton's problem. If he sold that hotel, he could build the Beverly Hilton. The sale netted him a neat profit; he sold The Plaza for fifteen million dollars, more than twice what he paid for it, and the Sonnabend interests took title in the name of the Fifty-ninth Street Corporation. One of the terms of the sale was that Hilton would be given a lease to operate the hotel for two and a half years.

Hilton also obtained a unique clause in the sale contract, an irrevocable option to purchase a one-half interest in the land under the hotel between October 1, 1965, and March 31, 1966, for the modest sum of $400,000. Before the option expired, canny Hilton made another neat profit by selling the option to another hotel-operating group, for $3,600,000.

Just about the time Hilton's lease on The Plaza was about to expire, in March 1956, the Department of Justice's antitrust division was charging Hilton with monopolizing the convention business in several American cities, including New York and Washington. To obtain a consent decree settling the case, Hilton had to sell some of his properties, and Sonnabend made a proposal to buy the Mayflower Hotel in Washington and the Roosevelt Hotel in New York. But Sonnabend had to offer an inducement in a deal that was something of a horse trade. The inducement was an extension of Hilton's Plaza lease up to 1960.

In 1954 Sonnabend had been invited to become president of the Childs Company, which was reporting serious annual losses on its chain of medium-price restaurants. Admiral John Bergen, chairman of the board, and Irving Felt, chairman of the executive committee, believed that Sonnabend could turn the losses into profits and obtain for Childs important acquisitions that would make it a company of substance. Childs' listing on the New York Stock Exchange had great appeal for Sonnabend.

In 1955 Childs stockholders approved the "acquisition of the operations of three Sonnabend-operated hotels," and the purchase of The Plaza fee subject to the Hilton lease. The name of the Childs Company was changed to the Hotel Corporation of America, which took title to The Plaza in 1956.

The Plaza made real estate headlines again in 1958. Hotel

Corporation of America, which had paid $16 million to buy the Plaza, was selling the hotel, building, lands and furnishings, for the largest price ever paid for a single hotel: $21 million. The purchaser was Lawrence A. Wien, New York lawyer and investor, and behind him was the wealthiest real estate group in the country, with investments of $500 million, five times the size of Atlas Corporation holdings when Odlum backed Hilton. The Empire State Building was but one of their properties.

Sales terms were made subject to mortgages of $15 million, the remaining $6 million to be paid in cash. Hilton's lease would be expiring in a few years, and the Wein interests gave HCA a lease to operate the hotel for twenty-five years and an option to repurchase the hotel in 1971. Hilton was still holding his option to purchase one half of the land at the time of the sale.

The sale of The Plaza strengthened Sonnabend's position by giving him the cash to liquidate remaining bank indebtedness, discharge arrears on preferred stock and to finance HCA hotel expansion.

By the time the second Hilton lease expired, in 1960, and HCA was to take up its own lease, they had a very sick hotel on their hands, perilously near to collapsing after having survived two wars and two depressions and having enjoyed a post-World War Two prosperity. While many were the speculations regarding the decline, the sad fact was that The Plaza was in a bad way.

In the first year of the takeover, sales declined over eight million dollars, and operation profits were 50 percent of what they had been a few years earlier. The year 1961 was a crucial one, and it was even suggested that the hotel be sold, to be replaced by an office building.

Sonnabend, who made his reputation and his millions by his skill in reorganizing moribund corporations, had a positive genius for mixing red and black and coming up with pure black. The Plaza was the flagship of his fleet of hotels, and his pride in it equaled that of Fred Sterry. Like Sterry in the crisis of 1907–8, he was determined to keep it from foundering. With a deep appreciation of the great tradition of the fine old hotel, and courage and confidence in the future, he proceeded to pour millions into the property—repairing, restoring and redecorating. He pumped new blood into its veins with modern projects and improvements that soon were bringing in profits without in the least destroying The Plaza's traditional aura.

A testimonial to his success was in the award presented to HCA by the New York Board of Trade in June 1965—"for maintaining and refurbishing the Plaza Hotel while retaining its distinctive charm and appeal." It was the first time the ninety-five-year-old, twelve-hundred-member trade organization recognized the contribution of commerce to art in its architectural achievement awards.

Today, as the dowager queen of American hotels celebrates her sixtieth birthday, she is healthy, wealthy and wise in the ways of a modern jet world. If any one man can be credited for the rejuvenation, it is A. M. Sonnabend.

He did not stop there. He continued to acquire hotels and motels, and Hotel Corporation of America was soon operating the third largest hotel chain in the country, with seventeen motor hotels as well as regular hotels in cities from Houston to London, from Winnipeg, Canada, to San Juan, Puerto Rico.

Suddenly everybody was talking about Sonnabend, and financial writers bombarded him for interviews. Whether modesty or his sense of humor inspired him, he told reporters that he had no special talent except that "I was always pretty good at squash."

Sonnabend's career was no "rags to riches" story; neither was he born with the silver spoon in his mouth. His father, Joseph Sonnabend, landed in Boston, an immigrant from Austria, at the age of eleven. By the time he was eighteen, Joseph owned a thriving little jewelry store in Boston. Two sons and two daughters were born to Joseph and his wife, and the family enjoyed a comfortable middle-class life. Abraham, the eldest son, early in life displayed the "will to do" that in later years brought him business fame and financial fortune. He worked his way through Harvard, completing his four years in three. With endurance he applied himself to field work in economics and reached the top of his class in 1917.

An ensign and aviator in the Navy in World War One, "Sonny"

Sonnabend, as he was called, returned to Boston at the end of the war and with a loan of $5,000 first went into the paper business and later into the real estate business. Within a year he had repaid the loan and had $20,000 in capital, and by 1920 felt financially secure enough to marry Esther Lewitt. By 1927 he had pyramided his holdings to a net worth of $350,000.

The years between 1927 and 1929 were heady, and fluctuating, the real estate market down, the stock market up. Everyone was wildly speculating in Wall Street, as stocks took dramatic rises. A. M. Sonnabend, shrewd and conservative, was one who did not succumb to the intoxication of the Wall Street market frenzy.

Sonnabend still had considerable real estate in Boston at the time of the Wall Street holocaust of 1929 and like everyone else suffered in the ensuing depression. He always remembered what his father had told him: that no matter what happened to business, people had to have a place to live, if nothing else, and he decided to gamble on lowering his rents in order to keep his tenants from moving elsewhere. But there was one stipulation: in order to get the reduced rents, they would have to take long leases.

Few refused, and Sonnabend kept his buildings full while others were emptying, thus winning the confidence of Boston bankers. They carried him along, and as they foreclosed other properties they offered them to Sonnabend, who was able to take advantage of the opportunities. As the economic situation eased in time and things started looking up, Sonnabend was soon prospering again, and by the beginning of World War Two he was one of the biggest apartment-house owners in Boston.

While Sonnabend had operated apartment hotels since the early thirties, his first real interest in the hotel business came in 1938, when a summer hotel in Swampscott, Massachusetts, became available. With a group of others he purchased the Preston Beach Hotel. This established something of a pattern for future hotel acquisitions with partners. In 1944 Sonnabend and seven partners purchased four Palm Beach properties—the Biltmore and Whitehall Hotels, the Palm Beach Country Club, and the Sun and Surf Club.

Interestingly enough, Hilton soon came into the picture. A little more than a year later, Connie Hilton bought the Biltmore for almost as much as the group had paid for the whole package. Some years later the other three properties were sold at great profits. By now the hotel business was in Sonnabend's blood; by now he was in the Big League. The acquisition of The Plaza made him proud owner of one of the world's most famous hotels.

The years 1960–61 were a test of A. M. Sonnabend's courage and acumen. Conditions in April 1960, when HCA took over operation of the hotel, were about as serious as they had ever been in the long—sometimes rich, sometimes turbulent—life of The Plaza. A. M.'s second son Paul recalls: "We were desperately concerned over whether we could bring the hotel back. The place was going to seed . . . businessmen didn't want to come here." Within a few years, as the result of an intensive campaign of wooing, Paul was to see businessmen overrunning the hotel.

Millions were needed to supply plasma for the ailing Plaza, and A. M. Sonnabend saw to it that those millions were available. A long-range program that would extend over a period of four years, at an ultimate cost of nine million dollars, was set in motion. Every facet of operation was involved: physical improvements, an advertising campaign, new restaurants and function rooms, improved service, and an aggressive merchandising program. By this time A. M. Sonnabend stepped from president of HCA to chairman of the board, and Roger Sonnabend, A. M.'s oldest son, was named president.

Neal Lang was the first to tackle the job of Plaza manager for the Sonnabends. Like A. M., he had been waiting in the wings until the Hilton lease expired. His hotel background was excellent, and among the posts he held were that of general manager of the Roney Plaza in Miami Beach, and also of the Sheraton Astor in New York. Sonnabend hired him in 1955 as general manager of the Edgewater Beach Hotel in Chicago, which he then owned, and sped him westward with a large party at The Plaza. Astute columnists saw the portent and predicted that as soon as Hilton departed, Lang would come east to run the hotel.

Real estate deals delayed the day, and Lang was brought back in 1957 to manage the Roosevelt, which Sonnabend had acquired. Finally, in 1960, he moved into the prized post at The Plaza. With him he brought as food and beverage manager the venerable Semy Ernest, who had served in that capacity at the Edgewater and the Roosevelt. A wisp of hair, gentle blue eyes, a white moustache, Old World manners, Mr. Ernest was a veteran of fifty years in the business, the Grand Old Man of the hotel industry. He did much to help the recovery of The Plaza with his special knowledge and experience; the respect in which he was held by food suppliers and their trust in him was a plus factor for the hotel at a time when it needed all the moral, as well as financial, support it could get.

When Neal Lang entered the Plaza picture, there was a marked change in the atmosphere behind the scenes. Lang was a strict disciplinarian and was not noted for tact and diplomacy. "My father said it is better to do a good job than to be a good guy," he observed. Perfection was Lang's fetish, and he was uncompromising in his efforts to achieve it. Every department of operation came under his keen perusal, was carefully scrutinized, carefully analyzed. Memos poured from his office with instructions, criticisms and queries. That he was not entirely popular with the staff was a matter of complete unconcern to him.

The twist was not Lang's idea of the proper dancing in the Persian Room. Veteran Emil Coleman, who was to become a fixture as the orchestra leader there until his death a few years ago, saw that times were changing, and played the twist one night. The incident brought the following memo from Lang, which reminded many of the banning of the turkey trot years earlier:

Subject: THE TWIST.

> The management of the Plaza prefers not to become involved in the enthusiasm for the twist currently being displayed in Manhattan. When Mr. Coleman inadvertently played this type of music last evening I took the liberty of asking him to discontinue it. This note is merely to establish The Plaza's policy on this particular subject.

It has been admitted by all, including Paul Sonnabend, that Neal Lang came to The Plaza at its most trying and difficult time and that he had a tough job to perform. Rumor had it that one of the reasons for the hotel's depleted business was Hilton's diverting the flow of reservations to funnel them into the Savoy-Hilton, which he owned. The customary summer slump but added to the loss of business. It was the same story in 1961, and the Sonnabends believed measures had to be taken for a new dynamic and aggressive marketing program and a change in rate structure. They felt that the hotel's reputation and character would be enhanced by such a program. The issue really was whether a great prestige hotel could be commercialized and still retain its prestige. To Paul Sonnabend, as president of The Plaza, fell the task of implementing such a program with Lang. New York luxury hotels normally take a drastic drop in occupancy during the torrid months, and it was Paul's firm belief that inducements should be held out to interest new customers and win back old friends by more reasonable rates. If high-priced suites were going to be unoccupied anyway, why not entice guests by offering them at a lowered rate? Better diminished income than no income. Lang was strenuously against it; he felt that the character of the hotel would suffer. Even if it meant red ink on the ledger he felt rates should be kept up in order to preserve the standard.

One thing led to another, and Lang, never noted for his meekness, blew a gasket and threatened to resign. Previous similar threats had been smoothed over by A. M. Sonnabend, who liked Lang and respected his ability, a liking and respect shared by Admiral Bergen and Irving Felt. This time, however, Lang's resignation was accepted, reportedly to Lang's surprise. He has since admitted to intimates that he was sure he would not be permitted to resign.

That was in the spring of 1962. A. M. Sonnabend farewelled Lang with a gift of a thousand-dollar watch and a twenty-thousand-dollar bonus.

To fill the breach, pending finding a successor to Lang, Paul Sonnabend stepped into the vacancy and proved himself to be the astute son of an astute father, an important factor in The Plaza's quick recovery.

Father Sonnabend had seen to it that his sons were trained for the business. He had taught Roger the hotel business at the age of twenty-one. A graduate of Massachusetts Institute of Technology who served in the Navy during World War Two, Roger was sent to the Nautilus Hotel and Beach Club, in Atlantic Beach, as assistant manager, to open up the hotel pending the arrival of a general manager. The general manager never arrived, and Roger telephoned his father to ask what he wanted done with "this relic."

"I want you to manage it! She's yours, and with her you sink or swim as a hotelman" said Father. Roger turned out to be a good swimmer. Within a year he had the Nautilus in the black and had proved himself to his father. By 1956, at the age of thirty-one, he was made executive vice president of the Hotel Corporation of America.

Brother Paul was thirty-two when he was elected a vice president of the corporation in 1959. Knowing that the hotel business was to be his career, he had entered the Cornell University Hotel School, after prepping at Phillips Exeter Academy, and received his bachelor of science degree in 1950. His first job after graduation was managing some HCA properties in Boston. Following Lang's resignation from The Plaza, he became president of the hotel.

A chip off the old block, Paul immediately plunged into the job of building up the rooms business, with special emphasis on appeal to the businessman. His first move was to hire a new advertising agency. While aware that the agency the hotel had retained for years was among the finest in the country, he felt that what The Plaza needed at this particular time was a fresh new approach—fresh indeed, judging from the subsequent campaign—and a smaller company that could devote the major part of its time to The Plaza.

He selected a Philadelphia agency, the Lavenson Bureau of Advertising, headed by James Lavenson, a brilliant, imaginative young man from whose agile mind tumbled ideas that not only helped lure business but made advertising history and won prizes in its field. Lavenson has since sold the agency to become an executive of Hotel Corporation of America.

Lavenson set right out to launch a unique mail advertising campaign designed to bring the "new" Plaza to the attention of the nation's thirty thousand top executives in a most unusual and intriguing way. Businessmen across the country soon got into a game of corresponding with one Mary O'Sullivan, whose first letter, on Plaza-engraved stationery, began:

> Dear Mr. Doe:
>
> I'm the chambermaid. I have my own stationery. I take care of the rooms at the Plaza. . . . I like the rooms. . . . You can eat in the Persian Room, but you can't lie down there.

The next letter, to the same thirty thousand executives, was signed by Paul Sonnabend, who wrote:

> Dear Mr. Doe:
>
> I have a problem. It's like this. Recently one of our chambermaids, Mary O'Sullivan, wrote a sales letter. (A privilege that I usually reserve for myself, as I am rather good at it.) But after all, it made her happy and I'm a big one for employee morale. . . . We have company picnics, bowling leagues, elevator races, and all that.

The point was, however, that she had slighted the Persian Room. What should he do about it? He asked: "Fire Mary O'Sullivan, sentence her to six months in the laundry? Bar her from the Persian Room?"

By now Mr. Doe was really in for it. The next letter read:

> It's me, again, the chambermaid. Remember? How are you? I'm fine, but a lot has happened here recently. Mr. Sonnabend, our managing director, found out that I wrote you and almost fired me.

A new name came into the act with a letter dated July 8, 1963, reading:

> Dear Mr. Doe: It's not true! Mary O'Sullivan will *not* sing in the Persian Room this summer. She must have started this rumor herself. Recently she started calling her uniform a bunny costume.

This was signed by Alphonse W. Salomone, who had just been appointed the Plaza's new manager and vice president.

The letters brought hilarious reaction, and replies in kind, from thousands of amused recipients. Behind it all was the ad lib wit of Jim Lavenson and a corps of unsung copywriters, but Mary O'Sullivan was for real, as real as an Irish reel, and she embodied the personality of more than two generations of Irish chambermaids at The Plaza.

The response to the whole pixie idea, in reservations as well as letters, was gratifying and overwhelming. The lines in front of the cashier windows grew longer, and The Plaza was impelled to issue a folder on "How to Make a Quick Getaway."

The hotel was well on the way to recovery. Arthur Dooley, who had come to The Plaza from the Roosevelt with Neal Lang, was acting as a transitory manager, pending completion of a new HCA hotel, the Hotel America in Hartford, where he was to be general manager.

Paul Sonnabend found his new manager in Alphonse Salomone, and it was like coming home again for Salomone. Nor was the Plaza any new challenge for him. He had served there in the Hilton administration and won immortality of a sort as the only nonfictional character in the book *Eloise*.

Handsome, soft-voiced Salomone was born in Winnipeg, Canada, and reared in Knoxville, Tennessee, where his father was in the marble business. The hotel business had fascinated him ever since college days when, as a student at the University of Tennessee he got his first taste of it as an employee at the Andrew Johnson Hotel in Knoxville. He left college in 1942 to attend Officers Candidate School at Fort Benning, and served overseas as a second lieutenant with the 80th Infantry Division in France, and with the Third Army until the end of the war, by which time he had earned the oak leaves of a major.

Back to Knoxville and the Andrew Johnson Hotel he went, but new horizons were opening up. In 1947 he came to Hilton's Plaza as rooms manager; he left there in 1956 when Hilton sent him to the Caribe Hilton in Puerto Rico and in 1961 made him a vice president of Hilton International with duties in the Caribbean operation.

Paul Sonnabend tapped him for the job of Plaza manager in 1963. Dowagers beamed, and old-timers greeted his return with affection. Then Paul transferred from the HCA-operated Mayflower Hotel in Washington another rising young executive, George DeKornfeld, to serve as second in command to Salomone. For George DeKornfeld The Plaza had a special meaning and family sentiment. Just before the First World War a distinguished visitor from abroad who registered at The Plaza was the Hungarian Baron Paul DeKornfeld. George, who prefers that you "Call Me Mister," is Baron DeKornfeld's nephew.

It was a vigorous new team, and all sorts of vigorous things were beginning to happen as a massive and exciting program went into high gear. A floor-by-floor, complete redecoration was done, air-conditioning units were installed throughout, in guest rooms and function rooms; television controlled by a master antenna was provided for all rooms, and new function rooms were created to meet the demands of more and more gala social events.

In the former Rendez-Vous, a little theater-type cabaret bearing the unique name "Plaza 9" was created as a background for the satiric revues of Julius Monk, an impresario expressing civilized outrage at a world in orbit. Every time town houses were torn down or a threatening gesture made at Central Park, whenever professors and politicians made fools of themselves, they were demolished on stage with a new satire. Public absorption in talk of hallucinatory drugs inspired a skit depicting four professors fleeing Harvard, a gleam in their eyes, singing such lines as "Don't do the beguine, take mescaline, and the visions you'll have are sure to be obscene."

A sharp satirical ditty called "Barry's Boys" could have helped destroy Barry Goldwater's last chance of making a respectable showing against Lyndon Johnson in the 1964 Presidential elections, and Monk's fans refused to let it die with the Republican contender's political hopes. Mary McCarthy's *Group* got sardonic treatment; a supersuave James Bond was challenged by a girl spy.

The critics raved and the customers kept coming. They were jammed together at little tables, and they loved it. Again The Plaza had a financial hit on its hands.

Alphonse Salomone had barely removed his hat as the new manager, when he plunged into a project that has become an extension of enchantment in a nostalgic atmosphere. A "Palm Court After Eight" came into being and gave truth to the old French proverb that the more things change, the more they are the same. This was the same Tea Court sacred to the memory of the elegant Edwardians, later the popular haunt of the thirties as the Palm Court, still later, the luncheon setting for calorie-conscious ladies who nibbled on salads; the place where, as *New York Times* society editor Russell Edwards wrote, "Nobody raises an eyebrow if you order tea at cocktail time."

All very fine and dandy—but after 8 P.M. the Palm Court presented a dismal, dark, yawning chasm in the most conspicuous area of the hotel, smiting the eye as one arrived from the Fifth Avenue entrance. To say nothing of its being a dead loss of space to management.

Coffeehouses were the new rage in New York and other cities; store fronts, steps down, and simple candlelight appealed to the long-haired youngsters. For the elite, however, who preferred a nonbeatnik atmosphere after dinner or the theater, for coffee and dessert, for a nightcap but not nightclub, there was virtually no place to go. Salomone envisioned New York's first luxury-class after-dinner coffee and dessert room specializing in coffees of all nations and pastries of the yummiest Viennese, German and French variety. Drinks, of course, too.

The result was a transformation of the Palm Court into an enchanting continental setting, a merging of the old and the new, with a new-old name, "Palm Court After 8."

Nothing changed, they didn't gild the lily, yet somehow change was evident. It wasn't done with mirrors, for they were already there, but with clever manipulation of lights. A new mood descended upon the room when ceiling lights were dimmed and subtle new illumination brought out the gleaming beauty of the four famed caryatids, representing the four seasons, and the great crystal hurricane lamps. A gold-and-white-striped awning lowered on the lobby "windows" outside created an intimate atmosphere within, and for the first time in its history The Plaza employed waitresses. Some columnists who heard the hotel was about to introduce "Petty Girls" as waitresses envisioned girls of the sexy dimensions drawn by illustrator George Petty. Not at all; the Plaza's answer to bunny girls were pretty maids in the Victorian costumes and winglike aprons drawn by Mary Petty in her *New Yorker* cartoons.

The soft glow of orchids and lilies floating in large wax-filled brandy snifters lighted from within made every woman look beautiful, and the strains of soft music in the background made every man feel romantic. The new room was a fabulous success from the beginning, socially and financially. For the investment of a mere $15,000 the Plaza added $200,000 annually to its gross.

Rogers Whitaker in the *New Yorker* said of it "... the light that begins at eight to play on the statuary ... is royal purple ... perfectly appropriate to the palace it becomes, a palace with the courtly violin of Gunnar Hansen and a dozen ladies-in-waiting laden with Linzer Torte, Irish coffee and spirits." Clementine Paddleford in her syndicated food column described it as the "most fashionable uptown coffeehouse in New York."

The next major Plaza project was to establish Trader Vic's Restaurant in the hotel at a cost of one million dollars. The news created a mild sensation, and not everyone was happy. Plaza aficionados could not visualize thatched roofs, war clubs, dugout canoes and carved wooden gods in the midst of the Plaza's Edwardian splendor.

They needn't have worried. Moving Trader Vic's into a basement area occupied mostly by storage space and a barbershop would be no intrusion on the established architecture—any more than the "Plaza 9" was. Like the latter spot, it would have its own entrance on Fifty-ninth Street, and an unobtrusive stairway leading down from the lobby within.

Victor Bergeron, whose New York Trader Vic's was being forced to move as a result of the sale and demolition of the Savoy-Plaza, had a fine appreciation of The Plaza's prestige and outdid himself to make this the jewel in his chain of restaurants. In twelve thousand square feet of space he created his own South Pacific. In the corridor approach nestled a fifty-four-foot outrigger canoe used in the film *Mutiny on the Bounty.* Agents combed Tahiti and other Pacific islands for exotic carvings. Tigerskins from India, masks from New Guinea, and Chinese smoke ovens added atmosphere. Three dining room areas and a bar were equipped to serve 350 people at one time, from lunch through dinner and supper until 1 A.M. The menu started somewhere in the South Seas and stretched to include the most bizarre of native rum drinks. New Yorkers as well as tourists flocked to dine on such delicacies as Tahitian and Samoan fish and eagerly pull apart fortune cookies.

Another bonanza. Success and popularity were instantaneous. In place of a barbershop paying fourteen thousand dollars a year rental, there was a fabulously picturesque restaurant that, while costing one million to establish, was expected to gross over two million dollars annually—and did.

There was still more to come. Additional function space was needed to meet a growing demand. To do so, the Baroque Suite, which was the first Plaza ballroom and had been reduced to a series of rooms with the building of a new ballroom in 1921, was restored to its original dimensions. The room, all gold and white and crystally, was finished just barely hours before its first great function, the Easter Sunday fashion-show luncheon of the Easter Seal Society in April 1965, and already it was booked for months in advance. Again The Plaza hit pay dirt with a second ballroom that could accommodate up to five hundred people.

Business kept improving. In 1964 the occupancy rate had reached 81 percent, five points above the New York City average and 20 points higher than the national average. Gross operating profits reached three and a half million and while the net operating profit that year was a modest $518,000, still—it was a profit.

The Plaza was firmly in the black again, and while it was not A. M.'s most profitable endeavor, it was perhaps his greatest triumph. Forecasts based on whatever it is hotels base their forecasts indicated that the next year the net profit would reach one million dollars.

But A. M. Sonnabend did not live to see that forecast come true. Suddenly, on February 11, 1964, he died of a heart attack in Palm Beach. With news of his death, the public learned of many benevolences he had been quietly and unassumingly carrying on all along, countless unpublicized philanthropies and relief organization projects. In behalf of human understanding he organized the Institute of Human Relations of the American Jewish Committee. He also established the Sonnabend Foundation to help in charitable causes without regard to race or creed.

The death of A. M. Sonnabend was a wrench, but his empire would not suffer. His three sons, Roger, Paul and Stephen, trained and seasoned in their father's image, would carry on for him.

The Plaza, for one, was still in good hands.

CHAPTER SEVENTEEN

Social Citadel

THE Battle of the Ballrooms" was the headline of a *New York Times* story in June 1963, the day before the mammoth glass-and-chrome New York Hilton hotel threw open its streamlined doors.

A whole segment of Americana was contained in that five-word headline; behind it was imbedded the history of the phenomenal growth and transformation of the American hotel from a place designed merely to provide food and shelter for travelers to a veritable social citadel. For more than a year before it opened, the Hilton, with the biggest ballroom in town, was making a strong and successful bid to capture a large part of New York's colossal business in banquets, charity balls, dances, wedding receptions, and other social functions.

If the history of Greece, wrote Gene Fowler, is in its temples, that of the United States is in its hotels. From the smoky little ordinaries, the inns and taverns of Colonial days, to the more comfortable hotels of a later century, serving mainly that new railroad-developed breed, the traveling salesman; from the ornate, marble structures of the fabulous Gilded Age to the chrome, concrete and glass towers of the sixties, the hotel industry has run parallel with the industrial growth and economic changes of the country. From this emerged an entirely new social way of life, and a new social structure of mass entertaining as phenomenal as mass production in industry. And, as in industry, the competition for the business is keen.

When our country was very young, there wasn't a ballroom in New York large enough for the First Presidential Inaugural Ball held a week after George Washington took the oath of office at Federal Hall on Broad Street. The Long Room at Fraunces Tavern was too small, and New York's first "modern" caravansary, the City Hotel, was not erected until 1794. The sponsoring Dancing Assembly had to hold the event in its rooms on the east side of Broadway, near Wall Street.

"Little Old New York" was considered a boom town of some thirty thousand inhabitants in 1794 when the City Hotel opened, the first inn to call itself a "hotel." It became popular immediately as a social center for men, haunt of the artistic and literati of the day, a meeting place for James Fenimore Cooper's famous "Bread and Cheese Club," and for another group headed by Colonel Nick Saltus and referred to simply as "The Club." In time this became the Union Club and New York's first private membership club; later it had a building of its own.

The city continued to boom as the nineteenth century rounded the turn and soon began to feel the strong impact of railroad development and a demand for more hotels to provide service beyond mere bed and board for travelers pouring into New York. Men brought their wives, and they wanted social diversion. By the late nineteenth century, Manhattan could boast countless hotels of the so-called "luxury" type. By 1900, New York, with the largest hotel population of any city in the world, was continuing to build hotels with lavish new features and innovations. They lured the elite with tearooms for the ladies, Turkish baths for the gentlemen, orchestras to provide chamber music during dinner, and roof gardens for summer dining in a pre–air-conditioned era. Of the last named, one of the most popular was atop the Astor Hotel, where guests dined and danced under the stars overlooking Times Square's fairyland of lights. This famed hostelry has gone the way of so many other New York hotels, doomed to make way for a high-rising office building.

The leading New York hotels before and at the turn of the century were the Hoffman House, the Fifth Avenue Hotel, the Holland House, the Windsor, the Buckingham, in the shadow of St. Patrick's Cathedral, where Saks Fifth Avenue now stands; the fabled first Waldorf-Astoria, the first Plaza, the old Netherlands and the old Savoy. As the city grew in population and in the vast numbers of out-of-town visitors, New York's horizon changed dramatically, silhouetted with countless great new hotels as well as apartment house and offices: the Knickerbocker, the Belmont, the Astor, the St. Regis, the Gotham, the Pierre, the Sherry-Netherland and the Savoy-Plaza; the Vanderbilt on the site of the Cornelius Vanderbilts' earlier home at Thirty-fourth and Park; the incomparable Ritz Carlton, the new Waldorf-Astoria, the fine Ambassador, renamed the Sheraton East; and, of course, the fabulous Plaza. Sadly, all but The Plaza, the Pierre, the St. Regis, the Gotham, and the Sherry-Netherland have vanished, while the Vanderbilt escaped extinction by being turned into an apartment house.

A distinctive feature of all these hotels was their large ballrooms, and soon all were politely competing for the fast-growing number of private parties and charity balls which have enlivened the social scene during the past fifty years.

The most exclusive dances in the mid- and late nineteenth century, and, to many who couldn't make it, the most snobbish, were those of the "Patriarchs," run by Ward McAllister. The Petronius of society was more drastic in blue-penciling this list than Mrs. Astor's "Four Hundred," by limiting the attendance to 250. Equally exclusive, with lineage going back to the seventies, were "The" Assemblies. The ballroom at the old Madison Square Garden designed by Stanford White, or the gold-and-white music and dancing room on the second floor of Delmonico's at Twenty-sixth Street were the settings for these sacrosanct dances. No hotels competed for their business; no hotels had ballrooms worthy enough.

The Assemblies, by invitational subscription only, were as exclusive as a blue-penciled list could make them, but they were subscription parties nevertheless. Private parties were always held in the home.

New York, circa 1907, was a city of private residences, and one doesn't have to be as old as Methuselah to recall a Park Avenue without a single shop. Madison Avenue was a long narrow vista of brownstones with projecting stoops and Victorian bays and bulges, and Fifth Avenue, even below Fifty-ninth Street, was mansion-lined on both sides. The Vanderbilts alone had seven town houses between them in an area extending from Fifty-second to Fifty-eighth Street.

The status symbol for the moneyed moguls was a ballroom in one's town house or country estate, and "genteel people" of less opulence had the front parlor for gala occasions. Entertaining in public just wasn't done; it was unthinkable that ladies would dine in so public a place as a hotel in "full evening" attire.

The splendiferous Waldorf-Astoria was the first hotel to break down the prejudice. Feminine society took the stylish new caravansary to its gem-bedecked bosom, and the first tentative step toward hotel entertaining was made by a group of fashionable ladies following the example of Mrs. William Astor. Of course she had a motive; her son, John Jacob Astor, had built the Astor half of the Waldorf-Astoria. But it was an innovation, and for the first time ladies of position were to be observed dining and entertaining in a public room attired in fine evening clothes. The fact that jeweled dog collars and diamond stomachers usually embellished these ladies but added to the fabulous sight of them. Never was a place so well nicknamed as "Peacock Alley," where the elect, in truth, strutted in peacocklike splendor.

But not until the opening of The Plaza did society of the Edwardian era embrace, en masse, the custom of giving large dinners and dances in a hotel. Society has always been a pacesetter for fashions and customs, and the press helped by rapturously reporting the presence of the social and financial greats at these affairs.

With mounting taxes, a new problem in the home, "the servant problem," and the social encroachments of an army of large hotels, wealthy dowagers dismantled their ballrooms and scrapped their little gilded chairs. Their daughters and granddaughters were now coming out in hotel ballrooms.

There was another new trend, influenced by Mrs. George Jay

Gould's appearance in a private theatrical. Suddenly amateur theatricals became the rage from Manhattan to the hinterlands. Plays and playlets, musicales, *tableaux vivants,* readings—"Culture for Cash"—were being held all over town, in ballrooms which boasted a stage.

Virginia-born Lady Astor, one of the three beautiful Langhorne sisters, even made a special trip from England to stage-manage and appear in a series of *tableaux vivants* at The Plaza for the benefit of the poor whites in the mountains of Virginia. Mrs. Nicholas F. Brady portraying a Romney, Mrs. Charles Ingram a Botticelli, appeared in a series called "Modern Portraits by Old Masters," standing rigidly in a gilded "frame" on stage. If you were "permitted" to subscribe to the Musical Mornings of Albert Morris Bagby, a dapper little man who was something of a darling of society, you were definitely "in." You were "in," too, if you were a devotee of The Plaza's weekly Artistic Mornings conducted by Sam Piza, a grandson of the late President Juan Rafael Mora of Costa Rica. The Southampton crowd took to its heart genial, stocky little Rafaelo Diaz of the Metropolitan and his Mornings of Music, and Geraldine Farrar and Alma Gluck participated in a series known as Chansons in Crinoline—in the proper crinoline dresses, of course.

All of these were properly "covered" in the society columns, and Fred Sterry made certain that those events which took place at The Plaza received the maximum publicity. Nobody appreciated the sweet influence of the press, particularly the society press, more than he and, always the innovator, he made life easier for a whole generation of society editors by sending them daily items of news concerning the activities of his socially exalted tenants and guests. The Plaza was the first hotel in New York to employ a full-time publicity director in an era when most reporters had to do their own leg work, get out and dig for their copy, and when the wire services were far more minimal than now. Since New York, years back, boasted about twelve newspapers as against a meager four today, it made for a lot of "society news" coverage.

The difficult chore of covering New York's hotels in the early 1900's and the twenties was revealed by veteran newsman Albert Stevens Crockett in an article he wrote in 1951 for the *Hotel Ga-*

zette. Crockett, who in 1965, at the age of ninety-three, was honored by the Overseas Press Club, told of his job on the morning *Sun,* making his own assignments and devoting attention mainly to hotels.

"Thus began a period of intensive hotel coverage, seeking humorous and human interest stories and news. Even at the beginning of the century," he wrote, "it would have proved impossible for one man to have covered all New York hotels, though quitting time seldom came before eight, and was often midnight. Some idea of what one newspaper published about New York hotels, with stories turned up in the course of three years, is suggested by the fact that . . . my weekly space measured seventeen columns, an average of almost three columns a day."

Other hotels followed Sterry's example, and today every hotel of consequence has its own press agent and public relations counsel. Coincidentally enough, the publicity director for The Plaza in the late thirties and early forties was Albert Crockett's stepson, Kirk Crockett.

Prince Serge Obolensky was, of course, the most glamorous of The Plaza's, and the town's, publicists; Edward Seay, who came after Obolensky and remained for thirteen years before leaving to join Hilton at the Waldorf-Astoria, was one of the most meticulous and best liked; Kirk Crockett saw to it that two United States Realty Hotels, The Plaza and the Savoy-Plaza, got their share of publicity, but by far the most energetic was a lady, Caroline Harding, hired by Sterry as his first full-time publicity director. Miss Harding's press output, in the twenties particularly, when the social game was being played with furious abandon, was staggering. Memoranda in her handwriting in Plaza files noted that from September 25 to October 2, 1922, the Plaza was mentioned 121 times in the city's newspapers; 119 times from October 2 to October 9; 112 items appeared from October 9 to October 16, and 117 items were clipped from the papers from October 16 to 23. All in all Plaza items in the society columns of New York's leading papers numbered 469 in a month's period—exclusive, as Miss Harding explained, of several papers she did not bother to read because "of no particular use to The Plaza."

Granted there were many more newspapers in the twenties than at any other period in New York, this total is awe-inspiring. It is doubtful if an Ivy Lee, a Steve Hannigan, an Edward Bernays could have matched it.

For making their jobs easier, Sterry was, of course, the darling of the press, but publicity aside, he was one of the most popular men in the hotel business, a man's man as well as the delight of feminine socialites. He was recognized as a gentleman of his word which, once given, was faithfully kept. A case in point concerns socially prominent Mrs. Matthew Akers of Louisville, Kentucky, who coveted Sterry's two favorite horses, Mint and Julep. He had vowed never to sell them, but Mrs. Akers wanted them and pressed him to name his price—any price. Unwilling to offend and unwilling to sell, Sterry named a sum he considered outrageously high in the belief no one, not even the very rich Mrs. Akers, would pay such a price.

That night Mrs. Akers placed her check on his plate at dinner. Sterry was devastated. The horses meant more to him than money, but his word meant more to him than anything else. Mint and Julep became the property of Mrs. Akers.

Years later his daughter, Mrs. Hanford Meade Twitchell, who as Virginia Sterry was one of New York's popular debutantes of the twenties, recalled the story, and spoke of the challenge of trying to keep up with him on his daily morning horseback rides through the Park on either of his beloved horses.

Only one other hotel in New York could match The Plaza in the matter of great social functions, particularly debutante festivities —with its natural aftermath of society-page publicity—and that was the Ritz Carlton. Fred Sterry was fully aware of this, and Henry Sell, editor of *Town and Country,* recalled to the author a day when he was lunching in the Oak Room with acid society scrivener Maury Paul, the Cholly Knickerbocker of Hearst's *New York American,* when they were joined by Sterry. "It's always so nice to have you here," said the genial boniface, adding with personable frankness, "You must come more often, as my guests. We've always got news—and it's easier to spell P-l-a-z-a than R-i-t-z C-a-r-l-t-o-n."

And indeed it was at The Plaza that Maury Paul accidentally came upon a story that was one of the greatest front-page scoops by this master of society scoops. While lunching in the Edwardian Room one day he spied two friends at a nearby table, debutante Charlotte Demarest, who was to be married to millionaire George Burton the very next day, and the half-American Hungarian Count Edward Zichy. As he joined them he was flabbergasted when they told him they had just discovered they were in love, and were to be married that afternoon. From that moment Maury never left them; he drove them to City Hall, witnessed the marriage (blood tests were apparently not necessary then), took them to dinner, later to the popular supper club, the Montmartre, and then saw them to The Plaza in the late, late evening—but in plenty of time to make his front-page deadline. The city editor, forewarned by telephone, held the presses for the copyright story, and that's how George Burton learned the next morning that his bride-to-be had eloped with another.

A city wept when the Ritz Carlton, one of America's truly great hotels, was torn down and later was replaced by a Madison Avenue office building. And it would weep two decades later when other luxury hotels went the way of the Ritz. After its demise The Plaza was the natural heir to a large part of the gala functions held there.

The new ballroom which replaced the original ballroom in 1921, and which was as elegant as the first, with balconies but a stationary stage, immediately became the scene of some of Manhattan's most glamorous debutante balls. The first of the galas that year was the coming-out party in honor of Joan Whitney, daughter of Mr. and Mrs. Payne Whitney and granddaughter of the munificent magnifico, William C. Whitney. As was to be expected, the Whitneys outdid themselves to make the debut a memorable occasion. The entire second floor of the hotel was reserved for the seven hundred guests invited to the supper dance, and no less than forty dinners preceded the ball. The debutante, who became Mrs. Charles Shipman Payson, was to make sports history in later years as owner of the Mets Baseball team. Her brother, John Hay Whitney (the Hay in the name is for their grandfather, John Hay, Secretary of State during the McKinley and Theodore Roosevelt administrations) contributed to the nation's history as Ambassador to the Court of St. James's.

It was the Christmas season, and the guests danced in a forest of evergreens to the continuous music of two orchestras; they consumed a midnight supper, and stayed on for breakfast at 4 A.M.

Reported the *New York Herald* on December 21, 1921: "Although given in a hotel, Mr. and Mrs. Whitney's party had all the characteristics of an entertainment in a private home." No accolade could have given better expression to the Plaza aura.

Grand and glorious as it was, Joan Whitney's coming-out ball could not begin to compare in magnificence with the debut of Marjorie Gould, daughter of Mr. and Mrs. George Jay Gould, in the original ballroom in January 1909. The ball, a dinner dance, ranks still as the most lavish debutante party in the history of The Plaza, scene of sixty years of elegant coming-out dances.

The *New York Journal* informed its readers the next day that the Plaza ballroom had been transformed into a fairyland, with headlines proclaiming, NEW STANDARD SET FOR LAVISHNESS AND ELEGANCE.

"The ballroom never looked so beautiful. Only an artist can describe the wealth and beauty of the flowers and the way they were arranged." And the writer then went on to compete with an artist by devoting columns of linotype to a description not only of the decorations, but of the gowns and jewels of the feminine guests, the dinner menu, the music, and to publishing the names of the entire list of guests. Nahan Franko, the Plaza's orchestra leader, composed and dedicated to the debutante "The Marjorie Waltz."

The *Journal* reported that three tall white rose bushes were arranged in the center of Miss Gould's table, set for fifty guests, above a sunken garden of lilies of the valley, some 5,500 in number. Mr. and Mrs. Gould each also presided at tables for fifty, but the decorations at their tables were mauve orchids, "for both Mr. and Mrs. Gould are very fond of the costly cattleyas." It was estimated that fully 1,500 of these blooms were used in decorating the other tables. At opposite ends of the room were two tables which the debutante's brothers, Jay and Kingdon, headed.

"As Miss Gould stood beside her mother," went on the ecstatic reporter, "I could well understand why American beauty rose was chosen as the color of her gown. Miss Gould is probably the only debutante in society history who did not don white for her coming-out ball. Not a jewel did this daughter of wealth wear; in her hair nestled one big American beauty rose."

As guests made their way to the ballroom, after being received in the State Suite by the debutante and her mother, they passed through a line of liveried footmen up from Georgian Court, the Gould estate in Lakewood. The cotillion was led by Phoenix Ingraham, dancing with the guest of honor. Favors for the men were gold pocketknives, cigar cutters and key rings, all gold; favors for the ladies included, among other things, gold-bangled bracelets in dainty silver boxes stamped with Miss Gould's monogram and the date. In later years the author, visiting Mr. and Mrs. Gould's granddaughter, Mrs. Guy Martin and her husband at their Georgetown residence, was shown one of these little heart-shaped boxes, a cherished memento.

"It was estimated that the combined bank accounts of the guests would total $1,500,000,000," reported the *Journal,* and the published list of the guests certainly tended to confirm this.

They don't give many parties like that any more, except perhaps by Fords and Du Ponts, who in later years made headlines with the coming-out parties for their daughters. The twenties did, however, see a large outburst of festive coming-out balls—for Barbara Hutton, for Doris Duke, for Cathleen Vanderbilt, who made her debut in the Plaza ballroom at a large dance given by her grandmother, Mrs. Frederic Neilson, in 1923. During that Christmas season Mr. and Mrs. Bernard Baruch gave a large dance there to introduce their daughter Renée.

The glitter and gilt of society in the Golden Age yielded to the alchemy of time, with its wars and economic changes. The first families of New York celebrated the end of World War Two and the end of wartime retrenchment by welcoming the largest group of debutantes in history, but few were the individual parties. The majority came out at debutante cotillions, the mass debutante balls which took the place of individual coming-out dances after war broke out.

The most exclusive of the debutante events, the Junior Assemblies, as well as the equally fashionable Junior League Debutante Ball, the Grosvenor Debutante Cotillion, and the Gotham Ball, are deeply imbedded in the tradition of The Plaza, and each has its special night during Thanksgiving week each year. The Junior League starts the balls rolling on Thanksgiving Eve; the next night marks not only the end of a perfect holiday but the beginning of an enchanted evening for Catholic debutantes at the Gothams, where they are received in the Grand Ballroom by His Eminence, Cardinal Spellman. Beneficiary of the Gothams is the Cardinal's pet charity, the New York Foundling Hospital, founded in 1869, one of whose first Auxiliary Board members was Mrs. John V. Bouvier, grandmother of Mrs. John F. Kennedy. Friday night brings the first of two Junior Assemblies (the second is held during Christmas week), and the Grosvenor Debutante Ball on Saturday night winds up the week's glamorous festivities.

The Plaza was the setting for the first International Debutante Ball in 1954, which served to introduce the daughters of Ambassadors to the United States and to the United Nations, as well as eligible young women from large cosmopolitan centers. Eventually the ball assumed such large proportions that it outgrew The Plaza ballroom with its dinner-dance capacity of six hundred.

A professional boxing match in The Plaza's new ballroom was the "attraction" dreamed up by the irrepressible Maury Paul as entertainment feature for one of his famous "Cholly Knickerbocker" Balls, given for the benefit of the *New York American* Christmas Fund in the mid-twenties. A. J. Drexel Biddle, Sr., father of "Tony" Biddle, Jr., and a great amateur boxer, supervised this production number, in a boxing ring set up in the center of the handsome gold-and-white ballroom. The names of the tin-ear heroes of the squared circle are lost to history, but the author who was present recalls that from the moment they went for each other, they had the elegant crowd of bejeweled women and white-tied gentlemen on the edge of its collective fanny. It looked like nothing so much as the first fifteen rows of a big Madison Square Garden fight in the good old days when Tex Rickard corralled the elect, and debs and dowagers forgot their Farmington manners, howling and yelling for blood like fight fans everywhere.

The *American,* the next morning, reported that among those present were Mrs. George Washington Kavanaugh, Cobina Wright, Mrs. Reginald C. Vanderbilt, and sundry other Vanderbilts as well as Drexels, Biddles, Chryslers, Belmonts, Rhinelanders and Pells. The identity of the lady wearing an emerald necklace who yelled, "Swat him in the kisser," will remain the author's secret.

Traditionally benefits for the Soldiers' and Sailors' Club have been held at the Plaza, and a particularly outstanding one was the Belmont Futurity Ball in 1951. Contributing to its success was the noted artist Raoul Dufy. Dufy, famed for his paintings of race tracks and thoroughbreds, was in this country that year being treated for arthritis, yet he made a special trip to Belmont Park to do a watercolor of the track with the thoroughbreds in action. On completion it was donated to the committee to be auctioned at the benefit. Another year Walter Salmon, the racing owner, donated a two-year-old to be auctioned, and none other than the auctioneer of the Faston Tipton stables, whose horse sales at Saratoga are world famous, came down to do the "going, going, gone" honors. Guests at The Plaza rubbed eyes in disbelief when they saw a horse being led into the Palm Court, which was set up as a paddock; the feat was only eclipsed when Elsa Maxwell led a cow into the Waldorf Ballroom for one of her famed parties.

The Terrace Room, which was designed as a public restaurant when the Fifty-eighth Street addition was built, soon had to be converted for functions.

In this jewel of a setting, stars of stage and screen and television, as well as lesser entertainment luminaries cavorted every Saturday night for several years in the fifties at the Mayfair Dances, designed primarily for that fraternity. The dances were a revival of the famed parties of pre-World War One, which were held at the Astor Hotel. Paradoxically they were founded as a result of an edict by David Belasco that actors and actresses under his management were not to be seen or heard by the public, except on stage; he felt that the stars had more appeal when they kept aloof in their own theatrical heaven.

Jack Rumsey, then manager for Daniel Frohman, said, "OK, we'll get a club of our own and have private weekly dances." And thus was born the Mayfair Dance Club. The first party was held in September 1913, after a Saturday night's final weekly curtain on Broadway; in 1923 the dances moved over to the Ritz Carlton, by this time having attracted many socialites. The Crystal Room of the Ritz was approached by a magnificent staircase, and the ladies delighted in using it to make grand entrances. Joe Smith of Plaza tea-dance fame conducted his orchestra.

The dances came under the cloud of the Second World War and were discontinued, to be revived in 1956 through the efforts of Charles Columbus, onetime ballroom dancer and Fred Astaire's choreographer, with the help of actress Shirley Booth. A night in November of that year found more than two hundred notables swarming to the Terrace Room for the opening dance. Hope Hampton turned up in all her jewels, to be rivaled only by Liz Taylor, and her then husband, the late Mike Todd; Charlie Columbus did a cha-cha-cha with Shirley, Helen Hayes was surrounded by admirers, and Dorothy and Lillian Gish watched with nostalgia—they had been among the members of the original Mayfair Club. Earl Blackwell saw that it all got properly reported in the papers.

While the prestige is important to hotels like The Plaza, the St. Regis and the Pierre, which have a corner on the debutante market, the big money today is in banquet business and charity balls.

"Name a disease," said one cynic, "and there's a ball for it." He was not far wrong. Hundreds upon hundreds of dances are given each season in dozens of hotels, to raise money for foundations and organizations established to prevent, cure or ease more physical and mental ills than one can find in an AMA report. In addition, there are hundreds more designed to raise funds for schools, churches, synagogues, scholarships, and to help the poor and underprivileged and foreign-born.

In a society of inflationary dollars, the cost of some of these reaches the astronomical. Tickets run from $30 to $100 each, and no one blinks an eye. The spectacular annual April in Paris Ball has topped all charity balls with an admission price of $150 each; in 1966 the price went up to $175. The high price, far from affecting the attendance, made the ball a sellout. No doubt the patrons felt the added price gave them added affluence status. Expenses, of course, often run into tens upon tens of thousands, and many of the events can make money only if they are underwritten. Without the help of three sponsors, who underwrote one fourth of the total expense of putting on the April in Paris Ball one particular year—1960—the cost would have been $95,000. And that, to paraphrase the old saying "is a lot of hay."

With such a golden crop to be harvested, the competition among the fashionable hotels has been keen, often frenzied. The battle of the ballrooms was already long begun; by the time the New York Hilton opened, it had developed the proportions of total warfare.

Wrote observer of the social scene Charlotte Curtis in the *Times* the night before the Grand Opening: "The Hilton, newest of Manhattan's new hotel belles, has scored socially significant points in the battle of the ballrooms, but it has yet to best its older, already established sisters."

The Plaza, second oldest sister of them all, three years younger than the St. Regis, is still the belle of the ball and continues to dominate the hotel social scene.

CHAPTER EIGHTEEN

Here Dwells Tradition

For three generations of New Yorkers, the majestic Plaza, overlooking their own Manhattan oasis of the trees and lakes of Central Park, offered reassurance that a way of life would survive wars, depressions, even death. She was elegant, yet sturdy, bulwark against all that was brash and mediocre, removed in spirit from the frenzied modern pace, indifferent to encroaching high-rise steel and chrome, serenely secure in her fine heritage. The Plaza was The Plaza. Nothing could disturb her well-ordered existence.

Complacent appreciation turned to angry defense, certainty gave way to doubts as destruction threatened to destroy the last vestiges of historic New York in the early 1960's, in a zooming boom of land values that spelled doom for old-established buildings.

As building after building, hotel after hotel, landmarks which were part of New York tradition and history, were torn down to make way for giant office buildings, the hue and cry of protest could be heard from one end of the country to the other—even from abroad, where buildings are more and more cherished as they grow older.

Hotels in midtown Manhattan were the particular targets of destruction. The incredible news that the fine, still comparatively young Savoy-Plaza had been sold, to be demolished and replaced by a colossal General Motors office building, provided the first shock to an unsuspecting citizenry suddenly aroused to a realization of what was happening to their city.

With the Savoy-Plaza would go another fine hotel, the adjacent Hotel Madison. In succession came news of the death blow delivered to other hotels: to the exquisite Park Lane, the charming and conservative Chatham, the New Weston, a little frayed around the edges, but still in healthy condition; more shock upon shock when it was announced that the death warrant for the beautiful Park Avenue citadel, the Sheraton-East, had been signed.

All civic hell broke loose, and blistering editorials in the leading newspapers throughout the country expressed outrage at the destruction of lovely old hotels.

To the Savoy-Plaza The Plaza wrote "A Love Letter to an Old Friend," an ad appearing in the papers, in the spirit of a proper lady expressing condolences.

> This is New York. They say it's a city where nobody knows and nobody cares who lives next door, or across the street. Well, we know you. . . . We've known you since 1927 when you opened your shining new doors and dazzled everybody. Now we hear you'll soon be leaving the scene. . . . Many people will miss you.
>
> We've been rivals. But sometimes old rivals are best friends, so let your best friend say it: We'll miss you very much!

Everyone was up in arms, and if one constructive thing came out of this program of destruction, it was the indignation of an angry citizenry which brought about establishment of the New York City Landmarks Preservation Committee, a commission appointed to designate buildings, their immediate surroundings, and even entire districts which were to be singled out for preservation.

The Plaza had but recently been designated a New York City landmark by the New York Community Trust. This, however, was before the City Landmarks Preservation Committee was formed. It was a group working in collaboration with the Municipal Art Society, New York University, and a panel of individual experts.

Their program, begun in 1957, was the expression of civic pride by a private, public-spirited group.

In 1962, people who saw The Plaza and its surroundings as a beauty not to be desecrated began a successful battle against the city's acceptance of Huntington Hartford's offer to erect an outdoor café in Central Park, at Fifty-ninth Street, just across from the hotel. The same forces mobilized to save the doomed hotels. Fannie Hurst and others were crying, "Save Our Landmarks, Save the Savoy-Plaza."

It was too late. The dire deed was done, and soon the public was being informed of plans for the new General Motors Building. The first horrendous sketches released for publication, showing a towering new building eclipsing and overwhelming the lovely Grand Army Plaza, that pleasant little square of rare quality of ease and distinction, brought dismay to all who saw it. General Motors tried to alleviate public distress by announcing that Edward Durrell Stone, the noted architect, would be the coarchitect of the new building, a Cadillac among buildings, with a plaza of its own, facing the Grand Army Plaza, and playing fountains in the foreground.

It didn't ease the situation a bit. The British novelist J. B. Priestley gave expression to his disapproval: "The parts of New York . . . that ought to have been pulled down years ago, never seem to be touched but buildings that other cities would be delighted to possess are torn down just for the hell of it."

"It's not only other cities that wanted these buildings," commented columnist John Crosby in the *New York Herald Tribune*, "New York wanted them too. Find a New Yorker who didn't mourn the passing of the Ritz Hotel or the Murray Hill Hotel. Who won't mourn the passing of The Plaza."

The idea that the Plaza could be next never entered anyone's mind until the gray day when it was announced that the Savoy-Plaza was sold. The Savoy-Plaza was practically family kin to The Plaza, though a generation younger. It was one of United States Realty's projects, built under the direction of Harry Black, and designed in the luxury mold by the well-known architectural firm of McKim, Mead and White.

Ironically for Mr. Priestley, it was not a New Yorker, but a group of Britishers who arranged for the sale and destruction of the Savoy-Plaza. Behind it was London Merchants Securities, Ltd., and the front "man" was a woman, Britisher Cecelia Benattar.

If not exactly "for the hell of it," beautiful buildings were being destroyed for the fortunes to be made in real estate. It was the land that was so valuable, not the buildings. Tax laws, old and new, worked against preservation of the past. Realty prices spiraled to the point where a quick profit was more desirable than running an inn through periods of feast and famine. Occupancy rates in hotels were declining; a contributing factor was a jet age of travel that could speed a businessman from Chicago to New York, and back that same day. Motels made further inroads in occupancy, as pleasure-seeking travelers took to wheeling in their own cars on the broad ribbons of highways crisscrossing the nation.

Twice in its brief history the Savoy-Plaza was practically sold from under the operators because of financial difficulties. The depression caused the first owners, United States Realty, to sell. It became the property of Conrad Hilton who, with typical Hilton self-advertising, renamed it the Savoy-Hilton, a name that was retained when Hilton sold it in 1956 to William Zeckendorf of the Webb and Knapp Corporation. At one time, it was said, Connie tried to get the city to change the name of the area to Hilton Square, but even he couldn't pull that one off.

In 1963, Webb and Knapp, overextended on the real estate front, sold the hotel to the Savoy Fifth Avenue Corporation, the American arm of London Merchants Securities, Ltd., whose president was the thirty-four-year-old Mrs. Benattar—London-born, and a born real estate genius. It was leased to Western International Corporation, owners of a large chain of eminent hotels, and the marquee immediately blazed again with the name Savoy-Plaza.

Knowing General Motors' lease on their Broadway and Fifty-seventh Street building was due to run out in 1966, Zeckendorf tried to interest company executives in buying the site of his Astor Hotel, but met with no success. As their meeting was breaking up, Zeckendorf suddenly turned to George Russell, executive vice president, and said, "Hey, would you be interested in the Savoy-

Plaza on Fifth?" That was a stopper; they definitely were, and soon GM and London Securities, through Mrs. Benattar, were brought together and completed a deal that made front-page headlines. Zeckendorf earned himself a nice finder's fee.

General Motors acquired 50 percent of the Savoy Fifth Avenue Corporation, which owned the square block of property bounded by Fifth, Madison, Fifty-eighth and Fifty-ninth Streets. The Savoy-Plaza closed its doors, and in October, 1965, General Motors moved ahead to replace the hotel with a fifty-story glass office building.

The Plaza was prospering at a most gratifying rate, but prosperity did not quiet the rumors that it, too, was to be sold and torn down. The rumor gained impetus when Hilton, who still owned a $400,000 option to purchase one half of the land beneath the Plaza, sold it to two real estate investors, Alexander DiLorenzo, Jr., and Sol Goldman, who bought the St. Regis Hotel. They paid Hilton $3,600,000 for his option and immediately exercised that option. For a four-million-dollar total they were partners with Lawrence Wien in the ownership of one of the most valuable pieces of land in the city.

This was enough to start another batch of rumors about The Plaza's fate, but Paul Sonnabend, president of the hotel, immediately squelched them by emphatically declaring that HCA had no intention of letting the hotel go. "We will never give up The Plaza," said he. "My father loved this hotel. He achieved the ambition of his life when he got it."

HCA holds an option to repurchase The Plaza from the Wien interests between the end of 1970 and 1973, for $7.5 million cash and assuming a mortgage which would bring the total price to $22.5 million. Paul Sonnabend announced that HCA would definitely exercise the option—and the public had the first official reassurance that The Plaza would survive.

To an interviewer, Sol Goldman said, "People needn't worry; they can't tear down The Plaza without us. And we won't let them. She's a great hotel. Without The Plaza, we wouldn't have much left." Whether he meant for himself or the city was never made clear.

Shortly after the Savoy-Plaza Hotel was sold, HCA President Roger Sonnabend in his office in Boston, was informed by his secretary that some hotelmen from Seattle were in the outer office asking to see him. They had made no appointment, but as they later told Roger, they simply hopped on a plane to beard the hotel lion in his den, with an offer to buy The Plaza. One of the gentlemen was Edward E. Carlson, president of Western International. They wanted a prestige hotel in New York to take the place of the Savoy-Plaza which they had lost to General Motors, and offered $26 million for The Plaza.

This was $5 million more than the profit HCA had made when it was sold to the Wien interests, and a potential $3.5 million profit on the option to buy it back.

The offer was turned down. Western International could not buy The Plaza at any price, but out of the meeting came an interesting business arrangement. If HCA wouldn't sell, why not establish a joint marketing program, combining sales and marketing activities of the two corporations, to work for their mutual benefit? The combine was to be mainly an exchange of reservations services. Without affecting the independence of either hotel chain, the marketing merger would cooperate in the framework of the combined worldwide network of seventy-two leading hotels, to serve the traveling public. Forty-five western hotels, twenty-seven HCA hotels, in areas where neither was competing with the other, were involved in the cooperative working arrangements, hotels ranging from Anchorage, Alaska, to Tokyo, by way of London, in Mexico, Guatemala, Honolulu and thirty-five cities in continental United States.

The Lavenson advertising firm was carrying on in the same name and in Lavenson's image for The Plaza.

The reading public was enchanted when magazines and newspapers, at the height of the agitation engendered by the news of hotel destruction, published a Plaza ad that was reproduced by request in numerous architectural and hotel-trade publications.

"The Day New York Almost Vanished," a far-from-farfetched fantasy, first appeared as an ad in the *New York Times Magazine* in March 1965. The response was fantastic. Hundreds of readers wrote to the *Times* and to The Plaza. Publications on both sides of the Atlantic commented on it editorially. More than a hotel or even a city, a way of life was being threatened and with it, the charm and beauty and the art of generations. Realty was kin to fantasy in "The Day New York Almost Vanished." This was the text:

It didn't happen all at once.
They did it very gradually.
"We can't alarm the people!" they said.
So they removed a little house here and a great hotel there.
And then a few limestone banks
And all the cast-iron store fronts they could find.
And very quietly one night they stole a railroad station
And buried it in New Jersey.

A few people grumbled. Some found temporary shelter at the Dakota when Park Avenue disappeared. Others moved to Westchester. And some completely disillusioned out-of-towners went to Philadelphia instead. But most people were complacent. Until the day they discovered that their city had been entirely replaced by glass.

Then they complained. But it was too late. So the faces of the city grew grimmer than they had ever been before. Clocks stopped. And the glass began to crack.

Soon after this on one ghastly glittering morning, an observant executive walking to work paused on Fifth Avenue at Fifty-ninth Street to clean his heavy dark goggles. Squinting, he looked around. And gasped.

There was The Plaza where he had always remembered it. "It can't be," he said, and rubbed his eyes. He looked again. "It is there!" he said. And ran to work.

He called his wife. "We'll go there tonight, before it's too late, don't tell anyone!" he hissed. So she only told her very best friend. Soon everyone knew.

Crowds gathered. They wandered in the lobbies. They caressed the marble, admired the gilded cherubs. And the caryatids in the Palm Court where palms still swayed. They feasted in the baronial splendor of the Edwardian Room.

And discussed mergers over martinis and lunch in the Oak Bar.

That night they danced to *real* music again in the Persian Room. And laughed with Julius Monk in his red velvet world at " Plaza 9." The lucky ones who had made reservations retired upstairs, to spacious rooms where they were waited on hand and foot by manicurists and chiropodists and chambermaids and valets and waiters with trays and florists with roses. They loved it.

After all, people of taste are like everybody else. They're very grateful when great demands are met. And incurably sentimental.

Eventually word spread out of town. And out-of-towners came again to see a part of the city they thought had vanished. Some never left The Plaza. They didn't have to. They had the world on a golden chain.

The Plaza had thought of everything. It always does. It always will.

In the tiniest of small print, at the bottom of the ad, it said, "This advertisement is fantasy, of course. But then, so is life at The Plaza. Come live it."

From all over the country letters poured in. Stephen H. Green of Philadelphia said: "I am writing to congratulate you on your advertisement in the *Saturday Review*. I have never stayed at The Plaza, but I admire what it is and what it represents—graciousness and charm in a time when formless, faceless shapes are deemed more valuable, or at least more profitable. I hope that the fantasy which is in The Plaza will continue to cast light upon New York."

From Mrs. Stember of Stamford, Connecticut: "Please accept our congratulations on your most impressive ad. . . . It was refreshing. As born New Yorkers, who crossed the state line twenty-five years ago and come back every now and then to find a new building standing where once stood a recognized landmark, it was heartening to realize The Plaza was still there—where it belongs, in the heart of New York."

"What a perfectly wonderful ad in the *New Yorker*," wrote

Helen Heller of Washington. "I read every word and then reread it. My husband and I haven't been to The Plaza in years, not since courting days, but we'll hurry back sometime during the summer."

This was the public speaking, an out-of-town public with no allegiance to a bustling city, but with a deep appreciation of beauty in any form.

From the very beginning The Plaza set a pattern for elegance of architecture and social splendor unrivaled by any hotel in the country, yet its grace and prestige have endured throughout decades marked by wars, depressions, national tragedies, the blight of prohibition, changing customs, changing wealth, ascending taxes, declining manners.

From the cotillion to the bunny hug, to the Charleston, to the frug; from diademed dowager to dancing deb; from Lillian Russell to Eloise; from Elinor Glyn to Eleanor Roosevelt; from Groucho to Gromyko; from Billie Burke to Brigitte Bardot; from Caruso to Ringo; from High Society to Hollywood—through all phases of transition, The Plaza has managed always to be in tune with the times, its dignity unruffled, its good taste unimpaired.

The time is now, and the stately past has fused with the staccato present in an unbroken continuity of a perfectly mannered life. The late Lucius Beebe wrote: ". . . the world has grown gray and its brighter lights have been dimmed by the mediocrity and the fussy devisings of little men. But the lights of The Plaza, somehow and miraculously have been undimmed . . . they gleam in welcome across the asphaltine stretches of the wealthiest avenue in the world."

Whatever her future fate, if ever her lights are one day forever dimmed, The Plaza belongs to history, the last of the Big-Time Splendors.

Index

INDEX

INDEX

INDEX

INDEX

INDEX